When I Don't Desire GOD

Other Crossway Books by John Piper

Amazing Grace in the Life of William Wilberforce
Beyond the Bounds, co-editor
Bloodlines
Contending for Our All
Counted Righteous in Christ
Don't Waste Your Cancer
Don't Waste Your Life
Esther
Fifty Reasons Why Jesus Came to Die
Filling Up the Afflictions of Christ
Finish the Mission, co-editor
The Future of Justification
A God-Entranced Vision of All Things, co-editor
God Is the Gospel
God's Passion for His Glory
The Hidden Smile of God
A Hunger for God
The Innkeeper
John Calvin and His Passion for the Majesty of God
The Legacy of Sovereign Joy
Love Your Enemies
The Misery of Job and the Mercy of God
The Pastor as Scholar and the Scholar as Pastor, co-author
The Power of Words and the Wonder of God, co-editor
The Prodigal's Sister
Recovering Biblical Manhood and Womanhood, co-editor
Rethinking Retirement
Risk Is Right
The Roots of Endurance
Ruth
Seeing and Savoring Jesus Christ
Sex and the Supremacy of Christ, co-editor
Spectacular Sins
Stand, co-editor
Suffering and the Sovereignty of God, co-editor
The Supremacy of Christ in a Postmodern World, co-editor
A Sweet and Bitter Providence
Think
Thinking. Loving. Doing.
This Momentary Marriage
Velvet Steel
What Jesus Demands from the World
What's the Difference?
When the Darkness Will Not Lift
With Calvin in the Theater of God, co-editor

When I Don't Desire GOD

How to Fight for Joy

John Piper

CROSSWAY®
WHEATON, ILLINOIS

When I Don't Desire God

Preface © 2013 by Desiring God Foundation

Text Copyright © 2004 by Desiring God Foundation

Published by Crossway
    1300 Crescent Street
    Wheaton, Illinois 60187

Cover design: Tyler Deeb, Pedale Design

First printing 2004

Tenth-Anniversary Edition printing 2013

Printed in the United States of America

Trade paperback ISBN: 978-1-4335-4317-3
ePub ISBN: 978-1-4335-4429-3
PDF ISBN: 978-1-4335-4427-9
Mobipocket ISBN: 978-1-4335-4428-6

Library of Congress Cataloging-in-Publication Data
Piper, John, 1946-
    When I don't desire God : how to fight for joy / John Piper.
       p.   cm.
    Includes bibliographical references and indexes.
    ISBN 13: 978-1-58134-652-7
    ISBN 10: 1-58134-652-2
    1. God—Worship and love. 2. Desire for God. 3. Happiness—
Religious aspects—Christianity. 4. Praise of God. I. Title.
BV4817.P57   2004
248.4—dc22   2004016323

Crossway is a publishing ministry of Good News Publishers.

VP   28   27   26   25   24   23   22   21   20   19
18   17   16   15   14   13   12   11   10

Contents

Preface to the Tenth-Anniversary Edition

Ten years have passed since this book was first published. My daughter is not eight years old. She's an adult. My pastoral ministry at Bethlehem Baptist Church is not twenty-four years old. It ended sweetly at thirty-three. My marriage has ripened to forty-five. And I am not fifty-eight, but two years shy of three score and ten.

What is my perspective now on *When I Don't Desire God: How to Fight for Joy?*

First, desires still matter. Behind this book is the conviction that God is most glorified in us when we are most satisfied in him. In other words, huge things hang in the balance when the satisfaction of our desires is in question. Jesus warned that the "deceitfulness of riches and the *desires for other things*" destroy the fruit of God's Word (Mark 4:19). But if we say with the psalmist: "Whom have I in heaven but you [O Lord]? And there is nothing on earth that I desire besides you" (Ps. 73:25), then fruit abounds, and God is glorified as our supreme Treasure.

Second, the need to fight to be happy in God himself is still ironic and true. It's ironic because in the midst of a fight, the feelings are often painful, not pleasant. But Paul still says to Timothy: "Fight the good fight of the faith. Take hold of the eternal life" (1 Tim. 6:12). Faith includes the embrace of Jesus as our all-satisfying Treasure. Therefore, the fight for faith is a fight for joy. If we were perfect—if there were no remaining corruption in our hearts—there would be no fight. There would be no obstacles to overcome. We won't fight for joy in heaven. But we are not there yet.

Third, the fight lasts until our final breath. I am old now—coming up to my eighth decade. And I testify that the joy of faith is not automatic at any age. Sin remains a mighty force. Killing it remains a daily duty (Rom. 8:13). And the essence of sin is preferring anything more than God. That is the root we must sever (daily!)—desiring anything more than God. And we sever it with a superior pleasure. Paul was speaking as man at the end of his life when he said, "I have fought the good fight" (2 Tim. 4:7). So, while this book is a mere ten years old, the battle rages on till life here is over.

Finally, we are never left by God to fight alone. He came in Christ to purchase our final victory once for all. All the promises of God are yes in him (2 Cor. 1:20). And he comes by his Spirit daily. "the desires of the Spirit are against the flesh" (Gal. 5:17), so that "you will not gratify the desires of the flesh" (Gal. 5:16). We fight for joy by the Spirit, not alone (Rom. 8:13). He never leaves us. He works "in us that which is pleasing in his sight" (Heb. 13:21). And faith is what pleases him (Heb. 11:6)—faith, the embrace of our all-satisfying Treasure.

And just as this book was written by a fellow believer for your help in the fight for joy, so God means for you to fight the fight of faith with fellow combatants at your side. The fight for joy means being part of the Christian militia: "Take care, brothers, lest there be in any of you an evil, unbelieving heart. . . . But exhort one another every day . . . that none of you may be hardened by the deceitfulness of sin" (Heb. 3:12–13). My prayer is that this book will prove to be an arsenal of faith-sustaining, joy-awakening weapons that you and your comrades can use to fight for each other's joy.

In other words, from my perspective ten years later, the message of this book still matters; it is still true to our need as sinners; it will not be irrelevant till we are in the grave; and without the all-purchasing cross and the all-providing Holy Spirit, these words would be powerless.

I pray again, therefore, that through Christ, and by the Spirit, they will not be powerless in your life, but powerful in the awakening and sustaining of everlasting joy.

John Piper

Preface
and
a Prayer

I hope you will not be offended if I open this book by praying for you. There is a reason. When all is said and done, only God can create joy in God. This is why the old saints not only pursued joy but prayed for it: "Make us glad for as many days as you have afflicted us" (Ps. 90:15). To be satisfied by the beauty of God does not come naturally to sinful people. By nature we get more pleasure from God's gifts than from himself. Therefore this book calls for deep and radical change—which only God can give.

But if I didn't believe God uses means to awaken joy in himself, I would not have written this book. I hope you will read it and that the eyes of your heart will be opened to the infinitely desirable Person of God. He made himself known in his Son, Jesus Christ, who "is the radiance of the glory of God and the exact imprint of his nature" (Heb. 1:3). Seeing and savoring this glory is the spring of all endless joy.

Someone asked me why I didn't put Chapter Twelve at the beginning and then proceed to solve the problem. The title of Chapter Twelve is "When the Darkness Does Not Lift." The reason is that I am helpless to solve that problem. But God can. And he *will*, in due time, for all who have tasted his saving grace. "Weeping may tarry for the night, but joy comes with the morning" (Ps. 30:5). And when it comes, it comes from God, not from this book. Chapter Twelve is at the end because when I have done all I can do, the darkness may still not be lifted. I hope you will not despair but will turn to God in prayer. Which is what I do now for you:

Father, I pray that all who've read this far will have the motivation and the strength to read on to the end at least as far as would be helpful to their faith. I pray that they would read with understanding. And may they be discerning so that, if I have blundered, they would be sure to see the error and not follow me. Protect them from the evil one who would distort and then deceive. Give great assistance from your Spirit, and may they see more truth than I have seen. Oh, that the eyes of their hearts might be bright with the glory of Christ through these pages! Remove every blinding obstacle, and show them your glory! And thus give them more joy than all the gladness that the world can give. And by this joy in Jesus Christ, fit them to love and serve and sacrifice. And by this joy, with which they bear their cross, Lord, cause the earth to know what you are truly worth. In Jesus' name, I pray. Amen.

You had compassion on those in prison, and you joyfully accepted the plundering of your property, since you knew that you yourselves had a better possession and an abiding one.

HEBREWS 10:34

. . . looking to Jesus, the founder and perfecter of our faith, who for the joy that was set before him endured the cross, despising the shame, and is seated at the right hand of the throne of God.

HEBREWS 12:2

There have been times when I think we do not desire heaven; but more often I find myself wondering whether, in our heart of hearts, we have ever desired anything else. . . . It is the secret signature of each soul, the incommunicable and unappeasable want, the thing we desired before we met our wives or made our friends or chose our work, and which we shall still desire on our deathbeds, when the mind no longer knows wife or friend or work. . . . All your life an unattainable ecstasy has hovered just beyond the grasp of your consciousness. The day is coming when you will wake to find, beyond all hope, that you have attained it.

C. S. LEWIS
The Problem of Pain[1]

1

Why I Wrote This Book

Sustaining the Sacrifice of Love

Christian Hedonism is a liberating and devastating doctrine. It teaches that the value of God shines more brightly in the soul that finds deepest satisfaction in him. Therefore it is liberating because it endorses our inborn desire for joy. And it is devastating because it reveals that no one desires God with the passion he demands. Paradoxically, many people experience both of these truths. That certainly is my own experience.

The Liberating and Devastating Discovery

When I saw the truth that *God is most glorified in us when we are most satisfied in him*, I was freed from the unbiblical bondage of fear that it was wrong to pursue joy. What once had seemed like an inevitable but defective quest for the satisfaction of my soul now became not just permitted but required. The glory of God was at stake. This was almost too good to be true—that my quest for joy and my duty to glorify God were not in conflict. Indeed they were one. Pursuing joy in God was a nonnegotiable way of honoring God. It was essential. This was a liberating discovery. It released the energies of my mind and heart to go hard after all the soul-happiness that God is for me in Jesus.

But simultaneous with the liberation came the devastation. I was freed to pursue my fullest joy in God without guilt. Indeed, I was *commanded* to pursue it. Indifference to the pursuit of joy in God would be indifference to the glory of God, and that is sin. Therefore, my quest took on a seriousness, an earnestness, a gravity that I never dreamed would be part of pursuing joy. And then, almost immediately, came the realization that my indwelling sin stands in the way of my full satisfaction in God. It opposes and perverts my pursuit of God. It *opposes* by making other things look more desirable than God. And it *perverts* by making me think I am pursuing joy in God when, in fact, I am in love with his gifts.

I discovered what better saints than I have found before me: the full enjoyment of God is my ultimate home, but I am still far off and only on the way. Augustine put it like this in one of his prayers:

> I was astonished that although I now loved you . . . I did not persist in enjoyment of my God. Your beauty drew me to you, but soon I was dragged away from you by my own weight and in dismay I plunged again into the things of this world . . . as though I had sensed the fragrance of the fare but was not yet able to eat it.[2]

How Christian Living Became Impossible

This discovery was devastating to me. It still is. I was made to know and enjoy God. I was freed by the doctrine of Christian Hedonism to pursue that knowledge and that joy with all my heart. And then, to my dismay, I discovered that it is not an easy doctrine. Christian Hedonism is not a lowering of the bar. Out of the blue, as it were, I realized that the bar had been raised. Manageable, duty-defined, decision-oriented, will-power Christianity now seemed easy, and real Christianity had become impossible. The emotions—or affections, as former generations called them—which I was now free to enjoy, proved to be beyond my reach. The Christian life became impossible. That is, it became supernatural.

Now there was only one hope: the sovereign grace of God. God would have to transform my heart to do what a heart cannot make itself do, namely, want what it ought to want. Only God can make the depraved heart desire God. Once when Jesus' disciples wondered about the salvation of a man who desired money more than God, he said to them, "With man it is impossible, but not with God. For all things are possible with God" (Mark 10:27). Pursuing what we want is possible. It is easy. It is a pleasant kind of freedom. But the only freedom that lasts is pursuing what we want when we want what we ought. And it is devastating to discover we don't, and we can't.

The Most Common Question I Have Received

This is why the most common and desperate question I have received over the last three decades is: What can I do? How can I become the kind of person the Bible is calling me to be? The question comes from an aching in the heart that rises from the hope of great joy. People listen to the biblical arguments for Christian Hedonism, or they read *Desiring God: Meditations of a Christian Hedonist.*[3] Many are persuaded. They see that the truth and beauty and worth of God shine best from the lives of saints who are so satisfied in God they can suffer in the cause of love without murmuring. But then they say, "That's not who I am. I don't have that kind of liberating, love-producing, risk-taking satisfaction in God. I desire comfort and security more than God." Many say it with tears and trembling.

Some are honest enough to say, "I don't know if I have ever tasted this kind of desire. Christianity was never presented to me like this. I never knew that the desire for God and delight in God were crucial. I was always told that feelings didn't matter. Now I am finding evidence all over the Bible that the pursuit of joy in God, and the awakening of all kinds of spiritual affections, are part of the essence of the newborn Christian heart. This discovery excites me and frightens me. I want this. But I fear I don't have it. In fact, as far as I can see, it is outside my power to obtain. How do you get a desire that you don't have and you can't create? Or how do you turn the spark into a flame so that you can be sure it is pure fire?"

Conversion Is the Creation of New Desires

To answer that question, I have written this book. I long to be of help to believers and unbelievers who are seeing some of the radical heart-changes demanded by the Bible in the Christian life—especially that we must desire God more than anything. I am not interested in superficial, external behavior changes, which the Pharisees were so good at. "You Pharisees cleanse the outside of the cup and of the dish, but inside you are full of greed and wickedness" (Luke 11:39). These external changes are doable without divine grace.

I would like to help those who are beginning to see that salvation is the awakening of a new taste for God, or it is nothing. "Oh, *taste* and see that the LORD is good!" (Ps. 34:8). I want to help those who are starting to see that conversion is the creation of new desires, not just new duties; new delights, not just new deeds; new treasures, not just new tasks.

Far and wide people are seeing these truths in the Bible. They are discovering that there is nothing new about Christian Hedonism at all, but that it is simple, old-fashioned, historic, biblical, radical Christian living. It is as old as the psalmists who said to God, "Restore to me the joy of your salvation" (Ps. 51:12) and "Satisfy us in the morning with your steadfast love" (Ps. 90:14).

It's as old as Jesus, who gave to his people this virtually impossible command for the day of their persecution: "Rejoice in that day, and leap for joy, for behold, your reward is great in heaven" (Luke 6:23).

It's as old as the early church who "*joyfully* accepted the plundering of [their] property," because they "had a better possession and an abiding one" (Heb. 10:34).

It's as old as Augustine who described conversion as the triumph of sovereign joy:

> How sweet all at once it was for me to be rid of *those fruitless joys* which I had once feared to lose . . . ! *You drove them from me*, you who are the true, the *sovereign joy*. You drove them from me and took their place, you who are *sweeter than all pleasure*, though not to flesh and blood, you who outshine all light, yet are hidden deeper than any secret in our hearts, you who surpass all honor, though not in the eyes of men who see all honor in themselves. . . . O Lord my God, my Light, my Wealth, and my Salvation.[4]

It's as old as John Calvin, the great Reformer of Geneva, who said in his 1559 *Institutes of the Christian Religion* that aspiring after happiness in union with God is "the chief activity of the soul."

> If human happiness, whose perfection it is to be united with God, were hidden from man, he would in fact be bereft of the principal use of his understanding. Thus, also the chief activity of the soul is to aspire thither. Hence the more anyone endeavors to approach to God, the more he proves himself endowed with reason.[5]

It's as old as the Puritans, like Thomas Watson, who wrote in 1692 that God counts himself more glorified when we find more happiness in his salvation:

> Would it not be an encouragement to a subject, to hear his prince say to him, You will honor and please me very much, if you will go to yonder mine of gold, and dig as much gold for yourself as you can carry away? So, for God to say, Go to the ordinances, get as much grace as you can, dig out as much salvation as you can; and the more happiness you have, the more I shall count myself glorified.[6]

It's as old as Jonathan Edwards, who argued with all his intellectual might in 1729 that "Persons need not and ought not to set any bounds to their spiritual and gracious appetites." Rather, they ought

> to be endeavoring by all possible ways to inflame their desires and to obtain more spiritual pleasures. . . . Our hungerings and thirstings after God and Jesus Christ and after holiness can't be too great for the value of these things, for they are things of infinite value. . . . [Therefore] endeavor to promote spiritual appetites by laying yourself in the way of allurement. . . .[7] There is no such thing as excess in our taking of this spiritual food. There is no such virtue as temperance in spiritual feasting.[8]

It's as old as Princeton theologian Charles Hodge who argued in the nineteenth century that the true knowledge of Christ includes (and does not just lead to) delight in Christ. This knowledge "is not the apprehension of what he is, simply by the intellect, but also . . . involves not as its consequence merely, but as one of its elements, the corresponding feeling of adoration, *delight, desire and complacency* [= contentment]."[9]

It is as old as the Reformed New Testament scholar Geerhardus Vos, who in the early twentieth century conceded that there is in the writings of the apostle Paul "a spiritualized type of hedonism."

> Of course, it is not intended to deny to Paul that transfigured *spiritualized type of "hedonism"* if one prefers so to call it, as distinct from the specific attitude towards life that went in the later Greek philosophy by that technical name. Nothing, not even a most refined Christian experience and cultivation of religion are possible without that. . . . Augustine speaks of this in his *Confessions* in these words:

"For *there exists a delight* that is not given to the wicked, but to those honoring Thee, O God, without desiring recompense, the joy of whom Thou art Thyself! And this is the blessed life, to rejoice towards Thee, about Thee, for Thy sake." Conf. X, 22.[10]

It's as old as the great C. S. Lewis, who died the same day as John F. Kennedy and had a huge influence on the way I experience nature worshipfully.[11]

Pleasures are shafts of glory as it strikes our sensibility. . . . But aren't there bad, unlawful pleasures? Certainly there are. But in calling them "bad pleasures" I take it we are using a kind of shorthand. We mean "pleasures snatched by unlawful acts." It is the stealing of the apples that is bad, not the sweetness. The sweetness is still a beam from the glory. . . . I have tried since . . . to make every pleasure into a channel of adoration. I don't mean simply by giving thanks for it. One must of course give thanks, but I meant something different. . . . Gratitude exclaims, very properly, "How good of God to give me this." Adoration says, "What must be the quality of that Being whose far-off and momentary coruscations are like this!" One's mind runs back up the sunbeam to the sun. . . . If this is *Hedonism*, it is also a somewhat arduous discipline. But it is worth some labour.[12]

Lewis was so influential in my understanding of joy and desire and duty and worship that I will add another quotation from him as a tribute to the greatness of his wisdom. I hope my enthusiasm for Lewis will set you to reading him, if you haven't. He, of course, had his flaws, but few people in the twentieth century had eyes to see what he saw. For example, few saw, as he did, the proper place of duty and delight:

Provided the thing is in itself right, the more one likes it and the less one has to "try to be good," the better. A *perfect* man would never act from sense of duty; he'd always *want* the right thing more than the wrong one. Duty is only a substitute for love (of God and of other people), like a crutch, which is a substitute for a leg. Most of us need the crutch at times; but of course it's idiotic to use the crutch when our own legs (our own loves, tastes, habits, etc.) can do the journey on their own![13]

The point of citing all these witnesses is that lots of people, with good reason, are being persuaded that Christian Hedonism is simple, old-fashioned, historic, biblical, radical Christian living, not some new spiritual technique. They are discovering that *God is most glorified in us when we are most satisfied in him.* Which means they are finding that their desires, not just their decisions, really matter. The glory of God is at stake. And many, with tears, want to know: What do I do when I don't desire God? God willing, I would like to help.

It Will Not Be an Easy Journey toward Joy

I take this task seriously. Our journey in this book is not across easy territory. There are dangers on all sides. Spiritual desires and delights are not commodities to be bought and sold. They are not objects to be handled. They are events in the soul. They are experiences of the heart. They have connections and causes in a hundred directions. They are interwoven with the body and the brain, but are not limited to the physical or mental. God himself, without body or brain, experiences a full array of spiritual affections—love, hate, joy, anger, zeal, etc. Yet our affections are influenced by our bodies and brains. No one but God can get to the bottom of these things. "For the inward mind and heart of a man are deep!" (Ps. 64:6); and not just deep, but depraved: "The heart is deceitful above all things, and desperately sick; who can understand it?" (Jer. 17:9).

So the answer to the question, "What should I do when I don't desire God?" is not simple. But it is crucial. The apostle Paul said, "If anyone has no love for the Lord, let him be accursed" (1 Cor. 16:22). Love is not a mere choice to move the body or the brain. Love is also an experience of the heart. So the stakes are very high. Christ is to be cherished, not just chosen. The alternative is to be cursed. Therefore life is serious. And so is this book.

The Aim Is Not to Soften Cushions, but to Sustain Sacrifice

The misunderstanding of this book that I want most to avoid is that I am writing to make well-to-do Western Christians comfortable, as if the joy I have in mind is psychological icing on the cake of already superficial Christianity. Therefore let me say clearly here at the beginning that the joy I write to awaken is the sustaining strength of mercy, missions, and martyrdom.

Even as I write this sentence Christians are being hacked to death outside Kano, Nigeria. Yesterday a twenty-six-year-old American businessman was beheaded in Iraq by terrorists. Why him? He just happened to be in the wrong place at the wrong time. This kind of death will increase especially for Christians. In Sudan water is systematically withheld from Christians as they die of thirst and malnutrition, while desperate attempts to visit wells are met with murder, rape, or kidnapping. Fresh reports come every month concerning the destruction of Christian churches and the arrest of pastors in China. In the last decade over five hundred Christian churches have been destroyed in Indonesia. Missionaries are at risk all over the world.

When I address the question, "What should I do if I don't desire God?" I am addressing the question: "How can I obtain or recover a joy in Christ that is so deep and so strong that it will free me from bondage to Western comforts and security, and will impel me into sacrifices of mercy and missions, and will sustain me in the face of martyrdom?" Persecution is normal for Christians. "All who desire to live a godly life in Christ Jesus will be persecuted" (2 Tim. 3:12). "Beloved, do not be surprised at the fiery trial when it comes upon you to test you, as though something strange were happening to you" (1 Pet. 4:12). "Through many tribulations we must enter the kingdom of God" (Acts 14:22).

In the New Testament this sobering truth does not diminish the focus on joy—it increases it. "We *rejoice* in our sufferings, knowing that suffering produces endurance" (Rom. 5:3). "Blessed are you when others . . . persecute you. . . . *Rejoice* and be glad, for your reward is great in heaven" (Matt. 5:11-12). "Count it all *joy*, my brothers, when you meet trials of various kinds, for you know that the testing of your faith produces steadfastness" (Jas. 1:2-3). "They left the presence of the council, *rejoicing* that they were counted worthy to suffer dishonor for the name" (Acts 5:41).

The fight for joy in Christ is not a fight to soften the cushion of Western comforts. It is a fight for strength to live a life of self-sacrificing love. It is a fight to join Jesus on the Calvary road and stay there with him, no matter what. How was he sustained on that road? Hebrews 12:2 answers, "For the *joy* that was set before him [he] endured the cross." The key to endurance in the cause of self-sacrificing love is not heroic willpower, but deep, unshakable confidence that the joy we have tasted in fellowship with Christ will not disappoint us in death. Sacrifices in the path of love were sustained in the New Testament not by willpower, but by joyful hope. "You had compassion on those in prison, and you *joyfully* accepted the plundering of your property, since *you knew that you yourselves had a better possession and an abiding one*" (Heb. 10:34).

The aim of this book is not to salve the conscience of well-to-do Western acquisition. The aim is to sustain love's ability to endure sacrificial losses of property and security and life, by the power of joy in the path of love. The aim is that Jesus Christ be made known in all the world as the all-powerful, all-wise, all-righteous, all-merciful, all-satisfying Treasure of the universe.

This will happen when Christians don't just *say* that Christ is valuable, or *sing* that Christ is valuable, but truly experience in their hearts the unsurpassed worth of Jesus with so much joy that they can say, "I count everything as loss because of the surpassing worth of knowing Christ Jesus my Lord" (Phil. 3:8). Christ will be glorified in the world when Christians are so satisfied in him that they let goods and kindred go and lay down their lives for others in mercy, missions, and, if necessary, martyrdom. He will be magnified most among the nations when, at the moment Christians lose everything on earth, they say, "To live is Christ, and to die is gain" (Phil. 1:21).

"Therefore let us go to him outside the camp and bear the reproach he endured. For here we have no lasting city, but we seek the city that is to come" (Heb. 13:13-14). This we will do for the joy that is set before us. And this joy will hold us and keep us, if we have tasted it and fought to make it the supreme experience of our lives. Christ is supremely glorious and supremely valuable. Therefore he is worth the fight.

It was when I was happiest that I longed most. . . . The sweetest thing in all my life has been the longing . . . to find the place where all the beauty came from.

C. S. LEWIS
Till We Have Faces[1]

The very nature of Joy makes nonsense of our common distinction between having and wanting. There, to have is to want and to want is to have. Thus, the very moment when I longed to be so stabbed again [with Joy], was itself again such a stabbing.

C. S. LEWIS
Surprised by Joy[2]

O God, you are my God;
earnestly I seek you;
my soul thirsts for you;
my flesh faints for you,
as in a dry and weary land
where there is no water.

PSALM 63:1

Then I will go to the altar of God,
to God my exceeding joy.

PSALM 43:4

2

What Is the Difference between Desire and Delight?

Discovering How Both and Neither Is the Goal

In this book I will use many words for *joy* without precise distinctions: happiness, delight, pleasure, contentment, satisfaction, desire, longing, thirsting, passion, etc. I am aware that all of these words carry different connotations for different readers. Some people think of *happiness* as superficial and *joy* as deep. Some think of *pleasure* as physical and *delight* as aesthetic. Some think of *passion* as sexual and *longing* as personal. So I signal from the outset that the Bible does not divide its emotional language that way. The same words (desire, pleasure, happiness, joy, etc.) can be positive sometimes and negative sometimes, physical sometimes and spiritual sometimes. That is the approach I take. Any of these words can be a godly experience of the heart, and any of them can be a worldly experience of the heart. I will try to make plain what way the words should be taken in any given context.

But one of the most urgent questions demanded by the title and subtitle of this book is the difference between *desire* and *joy*, or between desire and delight. The title speaks of desire: *When I Don't Desire God*. But the subtitle speaks of joy: *How to Fight for Joy*. How are the two different and related? The Bible teaches us to *desire* God and to have *joy* in God, or *delight* in God. It illustrates both. Godly people are seen yearning, longing, hungering, thirsting, and fainting for God. They are also seen enjoying, delighting in, and being satisfied in God. So we will look first at how the Bible expresses these two kinds of emotions—desiring and enjoying—and then we will ask what the difference is.

Examples of Desiring God

The God-entranced psalmist, Asaph, says, "Whom have I in heaven but you? And there is nothing on earth that I desire besides you. My flesh and my heart may fail, but God is the strength of my heart and my portion forever" (Ps. 73:25-26). Here is a desire for God so strong that it makes all others as nothing. From all the portions that earth and heaven can give, Asaph turns away and says, "God is my portion forever." Jeremiah said the same: "'The LORD is my portion,' says my soul, 'therefore I will hope in him'" (Lam. 3:24). David, the king, spoke in the same way: "I cry to you, O LORD; I say, 'You are . . . my portion in the land of the living'" (Ps. 142:5). "I say to the LORD, 'You are my Lord; I have no good apart from you.' . . . The LORD is my chosen portion" (Ps. 16:2, 5).

The longing psalmist expresses his desire for God with the image of a panting deer: "As a deer pants for flowing streams, so pants my soul for you, O God. My soul thirsts for God, for the living God" (Ps. 42:1). David pours out his heart with similar language: "O God, you are my God; earnestly I seek you; my soul thirsts for you; my flesh faints for you, as in a dry and weary land where there is no water. . . . Your steadfast love is better than life" (Ps. 63:1, 3).

The prophet Isaiah from time to time overflowed with words of longing for the Lord: "My soul yearns for you in the night; my spirit within me earnestly seeks you. For when your judgments are in the earth, the inhabitants of the world learn righteousness" (Isa. 26:9). The apostle Paul revealed the depth of his desire for Christ more clearly in his letter to the Philippians than in any other: "My desire is to depart and be with Christ, for that is far better. . . . Whatever gain I had, I counted as loss for the sake of Christ. Indeed, I count everything as loss because of the surpassing worth of knowing Christ Jesus my Lord. For his sake I have suffered the loss of all things and count them as rubbish, in order that I may gain Christ" (Phil. 1:23; 3:7-8).

Examples of Delighting in God

One of the most remarkable expressions of delighting or rejoicing in God is found in Habakkuk 3:17-18. My wife Noël and I used this in our wedding ceremony to express our expectation that life would be hard, but that God would be our all-satisfying portion. "Though the fig tree should not blossom, nor fruit be on the vines, the produce of the olive fail and the fields yield no food, the flock be cut off from the fold and there be no herd in the stalls, yet I will rejoice in the LORD; I will take joy in the God of my salvation." In other words, when all the supports of human life and earthly happiness are taken away, God will be our delight, our joy. This experience is humanly impossible. No ordinary person can speak in truth like this. If God alone is enough to support joy when all else is lost, it is a miracle of grace.

The psalmists speak repeatedly of the joy, delight, and satisfaction that they have in God. "I will go to the altar of God, to God my *exceeding joy*" (Ps. 43:4). "Let those who *delight* in my righteousness shout for joy and be glad" (Ps. 35:27). "Great are the works of the LORD, studied by all who *delight* in them" (Ps. 111:2). "As for me, I shall behold your face in righteousness; when I awake, I shall *be satisfied* with your likeness" (Ps. 17:15).

In both Old and New Testaments we are commanded to rejoice or delight in the Lord. "Delight yourself in the LORD" (Ps. 37:4). "Rejoice in the Lord always; again I will say, rejoice" (Phil. 4:4). In the Old Testament, to be converted from worldliness to godliness was to discover the truth of Psalm 16:11: "You make known to me the path of life; in your presence there is fullness of joy; at your right hand are pleasures forevermore." In the New Testament, conversion meant discovering that Jesus was a treasure of such surpassing worth that joy would enable a new disciple to leave everything and follow him: "The kingdom of heaven is like treasure hidden in a field, which a man found and covered up. Then *in his joy* he goes and sells all that he has and buys that field" (Matt. 13:44).

What's the Difference between Desire and Delight?

Now let's bring these two emotions together. On the one hand, we have desiring, yearning, wanting, craving, longing, thirsting, etc., and on the other hand, we have joy, delight, pleasure, gladness, happiness, satisfaction, etc. What is the difference?

The first thought that comes to most of our minds (I tried this on my eight-year-old daughter) is that *delight* (with its synonyms) is what we experience when the thing we enjoy is present, not just future. But *desire* (with its synonyms) is what we experience when the thing we enjoy is not present but, we hope, coming to us in the future.

I think that's true, but oversimplified, for several reasons. One is that many desires are themselves pleasant. That is, the desire is itself a pleasure, not just a longing for a pleasure. Who could draw a line between the power of sexual desire and sexual pleasure? The desire is part of the satisfaction. We speak of climax not because that is the only pleasure, but precisely because it is not the only pleasure. All the desires leading to it and following after it are part of the one big pleasure.

Or who can draw a clear line between the excitement of desire that a child feels just before Daddy gets home and the pleasure the child feels as Daddy walks in the door? The desire is part of the pleasure of Daddy coming home and getting home and being home. So desire is inseparable from pleasure. It is part of it.

Another reason it's an oversimplification to say that in *pleasure* the thing enjoyed is present but in *desire* the thing enjoyed is not yet present is that desire would not exist if the thing enjoyed had not already been tasted. That's how the heart comes to feel something is desirable. Desire is awakened by tastes of pleasure. The taste may be ever so small. But if there is no taste at all of the desirability of something, then there will be no desire for it. In other words, desire is a form of the very pleasure that is anticipated with the arrival of the thing desired. It is, you might say, the pleasure itself experienced in the form of anticipation.

Are We on the Right Track?

There are pointers in the Bible that we are on the right track in these thoughts. For example, not only does the Bible say, "Rejoice in the Lord" (Phil. 3:1), it also says, "We rejoice in *hope* of the glory of

God" (Rom. 5:2). On the one hand, the object of our joy is the Lord, experienced here and now. "God's love has been poured into our hearts through the Holy Spirit who has been given to us" (Rom. 5:5). On the other hand, the object of our joy is future and not yet fully experienced. Nevertheless, even though the object of the joy is future, we hope for it—that is, we desire it with confidence—and this desire is joyful. "We *rejoice* in hope." The final joy of seeing the glory of God and being swallowed up in it has been tasted, and the desire for it is the very pleasure of that future enjoyment experienced now in the form of anticipation. This is what Paul means by the command, "Rejoice in hope" (Rom. 12:12).

Another evidence that we are on the right track in our understanding of desire and delight is found in the comparison between Psalm 1:2 and Psalm 19:10. Psalm 1:2 says of the man who is blessed, "His *delight* is in the law of the LORD, and on his law he meditates day and night." Psalm 19:10 says of the words of the Lord, "More to be *desired* are they than gold, even much fine gold; sweeter also than honey and drippings of the honeycomb." On the one hand, the Word of God is delighted in, and on the other, it is desired.

Yes, the Word of God is desired sometimes because it is not present and we would like to read it or hear it. But it is also true that when it is present and enjoyed, there is also in that very moment a desire for more of the Word and for a fuller understanding and enjoyment of the Word. And even when the Word is absent, the desire for it is also a form of delight in it. There is delight by memory and a delight by anticipation. So desire for and delight in God's Word are inseparable.

There Will Always Be More of God to Enjoy

For all these reasons, I will not try to build a wall between desire and delight, or between longing and pleasure. Sometimes I will speak of desiring God and sometimes of delighting in God. Sometimes I will speak of the inconsolable longing for God and sometimes the pleasures at his right hand. The difference between desire for God and delight in God is important mainly to make clear that finite creatures like us, who have a spiritual taste for the glory of God, will always want more of God than we presently experience—even in eternity. There will always be more of God to enjoy. Which means there will always be holy desire—forever.

In this age that is frustrating. We kick ourselves that our cravings for lesser things compete with God as the satisfaction of our souls. Rightly so. This is a godly grief. We do well to be convicted and penitent. We know that we have tasted pleasures at his right hand, and that our desires for them are pitifully small compared to their true worth. It is helpful at this point to be reminded that our desires—no matter how small—have been awakened by the spiritual taste we once had of the presence of God. They are an evidence that we have tasted. It is also helpful at this point to be reminded that our desires are only a tiny part of what is to come. The strength of our desire is not the measure of the strength of the final pleasure. That truth can rescue us from despair and keep us fighting in this fallen world for all the joy possible in God.

But the truth that the finite soul will always want more of God than it presently experiences will not be frustrating in the age to come. Then when we are perfected and have our resurrection bodies, the longings that remain will not be because sin is competing with God for our affections. Rather the reason will be that finite minds cannot receive the fullness of infinite greatness and glory. It must be given in (glorious but manageable) increments every day for eternity.

In the age to come, desire for more of God will never be experienced with impatience or ingratitude or frustration. All desire in the age to come will be the sweetest anticipation, rooted ever more deeply in the enlarging memories of joy and in the ever-gathering pleasures of gratitude. God will not take from us the pleasure of anticipated pleasures. He will heighten it. He will give us for all eternity the perfect intermingling of present pleasure and anticipation of future pleasure. Anticipation will be stripped of all frustration. Its ache will be a wholly pleasant ache.

God will be glorified both by the intensity of the present delight that we have in his beauty and by the intensity of the desires we have for more revelation of his fullness. The present pleasures will waken ever fresh desires, and the desires will signal ever greater future pleasures. Pleasures will be perfectly desired, and the desires will be perfectly pleasant.

What we experience here in this fallen age is a partial reflection of that. This is what we are moving toward. It is not yet here. We know that all too painfully. But our calling here is to fight for joy—ours and the joy of all peoples through Jesus Christ. The aim is that God's worth—his infinite desirability—be known and prized and praised in all the world. This is what we mean by God being glorified. He is most glorified in and through his people when we are most satisfied in him. The intensity of our pleasure and our desire bear witness of his worth to the world, especially when we are freed by this (present and hoped for) pleasure to leave the pleasures of this world for a life of sacrifice and love for others.

Neither Desire nor Delight Is Finally What We Want

It should be obvious from this, but may not be, that desire and delight have this in common: Neither is the Object desired or delighted in. God is. I make this obvious point because all of us from time to time speak loosely and say that the aim of our pursuit is *joy*. Or we say that we want to be happy. Those are not false or evil statements. A Christian means: I aim to pursue joy *in God* so that the infinitely valuable objective reality of the universe, God, will get all the glory possible from my life. "I want to be happy" may be Christian shorthand for "I want to know the One, and the only One, who is in himself all I have ever longed for in all my desires to be happy."

But the loose way of talking can be misleading. Both ways of saying it can be taken to mean: the object of our wants is ultimately a psychological experience of happiness without any regard to what makes us happy. In other words, they may mean: The final object of our pursuit is joy itself, rather than the beauty of what we find joy in. This is a very common mistake. Jonathan Edwards warned against it by observing that "there are many affections which do not arise from any light in the understanding. And when it is thus, it is a sure evidence that these affections are not spiritual, let them be ever so high."[3] Our goal is not high affections *per se*. Our goal is to see and savor "the light of the gospel of the glory of Christ, who is the image of God" (2 Cor. 4:4). The affections that arise from that light *are* spiritual. By this Christ-revealing light, we avoid the mistake of simply pursuing joy, not Christ.

C. S. Lewis devoted most of his autobiography, which he called *Surprised by Joy*, to exposing this error by narrating his own mistakes.

> You cannot hope and also think about hoping at the same moment; for in hope we look to hope's object and we interrupt this by (so to speak) turning round to look at the hope itself. . . . The surest means of disarming an anger or a lust was to turn your attention from the girl or the insult and start examining the passion itself. The surest way of spoiling a pleasure was to start examining your satisfaction. . . .
>
> I perceived (and this was the wonder of wonders) that . . . I had been equally wrong in supposing that I desired Joy itself. Joy itself, considered simply as an event in my own mind, turned out to be of no value at all. All the value lay in that of which Joy was the desiring. And that object, quite clearly, was no state of my own mind or body at all. . . . I asked if Joy itself was what I wanted; and, labeling it "aesthetic experience," had pretended I could answer Yes. But that answer too had broken down. Inexorably Joy proclaimed, "You want—I myself am your want of—something other, outside, not you nor any state of you."[4]

Why Then Make So Much of Fighting for Joy?

One might ask, in view of this danger, why I would lay so much stress on joy in the Christian life. Why not just talk about God, the object of joy, and leave the experiences to take care of themselves? There are three answers.

One is this: It is not John Piper who commands us to rejoice in the Lord; God does. God elevates this experience of the heart to the level of command, not I. And he does so with blood-earnestness. "Because you did not serve the LORD your God with joyfulness and gladness of heart, . . . you shall serve your enemies" (Deut. 28:47-48). "God threatens terrible things if we will not be happy."[5] The fight for joy is not a warfare I appointed. God did.

The second answer is that God is most glorified in us when we are most satisfied in him. Therefore, to make pretensions about honoring him more, while not calling people to the most radical, soul-freeing satisfaction in God alone, is self-contradictory. It won't happen. God is glorified in his people by the way we *experience* him, not merely by the way we think about him. Indeed the devil thinks more true thoughts about God in one day than a saint does in a lifetime, and God is not honored by it. The problem with the devil is not his theology, but his desires. Our chief end is to glorify God, the great Object. We do so most fully when we treasure him, desire him, delight in him so supremely that we let goods and kindred go and display his love to the poor and the lost.

The third reason we should make much of joy and the pursuit of joy in God is that people do not awaken to how desperate their condition is until they measure their hearts by Christian Hedonism—or whatever you may call it. I have found for thirty years that preaching and teaching about God's demand that we delight in him more than in anything else breaks and humbles people, and makes them desperate for true conversion and true Christianity. Oh, how easy it is to think we are what we ought to be when the emotions are made peripheral. Mere thoughts and mere deeds are manageable by the carnal religious mind. But the emotions—they are the weathercock of the heart. Nothing shows the direction of the deep winds of the soul like the demand for radical, sin-destroying, Christ-exalting joy in God.

But having made my defense, I say again: God and God alone is the final, ultimate goal of our quest. All that God is for us in Jesus is the Object of our quest for joy. When I speak of fighting for joy, I mean joy in God, not joy without reference to God. When I speak of longing for happiness, I mean happiness in all that God is for us in Jesus, not happiness as physical or psychological experience apart from God. Whether we are desiring or delighting, the end of the experience is God.

Fighting for that experience of God through Jesus Christ is what this book is about.

Always you renounce a lesser good for a greater; the opposite is what sin is. . . . The struggle to submit . . . is not a struggle to submit but a struggle to accept and with passion. I mean, possibly, with joy. Picture me with my ground teeth stalking joy—fully armed too as it's a highly dangerous quest.

FLANNERY O'CONNOR
The Habit of Being[1]

Not that we lord it over your faith, but we work with you for your joy.

2 CORINTHIANS 1:24

3

The Call to Fight
for Joy in God

*Taking God's Demand for Delight
Seriously*

Do these two things really go together? Fighting and joy? Fighting sounds so pressured and violent. Joy sounds more relaxed and peaceful. It just seems strange to talk about *fighting* for joy. You may as well talk about fighting to like hot fudge sundaes. Either you do or you don't, right? What's the fight? No, it's not that simple. Physical tastes like hot fudge versus caramel are morally neutral. It's not right or wrong to like the one over the other. But having a spiritual taste for the glory of Christ is not morally neutral. Not to have it is evil and deadly. Not to see and savor Christ is an insult to the beauty and worth of his character. Preferring anything above Christ is the very essence of sin. It must be fought.

The Essence of Evil

God defines evil this way when he says, "My people have committed two *evils*: they have forsaken me, the fountain of living waters, and hewed out cisterns for themselves, broken cisterns that can hold no water" (Jer. 2:13). God pictures himself as a mountain spring of clean, cool, life-giving water. The way to glorify a fountain like this is to enjoy the water, and praise the water, and keep coming back to the water, and point other people to the water, and get strength for love from the water, and never, never, never prefer any drink in the world over this water. That makes the spring look valuable. That is how we glorify God, the fountain of living water.

But in Jeremiah's day people tasted the fountain of God's grace and did not like it. So they gave their energies to finding better water, more satisfying water. Not only did God call this effort futile ("broken cisterns *that can hold no water*"), but he called it evil: "My people have committed two *evils*." They put God's perfections to the tongue of their souls and disliked what they tasted; then they turned and craved the suicidal cisterns of the world. That double insult to God is the essence of what evil is.

So preferring the pleasures of money or power or fame or sex over the "pleasures . . . at [God's] right hand" (Ps. 16:11) is not like preferring caramel to hot fudge. It is a great evil. Indeed it is the ultimate meaning of evil. Esteeming God less than anything is the essence of evil.

Heaven Hangs on Having the Taste of Joy in God

Therefore, it might not be so strange after all to think of *fighting* for this joy. Our eternal lives depend on it. A person who has no taste for the enjoyment of Christ will not go to heaven. "If anyone has no love for the Lord, let him be accursed" (1 Cor. 16:22). "Whoever loves father or mother more than me is not worthy of me, and whoever loves son or daughter more than me is not worthy of me" (Matt. 10:37). "Though you have not seen him, you love him. Though you do not now see him, you believe in him and rejoice with joy that is inexpressible and filled with glory" (1 Pet. 1:8). Loving Jesus, not just "deciding" for him or "being committed to him" or affirming all the right doctrines about him, is the mark of a true child of God. Jesus said, "If God were your Father, you would love me" (John 8:42).

Yes, I am assuming that loving Jesus includes the taste of joy in his personhood. I reject the notion that love for Christ is identical to mental or physical acts done in obedience to his Word. When Jesus said, "If you love me, you will keep my commandments" (John 14:15), he was describing the *effect* of love, not the essence of love. First there is love, then there is the effect—obedience. The obedience is not identical with love.

Jesus once described his coming like this: "The light has come into the world, and people loved the darkness rather than the light because their deeds were evil" (John 3:19). Here the issue of salvation is loving or hating the light. Love darkness, or love light. That's the crisis of the soul. But what is love for darkness? It's preferring darkness, liking darkness, wanting darkness, running to darkness, being glad with darkness. But all of that is what Jesus demands for himself: "Prefer my light, like my fellowship, want my wisdom, run to my refuge, be glad in my grace. Above all, delight in me as a Person." Look around on all that the world can give; then say with the apostle Paul, "My desire is to depart and be with Christ, for that is far better" (Phil. 1:23). That is what it means to love Christ. And to have no love for him is to be accursed.

Surely, then, this is worth fighting for. It may feel strange at first, but when we see what is at stake, no battle will seem more important. Loving Christ involves delight in his Person. Without this love no one goes to heaven. Therefore there is no more important struggle in the universe than the struggle to see and savor Christ above all things—the struggle for joy.

Not Only Love, but Faith Too Includes the Taste for Joy in God

To make this fight feel even more imperative I will go further and say that not only does *love* to Christ include the taste of joy in his personhood; so too does *faith* in Christ. I do not mean that faith and joy are equivalent or identical. Faith in Christ involves more than delighting in Christ. We trust him—bank on him—to be our righteousness and the sacrifice for our sins, and the propitiator of God's wrath, and our mediator with the Father. Faith depends on Christ alone for all that and more. But it does not involve less than the taste of delight in Christ himself.

Within saving faith there is the necessary element of a pleasing taste for the glory of Christ. Paul describes what happens in conversion as "seeing the light of the gospel of the glory of Christ, who is the image of God" (2 Cor. 4:4). This is what Satan desperately wants to hide from the eyes of our hearts—a spiritual sight of Christ's glory in the gospel. Not just facts, but the beauty of the facts. The saving response to this spiritual apprehension of glory in the cross of Christ must include a pleasing sense of Christ's beauty. It is inconceivable that faith would find Christ distasteful. It is inconceivable that the regenerate heart could look upon the glory of Christ in the gospel with indifferent or negative affections.

When Jesus says, "I am the bread of life; . . . whoever *believes* in me shall never thirst" (John 6:35), he is saying that "believing" in him includes a taste for the living water of his all-satisfying glory, so that the believing heart will never thirst again. That is, faith, having tasted the all-satisfying sweetness of the living Christ, will never forsake him in preference for the broken cisterns of the world. There may be temporary strayings and backslidings. There may be great soul-conflict. But once the soul has truly tasted the water of life and the bread of heaven, it will never finally forsake the Lord.

Believing means trusting Jesus not only as our all-sovereign Lord and all-sufficient Savior, but also as our all-surpassing Treasure. Trusting in Christ as our Treasure means seeing and savoring him as a Treasure. Christ is not our Treasure if we do not treasure him. And treasuring something means being glad to have it. Therefore saving faith involves no less than being glad to have Jesus himself for who he is.

It could not be otherwise, if the aim of God is to glorify his Son. If Christ is followed only because his gifts are great and his threats are terrible, he is not glorified by his followers. A defective lord can offer great gifts and terrible threats. And a person may want the gifts, fear the threats, and follow a lord whom they despise or pity or find boring or embarrassing, in order to have the gifts and avoid the threats. If Christ is to be glorified in his people, their following must be rooted not mainly in his promised gifts or threatened punishments, but in his glorious Person. Oh, it is true that "Great are the works of the LORD, studied by all who delight in them" (Ps. 111:2). I do not minimize the joy of seeing the works of the Lord. But his works are great because the Lord is great. And they will become idols of delight unless they point us to the Lord himself as our highest delight. The faith that honors Christ is the faith that sees and savors his glory in all his works, especially the gospel.

The Call to Fight for This

This means that the biblical passages that speak of the fight of faith apply to the fight for joy. In his first letter to Timothy Paul tells him, "Fight the good fight of the faith. Take hold of the eternal life to which you were called" (6:12). Faith is something that must be fought for, if it is to thrive and survive. This is how we take hold on eternal life—by fighting to maintain faith, with its joy in Christ. Satan seeks more than anything to destroy our faith. You can hear this in 1 Thessalonians 3:5, where Paul says, "When I could bear it no longer, I sent to learn about your *faith*, for fear that somehow *the tempter* had tempted you and our labor would be in vain." In other words, their *faith* is what Satan targets. If faith is going to endure, with its joy in God, we must fight.

What We Have Lost in the Western Church

One of the reasons that in the Western church today our joy is so fragile and thin is that this truth is so little understood—the truth, namely, that eternal life is laid hold of only by a persevering fight for the joy of faith. Joy will not be rugged and durable and deep through suffering where there is not resolve to fight for it. But today, by and large, there is a devil-may-care, cavalier, superficial attitude toward the ongoing, daily intensity of personal joy in Christ, because people do not believe that their eternal life depends on it.

The last two hundred years have seen an almost incredible devaluation of the fight for joy. We have moved a hundred miles from *The Pilgrim's Progress* where Christian labors and struggles and fights all his life "for the joy that was set before him" (Heb. 12:2) in the Celestial City. Oh, how different is the biblical view of the Christian life than the one prevalent in the Western church. It is an earnest warfare from beginning to end, and the war is to defend and strengthen the fruit-bearing fields of joy in God.

James 1:12 says, "Blessed is the man who remains steadfast under trial, for when he has stood the test he will receive the crown of life, which God has promised to those who love him." The person who will receive the crown of eternal life is the person who successfully endures trial—that is, the person who fights for joy in the pain of loss and gets the victory over the unbelief of anger and bitterness and discouragement.

Revelation 2:10 says to those who are being thrown in prison for their faith, "Be faithful unto death, and I will give you the crown of life." This is very different from the mood of Western Christianity. Here something infinite and eternal hangs on whether these Christians hold fast to the joy of faith while in prison. But today worship services, Bible studies, prayer meetings, and fellowship gatherings in many churches do not have a spirit of earnestness and intensity and fervor and depth because people do not really believe that anything significant is at stake in the fight for joy—least of all their eternal life. The all-important priority seems to be cheerfulness, even jollity.

Oh, that the church would waken to the warfare we are in and feel the urgency of the fight for joy. This is how we hold fast to eternal life. "Fight the good fight of the faith. Take hold of the eternal life" (1 Tim. 6:12). Faith has in it the taste of joy in the glory of Christ. Therefore the good fight of faith is the fight for joy.

A Good Fight

It will help us fight for joy if we realize why Paul calls it a *good* fight. First, it is a good fight because the enemy of our joy is evil. The enemy is unbelief, and the satanic forces behind it, and the sins that come from it. When you set yourself to combat the forces that try to make you delight in yourself or your accomplishments or your possessions more than in God, you oppose a very evil enemy. Therefore it is a good fight.

Second, it is a good fight because we are not left to our own strength in the fight. If we were, as Martin Luther says, "Our striving would be losing." In other words, when a child of God fights for joy in God, God himself is the one behind that struggle, giving the will and the power to defeat the enemy of joy (Phil. 2:12-13). We are not left to ourselves to sustain the joy of faith. God fights for us and in us. Therefore the fight of faith is a good fight.

Third, it is a good fight because it is not a struggle to carry a burden, but a struggle to let a burden be carried for us. The life of joy in God is not a burdened life. It is an unburdened life. The fight for joy is the struggle to trust God with the burdens of life. It's a fight for freedom from worry. It's a fight for hope and peace and joy, which are all threatened by unbelief and doubt about God's promises. And since freedom and hope and peace and joy are good, the fight to preserve them is a good fight.

Fourth, the fight of faith is good because, unlike most fights, it does not involve self-exaltation but self-humbling. Most fighting is not good because it is a proud attempt to prove our own strength at someone else's expense. But the fight for joy is just the opposite. It's a way of saying that we are weak and desperately need the mercy of God. By nature we do not like to admit our helplessness. We do not like to say, "Apart from Christ I can do nothing—I cannot even rejoice" (see John 15:5). But the very essence of faith is the admission of our sinful helplessness in the quest for eternal joy, and looking away from ourselves to God through Christ for the help and the joy that are in him alone. This kind of humility is good. Therefore the fight for joy is a good fight.

Fifth, the fight for joy is good because by it God is greatly glorified. When we devote ourselves to resist the idolatrous power of every craving, every desire, every pleasure that is not God, then God is exalted as the superior Treasure of our lives. Fighting against all alien joy shows that we know the infinite worth of God. Therefore the fight for joy is a good fight.

At the end of his life Paul said, "I have *fought the good fight*, I have finished the race, I have kept the faith" (2 Tim. 4:7). Keeping the faith for a lifetime is the result of fighting the good fight for a lifetime. And if faith includes at least the taste of joy in the glory of Christ, then this lifelong fight is a fight for joy—a very good fight.

Paul's Ministry: Working for Our Joy

It's no surprise, then, that Paul conceived of his entire ministry as helping people fight for joy. He says as much in two places. In 2 Corinthians 1:24 he says, "Not that we lord it over your faith, but we work with you for your joy." Notice two things. One is how joy and faith are almost interchangeable: "We don't lord it over your *faith*; we work with you for your *joy*." You would have expected him to say, "We work with you for your *faith*." But he says he works for their *joy*. That is what I am trying to do in this book. That is what I try to do every Sunday in the pulpit. That is what we should do for each other every day (Heb. 3:12-13). Maintaining joy in God takes "work"; that is, it's a fight against every impulse for alien joys and every obstacle in the way to seeing and savoring Christ.

The other place where Paul speaks of his calling in this way is

Philippians 1:25. He is wrestling with two competing desires: to depart and be with Christ, or to stay and minister to the churches. He concludes, "I know that I will remain and continue with you all, for your progress and *joy in the faith*." In other words, he expresses the summary of his ministry on earth as working to advance their joy! It is remarkable that Paul would sum up his entire ministry as working for our joy. So we should not draw back at the summons to work and fight for joy in God.

Back to the Tension between Fighting and Rejoicing

Now back to the question we began with: Do fighting and joy go together? I've tried to address one issue, namely, that the stakes are so high we should not be surprised that we must fight. Our souls hang in the balance. So I hope it sounds more fitting and crucial now when the summons comes: Take up arms and fight for joy in God. A manual in that war is what this book aims to be.

But another thing that makes fighting and joy seem incompatible is that joy is spontaneous and fighting is planned. Joy happens in the heart spontaneously. You don't get up in the morning feeling blue and then immediately experience joy simply because you decide to. If you are tired when you wake up, you can force yourself to throw your legs out of bed. But if you are gloomy and discouraged when you wake up, you cannot just start feeling happy. Joy is not in the power of the will the way physical motion is.

So how does the intentionality of the fight relate to the spontaneity of the joy? This is virtually the same question that I posed in the previous chapter and promised to try to answer here: How does the fact that joy is a free gift of God relate to our responsibility to have it?[2] One of the reasons we experience joy in God as spontaneous is that it's a gift. And one of the reasons we must fight for it is that we are responsible to have it. So the questions are virtually the same: How do we fight for something that is spontaneous? And, what can we do to obtain a totally free gift?

This entire book is meant as an answer to that question, but here I will simply offer a broad summary answer in three parts.

The Fight Itself Is a Gift

First, we embrace the truth that not only our joy in God, but also the fight for joy itself is a gift of God. In other words, God works in us to enable us to fight. Embracing this truth prevents us from thinking that the joy we fight for is ultimately our achievement. Joy remains a gift and continues to be spontaneous, even though we ourselves are engaged in its cause.

The evidence for this point is found in numerous biblical texts. For example, in 1 Corinthians 15:10 Paul says, "By the grace of God I am what I am, and his grace toward me was not in vain. On the contrary, I worked harder than any of them, though it was not I, but the grace of God that is with me." Paul worked hard. He did not say that God's grace made his work unnecessary. He said God's grace made his work possible. He worked, but "it was not I, but the grace of God that is with me." So the fight for joy is our fight, and we are responsible to do it. But when we have fought for joy with all our might, we say with the apostle Paul, "It was not I, but the grace of God that was with me." It was a gift.

Philippians 2:12-13 describes how Christian work is enabled by the work of God within us. "Work out your own salvation with fear and trembling, for it is God who works in you, both to will and to work for his good pleasure." God's work in us does not eliminate our work; it enables it. We work *because* he is the one at work in us. Therefore, the fight for joy is possible because God is fighting for us and through us. All our efforts are owing to his deeper work in and through our willing and working. This is why I say our fight for joy is a gift of God.

The same thing could be shown from Hebrews 13:20-21: "Now may the God of peace who brought again from the dead our Lord Jesus, the great shepherd of the sheep, by the blood of the eternal covenant, equip you with everything good that you may do his will, working in us that which is pleasing in his sight, through Jesus Christ, to whom be glory forever and ever. Amen." God works in us that which is pleasing in his sight. The fight for joy is owing to his working in us. When all is said and done, Paul says, "I will not venture to speak of anything except what Christ has accomplished through me" (Rom. 15:18). In this way the gift of joy remains a gift and remains spontaneous, even though we fight for it. All our fighting is a work of God, and when a work of God brings about joy in God, the joy is manifestly a gift.

We Fight to Put Ourselves in the God-Ordained Path of Blessing

Second, we understand that our fight for joy does not coerce God to give the gift of joy, but puts us in the path where he has ordained the blessing to come. I say it carefully, lest I sound as though joy can be demanded from the Almighty. It is a fruit of the Spirit that grows on the tree of faith (Gal. 5:22); it is not a wage God must pay for our work or for our fight. That God ordinarily gives joy when we walk in certain paths is no guarantee that he will do so according to our timetable.

We are like farmers. They plow the field and plant the seed and cut away weeds and scare away crows, but they do not make the crop grow. God does. He sends rain and sunshine and brings to maturity the hidden life of the seed. We have our part. But it is not coercive or controlling. And there will be times when the crops fail. Even then God has his ways of feeding the farmer and bringing him through a lean season.

We must learn to wait for the Lord. King David gave us an example of this in Psalm 40. "I waited patiently for the LORD; he inclined to me and heard my cry. He drew me up from the pit of destruction, out of the miry bog, and set my feet upon a rock, making my steps secure. He put a new song in my mouth, a song of praise to our God" (vv. 1-3). Here is a man after God's own heart (1 Sam. 13:14), who spent time in "the pit of destruction" and in "the miry bog"—where there was no song in his mouth. How long was he there? We are not told. What matters is what he did there. He waited for the Lord. He could not make the Lord come. He *could* wait and hope and trust that he would come. And he did come. He put David's feet on a rock and put a new song in his mouth.

Georg Neumark (1621-1681), the German hymn-writer, expressed this humble position in his great hymn, "If Thou But Suffer God to Guide Thee":

> God knows the time for joy and truly
> Will send it when he sees it meet
> When He has tried and purged thee duly

And found thee free from all deceit.
He comes to thee all unaware
And makes thee own His loving care.[3]

Two hundred years later Karolina Wilhelmina Sandell-Berg (1832-1903), known as the Fanny Crosby of Sweden because of the 650 hymns that she wrote, expressed the same humility under the mighty hand of God. In one of her best-known hymns, "Day by Day," she wrote:

He Whose heart is kind beyond all measure
Gives unto each day what He deems best—
Lovingly, its part of pain and pleasure,
Mingling toil with peace and rest.[4]

In obedience to God's Word we should fight to walk in the paths where he has promised his blessings. But when and how they come is God's to decide, not ours. If they delay, we trust the wisdom of our Father's timing, and we wait. In this way joy remains a gift, while we work patiently in the field of obedience and fight against the weeds and the crows and the rodents. Here is where joy will come. Here is where Christ will reveal himself (John 14:21). But that revelation and that joy will come when and how Christ chooses. It will be a gift.

We Fight to See

Third, we understand that the fight for joy is first and always a fight to see. Seeing the glory of Jesus Christ in the gospel awakens joy. And joy in Christ magnifies his worth. That is why Satan aims chiefly at blinding us from seeing Christ for who he is. He hates to see Christ honored. And Christ is mightily honored when the sight of his glory gives rise to the kind of gladness that cuts the nerve of sin and causes radical sacrifice in the cause of the gospel.

Paul tells us about this design of Satan in 2 Corinthians 4:4: "The god of this world has blinded the minds of the unbelievers, to keep them from *seeing the light of the gospel of the glory of Christ*, who is the image of God." If joy in Christ, with all the risk-taking love that flows from it, is to be stopped, then seeing the glory of Christ must be blocked. That is Satan's chief employment.

When we understand that seeing Christ is what leads to enjoying Christ, and that therefore the fight for joy is mainly a fight to see, we grasp how the fight does not undermine the fact that joy is a gift and a spontaneous experience. The joy that comes from seeing beauty is spontaneous no matter how hard one fought to see. The fighting does not cause the joy. Seeing causes the joy. And it does so freely. There is no coercion. No one stands before a beautiful sunrise and says, "Now I worked hard to get up this early; you owe me happiness by your bright colors." No. We stand there, and in humility we receive. And if the joy comes, it is a gift.

The essence of the Christian life is learning to fight for joy in a way that does not replace grace. We must be able to say at the end of our lives, "I have fought the good fight." But we must also say, "It was not I, but the grace of God that is with me." I have pursued Christ as my joy with all my might. But it was a might that he mightily imparted. We must fight for joy in such a way that we prove Jesus true when he said, "My yoke is easy, and my burden is light" (Matt. 11:30). We will succeed in this battle when we can say with Paul in Colossians 1:29 that we are "struggling with all his energy that he powerfully works within me." We struggle to bear the burden and carry the yoke. But he gives the power. All burdens are light to him. All yokes are easy to him. This too is something glorious to see in him. This too makes us glad in him. Trust him for this. Our joy in him will be the greater because we see him as the one who gives both the joy and the strength to fight for it.

Joy is never in our power and pleasure often is.
C. S. LEWIS
Surprised by Joy[1]

The fruit of the Spirit is . . . joy.
GALATIANS 5:22

For who sees anything different in you? What do you have that you did not receive? If then you received it, why do you boast as if you did not receive it?
1 CORINTHIANS 4:7

4

Joy in God
Is a Gift of God

*Doing Ourselves
What Must Be Done for Us*

The title of this chapter is good news for the hopeless and bad news for the self-reliant. Or to put it another way: it is liberating and devastating. It liberates from despair the person who knows that he cannot make himself desire what he does not desire. And it devastates the presumption of the person who thought that all his duties were in his own power.

A Half-Right Denial

One of the reasons people deny that delighting in God is essential is that they know intuitively that this delight is beyond their control, and they feel that something beyond their control cannot be required. They are half right. In the end, joy in God is a free gift, not a self-wrought human accomplishment. That's right. But it is not biblical to say that the only virtues God can require of me are the ones that I am good enough to perform. If I am so bad that I can't delight in what is good, that is no reason God can't command me to love the good. If I am so corrupt that I can't enjoy what is infinitely beautiful, that does not make me less guilty for disobeying the command to delight in God (Ps. 37:4). It makes me more guilty.

The Duty to Delight in God

The fact that joy in God is a duty is plain from the straightforward biblical commands to do it. "Rejoice in the Lord always; again I will say,
rejoice" (Phil. 4:4; see also Ps. 32:11; 37:4; 97:12; 100:1; Joel 2:23).
Matthew Henry, writing in the seventeenth century, speaks on behalf
of centuries of sober reflection on these words:

> *Rejoice in the Lord always, and again I say Rejoice* (v. 4). All our joy
> must terminate in God; and our thoughts of God must be delight-
> ful thoughts. *Delight Thyself in the Lord* (Ps. 37:4). . . . Observe,
> It is our duty and privilege to rejoice in God, and to rejoice in him
> always; at all times, in all conditions; even when we suffer for him,
> or are afflicted by him. We must not think the worse of him or of his
> ways for the hardships we meet with in his service. There is enough
> in God to furnish us with matter of joy in the worst circumstance on
> earth. . . . Joy in God is a duty of great consequence in the Christian
> life; and Christians need to be again and again called to it.[2]

Since joy in God is a duty, some say it can't be a gift. But consider
now what the Bible says about this. Then we will close this chapter by
asking why it matters.

We Don't Just Do Sins, We Are Sinners

Among those who believe the Bible to be the Word of God, it is a commonplace to say that "all have sinned and fall short of the glory of God"
(Rom. 3:23). That is a profound and all-important truth. But it's not the
whole story. The problem is not that we have all done *acts* that are sinful, but that we *are* sinful. N. P. Williams put it like this: "The ordinary
man may feel ashamed of doing wrong: but the saint, endowed with a
superior refinement of moral sensibility, and keener powers of introspection, is ashamed of being the kind of man who is liable to do wrong."[3]
Sin is not just something we do; it is a power deeply rooted in our nature.
When we are converted to Christ, the Holy Spirit is given to us, and by
his power we begin to overcome our fallen, sinful nature.

But by nature we are rebellious, disobedient, and hardened against
God. Thus the psalmist cries out, "Enter not into judgment with your
servant, for *no one living is righteous before you*" (Ps. 143:2). The

prophet Jeremiah bemoans the truth that "the heart is deceitful above all things, and desperately sick; who can understand it?" (Jer. 17:9). King David traced this condition back to his birth: "Behold, I was brought forth in iniquity, and in sin did my mother conceive me" (Ps. 51:5). This inborn corruption is so severe that Paul says, "I know that nothing good dwells in me, that is, in my flesh" (Rom. 7:18).

What Paul means by "flesh" is not his skin, but his natural self apart from the redemption of Christ and apart from the transforming work of the Holy Spirit. Another way Paul refers to the "flesh" is by calling it simply the "natural person"—that is, the person we are by nature, without Christ. So he says, for example, in 1 Corinthians 2:14, "The *natural person* does not accept the things of the Spirit of God, for they are folly to him, and he is not able to understand them because they are spiritually discerned." In other words, "the natural person," or "the flesh," is so resistant to spiritual reality that he can't understand or accept the things of God. This person will not delight in God. The natural heart is so corrupt in its desires that it cannot see or savor the beauty of Christ.

That's what Paul means when he says in Romans 8:7-8 that the mind of the flesh "is hostile to God, for it does not submit to God's law; indeed, it cannot. Those who are in the flesh cannot please God." Notice the word *cannot*. It's used twice. The natural person, the person defined by flesh, but not yet changed by Christ, is so hostile in mind to God's glorious authority (not submitting to his law) that he cannot delight in God or rejoice in his ways. He can do many religious and moral things, but his heart is far from God (Matt. 15:8), and he cannot make himself stop seeing the greatness and authority of God as undesirable.

How Then Are We Dead?

It is not surprising then to hear Paul describe us, in this fallen, natural, fleshly condition as "dead." That's what he says in Ephesians 2:4-5: "But God, being rich in mercy, because of his great love with which he loved us, *even when we were dead* in our trespasses, made us alive together with Christ—by grace you have been saved." The deepest reason why we cannot rejoice in the Lord is that by nature we are dead. That is, we have no spiritual sensitivity to the truth and beauty of the gospel of Christ. We are like the blind in the art gallery of heaven. Our deadness is not the deadness of the body. It's not even the deadness of the intellect or the will. It is the deadness of the spiritual ability to see reality for what it is.

Paul describes our deadness to divine beauty with phrases like "futility of mind" and "darkened in understanding" and "ignorance that is in us." And he traces it back to "hardness of heart." You see this in Ephesians 4:17-18: "You must no longer walk as the Gentiles do, in the *futility* of their minds. They are *darkened* in their understanding, alienated from the life of God because of the *ignorance* that is in them, due to their *hardness* of heart." Notice that hardness is deeper than ignorance. Ignorance is rooted in hardness, not the other way around. Therefore we are not excused. The problem with our ignorance of God's beauty is not innocent unawareness, but culpable hardness. Our hardness is our deadness, and our deadness makes us unable to submit to the command to love the Lord with all our hearts.

Because of this fallen, sinful, hardened, rebellious, futile, dead condition of our hearts, joy in God is impossible. Not impossible in a way that makes us less guilty, but more guilty. When the rich young ruler walked away from Jesus because he delighted more in his riches than in following Christ, Jesus said, "It is easier for a camel to go through the eye of a needle than for a rich person to enter the kingdom of God" (Matt. 19:24). The disciples were astonished at this. They knew that a camel *cannot* go through the eye of a needle. That's true. And humans cannot make themselves delight in Christ more than money. So Jesus answered, "With man this is impossible, but with God all things are possible" (v. 26).

Coming to Jesus for Joy Is a Gift of God

This was Jesus' way of saying that joy in God is a gift. Preferring Jesus to money is a gift of God. We can't produce it on our own. It must be given to us. When Jesus is presented to us as the most desirable Person, Lord, Savior, and Friend in the universe, we will not come to him on our own. Jesus said, "No one can come to me unless the Father who sent me draws him. . . . No one can come to me unless it is granted him by the Father" (John 6:44, 65). Coming to Jesus as the Treasure and Pleasure of our lives is "granted . . . by the Father" or it doesn't happen. We are too hard and rebellious in ourselves even to *see* Jesus as attractive, let alone leave all and come to him as our all-satisfying Joy.

Jesus said it another way: "That which is born of the flesh is flesh, and that which is born of the Spirit is spirit. Do not marvel that I said to you, 'You must be born again'" (John 3:6-7). Until we are born again by the Spirit of God, all we are is "flesh"—natural people with no spiritual life, no living taste buds in the soul for the sweetness of Christ. How then are we made alive? The next thing out of Jesus' mouth is, "The wind blows where it wishes, and you hear its sound, but you do not know where it comes from or where it goes. So it is with everyone who is born of the Spirit" (v. 8). The point is that the Spirit is free. He blows where he wills. We don't control him. He controls us. His life-giving work is pure gift. When you see Jesus as your Treasure, the Spirit has blown through your heart. Your joy in Jesus is a gift.

Is Repentance Too a Gift?

Someone may say, "This sounds like repentance. But isn't repentance something we do? Are you saying repentance also is a gift?" That's a good question. The transformation we've described is indeed repentance. Repentance refers to the experience of a changed mind. Once the mind was hostile to God, but now the mind is in love with God. Once the crucifixion of Christ seemed foolish, but now it is precious to us. It's the wisdom and power of God (1 Cor. 1:23-24). Once the mind trusted in human ability to achieve happiness and security, but now the mind despairs of itself and looks to Christ for hope and joy. Christ—and all that God is for us in him—has become our happiness and our security.

Yes, that is repentance. And, yes, repentance is a gift. We do not make ourselves into Christ-adoring people. We do not muster enough human wisdom or strength or willpower to deliver ourselves from the captivity of Satan's deceits. No, that is all a precious gift of God. Oh, he uses human means to bring it about. Otherwise I would not be writing this book. But in the end, no human means make the miracle of repentance happen. You can see both the means and the miracle in 2 Timothy 2:24-26: "The Lord's servant must not be quarrelsome but kind to everyone, able to teach, patiently enduring evil, correcting his opponents with gentleness. [That's the means. Now the miracle.] God may perhaps *grant them repentance* leading to a knowledge of the truth, and they may escape from the snare of the devil, after being captured by him to do his will." We teach and we love, but God grants repentance.

I pray that this book will be used by God as one of his many means to "grant . . . repentance." But in the end, it will be God, and not this book, or any book, that delivers a person from the captivity of the devil's deceit and opens one's eyes to see the superior worth of Jesus Christ. Then, when God grants repentance, he will prize Christ above all treasures and savor him above all pleasures. That is a gift. I pray for every reader who needs it: *Lord, grant them repentance.*

The Central Mystery of the Christian Life

But the question was asked above, "Isn't repentance something we do? If it's a gift of God, how do we do it?" Yes, repentance is something we do. After Peter preached a convicting message at Pentecost, the crowd cried, "Brothers, what shall we *do*?" To this Peter answered, "Repent" (Acts 2:37-38). He said more. But that's the point at issue here. Repentance is a command that we are responsible to obey.

Here we have arrived at the central mystery of living the Christian life. Christ has died for our sins and risen from the dead. Because of his blood and righteousness we are forgiven and counted righteous by God in Christ (2 Cor. 5:21; Phil. 3:9; Rom. 5:19). Therefore, Christ has become the Yes to all God's promises (2 Cor. 1:20). Everything promised by the prophets for the new covenant has been purchased for us infallibly by Christ. These new-covenant promises include, "The LORD your God will circumcise your heart . . . so that you will love the LORD your God with all your heart" (Deut. 30:6); and, "I will put my law within them . . . on their hearts" (Jer. 31:33); and, "I will remove the heart of stone from their flesh and give them a heart of flesh" (Ezek.11:19); and, "I will put my Spirit within you, and cause you to walk in my statutes" (Ezek. 36:27).

All of these new-covenant promises have been secured for us by Christ who said at the Last Supper, "This cup that is poured out for you is *the new covenant in my blood*" (Luke 22:20). The blood of Christ obtained for us all the promises of the new covenant. But look again at these promises. What distinguishes them from the old covenant is that they are promises for *enablement*. They are promises that God will do for us what we cannot do for ourselves. We need a new heart to delight in God. We need the Spirit of God whose fruit is joy in God. We need to have the law written on our heart, not just written on stone, so that when it says, "Love the LORD with all your heart," the Word itself produces the reality within us. In other words, we need the gift of joy in God. Left to ourselves, we will not produce it. That's what Christ bought for us when he died and shed the blood of the new covenant. He bought for us the gift of joy in God.

The Other Half of the Mystery

That is half the mystery of the Christian life—the most crucial half. The other half is that we are commanded to do what we cannot do. And we must do it or perish. Our inability does not remove our guilt—it deepens it. We are so bad that we cannot love God. We cannot delight in God above all things. We cannot treasure Christ above money. Our entrenched badness does not make it wrong for God to command us to be good. We ought to delight in God above all things. Therefore it is right for God to command us to delight in God above all things. And if we ever do delight in God, it will be because we have obeyed this command.

That is the mystery: we must obey the command to rejoice in the Lord, and we cannot, because of our willful and culpable corruption. Therefore obedience, when it happens, is a gift. The heretic Pelagius in the fourth century rejected this truth and was shocked and angered when he saw the way St. Augustine prayed in his *Confessions*. Augustine prayed, "Give me the grace [O Lord] to do as you command, and command me to do what you will! . . . O holy God . . . when your commands are obeyed, it is from you that we receive the power to obey them."[4]

The Christian Life Is All of Grace

That is a biblical prayer, and we will see many like it in the chapters to come (e.g., Ps. 51:12; 90:14; Rom. 15:13). It corresponds to the mystery of the Christian life. We must delight in God. And only God can change our hearts so that we delight in God. We are utterly thrown back on God. The Christian life is all of grace. "From him and through him and to him are all things. To him be glory forever" (Rom. 11:36).

In the next chapter I will talk about the kind of willing and doing involved in obeying the command to rejoice, when this rejoicing itself is a gift. We do not stop and become passive when we hear that joy is a gift. We act. How and why we act is the question we will take up in the next chapter. But first I promised that we would ask why the truth of this chapter matters.

Why Does Believing This Matter?

The first reason is that truth matters, and we should believe and embrace it whether we can see how it benefits us or not. This is what the Bible says about us and about joy in God. We can't produce it; God must give it. That is true, and we should believe and love the truth.

Second, when we believe this truth, our joy in God is multiplied because it is compounded with gratitude. In all our joy we are thankful to God, the Giver, that we delight in God.

Third, when we believe this truth, we will seek our joy from God with greater urgency than if we thought it was in our power. This truth sets us to praying as never before.

Fourth, believing this truth will prevent our strategies in the fight for joy from degenerating into technique and legalism. Technique cannot be paramount because God is sovereign. There are things we must do in the battle for joy. But if joy is a gift, it can never be earned. So legalism that tries to earn things from God is excluded. Not only that, but knowing that joy is ultimately a gift, and not a mere human achievement, also protects us from elevating technique and willpower too highly. Our strategies must be humble and dependent, followed by "May the LORD do what seems good to him" (2 Sam. 10:12). Our strategies to fight for joy are simply means of God's grace. And means of grace are always modest.

The Bible illustrates the modesty of means in numerous ways. "The horse is made ready for the day of battle, but the victory belongs to the LORD" (Prov. 21:31). "Unless the LORD builds the house, those who build it labor in vain. Unless the LORD watches over the city, the watchman stays awake in vain" (Ps. 127:1). "Many are the plans in the mind of a man, but it is the purpose of the LORD that will stand" (Prov. 19:21). If joy is a gift from God, we will use all his appointed means, but we will not trust in means, but in God.

Fifth, believing that joy in God is a gift of God will give all the glory to God. This is the goal of the Christian life—to live in a way that will show God to be most wonderful. The apostle Peter gives a principle in 1 Peter 4:11 for how to do that. He says, "Whoever serves, [let him serve] as one who serves by the strength that God supplies—in order that in everything God may be glorified through Jesus Christ." The strength to serve is a gift. God supplies it. When we believe that and lean on it consciously, we show God to be the glorious giver of the strength. The giver gets the glory.

We may paraphrase like this: "Let him who rejoices in the Lord, rejoice in the joy that God supplies, so that in everything—including our joy—God may be glorified through Jesus Christ." Therefore, believing that joy in God is a gift from God is essential in our calling to live for the glory of God. It shapes all our other strategies. It makes them humble. It makes them into acts of faith. In everything we do in our quest for joy we are praying and trusting the grace of God for a gift. May this truth liberate the despairing soul and humble the proud.

Man's proper happiness consists in the enjoyment of God; but it is not possible that man should enjoy God with only those things in him which he receives by the first birth. So that there is this necessity of man's being born again.

JONATHAN EDWARDS
"Born Again"
The Works of Jonathan Edwards[1]

The god of this world has blinded the minds of the unbelievers, to keep them from seeing the light of the gospel of the glory of Christ, who is the image of God.

2 CORINTHIANS 4:4

Oh, taste and see that the LORD is good!

PSALM 34:8

5

The Fight for Joy
Is a Fight to See

*Valuing God through the Eyes of the Heart
and the Ears of the Head*

There is more than one kind of seeing. Otherwise Jesus would not have said, "Seeing they do not see" (Matt. 13:13). It is possible to see in one way while not seeing in another way. The difference the Bible describes is that we have two kinds of eyes—eyes of the heart and eyes of the head. The apostle Paul prayed that you would have "the eyes of your hearts enlightened, that you may know what is the hope to which he has called you, what are the riches of his glorious inheritance in the saints" (Eph. 1:17-18). So there is such a thing as eyes of the heart. And there is a kind of knowing or seeing that comes through these eyes that is different from the seeing that comes through the eyes of the head.

Other Scriptures also link the heart and its eyes. Moses lamented that "to this day the Lord has not given you a *heart* to understand or *eyes* to see" (Deut. 29:4). They could still see with their physical eyes. God had not struck the whole nation blind. But they could not see with the eyes of their hearts. Seeing they did not see. So it was in the days of Ezekiel: "Son of man, you dwell in the midst of a rebellious house, who have eyes to see, but see not" (Ezek. 12:2). And Jeremiah too grieved over this spiritual blindness: "O foolish and senseless people, who have eyes, but see not" (Jer. 5:21).

Blind Like the Things We Make and Trust

The psalmist described the connection between this inner blindness and idolatry. "The idols of the nations are . . . the work of human hands. They have . . . eyes, but do not see. . . . Those who make them become like them, so do all who trust in them!" (Ps. 135:15-18). Make and trust a blind idol, and you become blind. Apply that principle to the modern world, and think of the idols of our own day. What do we make and what do we trust? Things. Toys. Technology. And so our hearts and our affections are formed by these things. They compress the void in our heart into shapes like toys. The result is that we are easily moved and excited by things— computers, cars, appliances, entertainment media. They seem to fit the shapes in our hearts. They feel good in the tiny spaces they have made. But in this readiness to receive pleasure from things, we are ill-shaped for Christ. He seems unreal, unattractive. The eyes of our hearts grow dull.

Paul said the same thing about the people of Israel in his own day, quoting the prophet Isaiah: "'This people's heart has grown dull . . . and their eyes they have closed; lest they should see with their eyes . . . and understand with their heart'" (Acts 28:27). In other words, the heart and its eyes are failing in their appointed task. In the book of Revelation, Jesus saw this happening in the church of Laodicea, who thought they needed nothing. He said to them, "You are wretched, pitiable, poor, *blind*, and naked." And he counseled them, "Buy from me . . . salve to anoint your eyes, so that you may see" (3:17-18).

This divine "salve" must be what Paul was praying for in Ephesians 1:18 when he asked the Lord that the eyes of our hearts would be enlightened to know our hope and inheritance and power. Without the work of our omnipotent internal Eye Surgeon we would remain blind and unable to see. Oh, how we need the gift of spiritual sight! Whatever joy we have without this sight would not be spiritual joy. It would not be a spontaneous response to seeing the beauty of Christ. And therefore it would not honor Christ. It would be superficial and fleeting.

Why Is Seeing So Essential?

Why is spiritual seeing so essential to joy in God? It's because spiritual seeing is the act of the heart that corresponds to the revelation of the glory of God for the enjoyment of his people. In other words, God's ultimate purpose for creating the universe and ruling the history of redemption is the manifestation of his glory for the everlasting enjoyment of a redeemed people. Jonathan Edwards, who has taught me as much as any man outside the Bible, said in his great book on *The End for Which God Created the World*, "It appears that all that is ever spoken of in the Scripture as an ultimate end of God's works is included in that one phrase, the glory of God."[2] That is why we exist—to see, and rejoice in, and reflect the value of the glory of God.[3] "Bring my sons from afar and my daughters from the end of the earth, everyone . . . whom I created for my glory" (Isa. 43:6-7). That's why we were created, and why we should do everything for the glory of God: "Whether you eat or drink, or whatever you do, do all to the glory of God" (1 Cor. 10:31).

God Is Glorified by Being Seen and Rejoiced In

In one of the most important statements I have ever read, Edwards said it like this:

> God glorifies himself towards the creatures also [in] two ways: (1.) by appearing to . . . their understanding; (2.) in communicating himself to their hearts, and in their rejoicing and delighting in, and enjoying the manifestations which he makes of himself. . . . God is glorified not only by his glory's being seen, but by its being rejoiced in . . . [W]hen those that see it delight in it: God is more glorified than if they only see it.[4]

God's aim in all that he does is to glorify himself. This involves both radiance from God and reflection from creation. His glory streams out from himself, and it streams back again in many ways, especially when he is treasured and enjoyed by his people. "The refulgence shines upon and into the creature," Edwards says, "and is reflected back to the luminary. The beams of glory come from God, and are something of God, and are refunded back again to their original. So that the whole is *of* God, and *in* God, and *to* God, and God is the beginning, middle and end."[5]

Seeing the Glory Is Foundational to Savoring the Glory

Nothing in the universe is more central than the radiance of the glory of God revealed in Christ for the enjoyment of his people. Therefore, the importance of *seeing* it for what it really is can hardly be exaggerated. For seeing it is foundational to enjoying it. And that joy is foundational for showing the worth of Christ in the world. It is foundational for the life of love and sacrifice and suffering that it sustains.

Therefore beneath the quest for satisfaction in Christ—which sustains the life of sacrifice for Christ—is always the quest to see the glory of Christ. All strategies in the fight for joy are directly or indirectly strategies to see Christ more fully.

The Fullness of the Glory Is Not Yet Seen

This connection between God's glory and our seeing demands that we understand the two kinds of seeing we have spoken about. For in one sense the glory of God is not yet visible, and in another sense it is. Paul says in Romans 8:18, "I consider that the sufferings of this present time are not worth comparing with the glory that is to be revealed to us." This means that the glory is not yet here to see. So he says in Romans 8:24-25, "Who hopes for what he sees? But if we hope for what we do not see, we wait for it with patience." And in this hope we rejoice: "Through [Christ] we have also obtained access by faith into this grace in which we stand, and *we rejoice in hope of the glory of God*" (Rom. 5:2).

This is the great global hope of all the prophets. "The *glory of the* LORD shall be revealed, and all flesh shall see it together, for the mouth of the LORD has spoken" (Isa. 40:5). "The time is coming to gather all nations and tongues. And they shall come and shall *see my glory*" (Isa. 66:18). Note well: they will *see* the glory of the Lord. Seeing corresponds to the great and final revelation of the glory of God. There is a glory of God that we hope for and do not yet see.

The Hope of Glory Is Sustained by the Glory We Have Seen

But that is not the whole story. The reason we hope for the revelation of God's glory is because we have indeed seen so much of it in Christ and in nature that our hearts are captured by it forever. The apostle Peter admits that in one sense we do not now see Christ. But listen to how he says it: "Though you have not seen him, you love him. Though you do not now see him, you believe in him and rejoice with joy that is inexpressible and filled with glory" (1 Pet. 1:8). We may groan at times because our seeing is so incomplete (Rom. 8:23). But for Peter the joy of what we *have* seen and the hope of what we *will* see are inexpressible and full of glory.

Therefore, Peter called Christians to be so enthralled with the hope of glory that they would be willing to make any sacrifice now for the sake of knowing and showing Christ: "Rejoice insofar as you share Christ's sufferings, that you may also rejoice and be glad *when his glory is revealed*" (1 Pet. 4:13). The final revelation of the glory of Christ will be the consummation of our joy. Every sacrifice will have been worth it. Indeed those who have suffered most for Christ will say, in one very true sense, "We never made a sacrifice. That slight momentary affliction was 'preparing for us an eternal weight of glory beyond all comparison'" (2 Cor. 4:17 AT).

The Revelation of God's Glory in Nature

The glory we have already seen, and the hope that we will see more, creates and sustains our joy now. There are magnificent revelations of it in nature—even if they pale in comparison to Christ. "The heavens declare the glory of God, and the sky above proclaims his handiwork. Day to day pours out speech, and night to night reveals knowledge" (Ps. 19:1-2). We know from Paul's strong words in Romans 1:20 that we have "seen" the "invisible" attributes of God in this universal display of divine glory. "For his invisible attributes, namely, his eternal power and divine nature, have been clearly perceived [= clearly seen, *kathoratai*] ever since the creation of the world, in the things that have been made." This is amazing. Paul says that when we look at God's display of his glory in nature (from the atom to the supernova) we all see clearly the glory of God. But seeing we do not see.

Why? Paul says it's because of the "ungodliness and unrighteousness of men, who by their unrighteousness *suppress the truth*" (Rom. 1:18). We see, but we suppress. We prefer mindless, moral-less, loveless theories of naturalistic evolution to the glory of God. Oh, how deep is our corruption! This is absolutely tragic. In one act of proud suppression we cut ourselves off from God and joy. Oh, what joys God means for his children to have in the beauties of nature! Not nature as an end in itself, but as an almost endless diversity of spectacular wonders, pointing always to God's magnificence.

"O Lord, how manifold are your works! In wisdom have you made them all; the earth is full of your creatures. Here is the sea, great and wide, which teems with creatures innumerable, living things both small and great. There go the ships, and Leviathan, which you formed to play in it" (Ps. 104:24-26). The Lord is lavish in creation, because his glory is infinite in beauty and diversity and greatness. Alas that seeing we do not see! And we consign ourselves to the kind of pleasures that sophisticated human animals can feel as their chemicals interact.

The Joy-Killing Blindness Can Be Healed

But that can change, and we should fight to change it with all our might. Our hearts can change so that when the desert blossoms like a crocus we "see the glory of the Lord, the majesty of our God" (Isa. 35:2). The change comes when we turn to Christ. Here the veil is lifted from the darkened heart. What Paul said about the Jewish people is true for all of us, whether we are reading the Bible or the book of nature: "Their minds were hardened. . . [The] veil remains unlifted, because only through Christ is it taken away. . . . When one turns to the Lord, the veil is removed" (2 Cor. 3:14-16).

Salvation is the purchase and provision of sight for the blind. God sent Christ into the world to die for our spiritual blindness, pay its penalty, absorb the wrath it deserves, and provide a perfect imputed righteousness for all who believe. This is the most beautiful display of God's glory that has been or ever will be. The divine glory we have been redeemed to see is most beautifully shown in the redemption itself. The all-glorious Christ is both the means and the goal of our salvation from blindness. His life, death, resurrection, and present reign in heaven are *both* the means by which we sinners regain our sight *and* the highest glory we are saved to see.

Why Blindness Is Removed Only in the Presence of Christ

This is why God has appointed that turning to Christ is the way our sight will be restored. The point of restoring the sight of the blind is that they might see and enjoy the glory of Christ. That is the reason we have eyes—both physical and spiritual. Therefore it would contradict the very purpose of seeing if God were to restore our sight by any other means than the revelation of the glory of Christ. If we were given eyes to see and there were no Christ to see, then the joy of our seeing would not glorify Christ. But the Spirit who wakens our inner sight was sent to glorify Christ. Jesus said, "When the Spirit of truth comes, he . . . will glorify me" (John 16:13-14). Therefore the Spirit will open the eyes of the blind only in the presence of the glory of Christ.

How Is the Glory of Christ Present to See?

But how can this be when Christ is in heaven and the glory of his redeeming work happened centuries ago? The answer is given by the apostle Paul in one of the most important gospel passages in the Bible:

> If our gospel is veiled, it is veiled only to those who are perishing. In their case the god of this world has blinded the minds of the unbelievers, to keep them from seeing the light of the gospel of the *glory of Christ*, who is the image of God. For what we proclaim is not ourselves, but Jesus Christ as Lord, with ourselves as your servants for Jesus' sake. For God, who said, "Let light shine out of darkness," has shone in our hearts to give *the light of the knowledge of the glory of God in the face of Jesus Christ*. (2 Cor. 4:3-6)

Here Paul defines conversion—which Satan does all he can to hinder—as "seeing the light of the gospel of the glory of Christ" (v. 4). He says it a different way in verse 6: It is the shining in our hearts of "the light of the knowledge of the glory of God in the face of Jesus Christ." These descriptions of conversion imply two things. One is that the gospel is the proclamation of the "knowledge" of Christ in such a way that its glory can be seen by the eyes of the heart. The other is that this "seeing" is the work of God, "shining in our hearts" the same way he did on the first day of creation when he said, "Let there be light." In other words, seeing the glory of Christ in the gospel is a gift.

Therefore when I said above that the Spirit will open the eyes of the blind only in the presence of the glory of Christ, I meant, only in the hearing of the gospel of Christ does God say in the heart, "Let there be light." *By means of* the glory of Christ in the gospel, and *for the sake of* the glory of Christ in the gospel, God restores our sight only in the presence of Christ in the gospel. In this way, when our eyes are opened and the light shines, it is Christ whom we see and enjoy and glorify.

Telling the gospel of Christ's death for our sins and his resurrection (1 Cor. 15:1-4) is a re-presentation of the glory of Christ once revealed in history. At that time the apostle John said, "The Word became flesh and dwelt among us, and we have seen his glory, glory as of the only Son from the Father, full of grace and truth" (John 1:14). In other words, the eternal "Word"—the Son of God—entered history and revealed "the glory of God in the face of Jesus Christ." So now when the Word of God is preached ("the gospel of the glory of Christ"), that same glory ("the light of the knowledge of the glory of God in the face of Jesus Christ") shines forth. Becoming a Christian means seeing this glory when we hear the gospel.

God Reveals Himself by His Word

This relationship between the Word of God and the glory of God— between hearing and seeing—is not new. In Exodus 33:18 Moses said to God at Mount Sinai, "Please show me your glory." He wanted to *see* the glory of God. God responded with a revelation of himself by the Word. He said, "I will make all my goodness pass before you and will proclaim before you my name 'The LORD'" (v. 19). And then he did that on the mountain with a full proclamation of the meaning of his name: "The Lord passed before him and proclaimed, 'The LORD, the LORD, a God merciful and gracious, slow to anger, and abounding in steadfast love and faithfulness, keeping steadfast love for thousands, forgiving iniquity and transgression and sin, but who will by no means clear the guilty, visiting the iniquity of the fathers on the children and the children's children, to the third and the fourth generation" (Ex. 34:6-7). That was God's deepest answer to Moses' request, "Let me see your glory." He proclaimed in words the essence of his gracious name.

Similarly God revealed himself to the prophet Samuel by the word. First Samuel 3:21 says, "And the LORD appeared again at Shiloh, for the LORD revealed himself to Samuel at Shiloh by the word of the LORD." This is what we want as human beings: We want a revelation of God himself. We want to say with Moses, "Show us your glory." And indeed a time is coming when "the glory that is to be revealed to us" will make all "the sufferings of this present time" seem as nothing (Rom. 8:18). But for now, in this age, God has ordained that primarily he reveals his glory to us "by the word of the LORD." Hearing is the primary way of seeing in this age.

Seeing the Glory Is What Happens When Hearing Succeeds

This relationship between the Word of God and the glory of God is remarkable, and we should grasp it firmly. God ordained that spiritual *seeing* should happen mainly through *hearing*. Christ is not visually present for us to see. He is presented today in the Word of God, especially the gospel. Paul said, "Faith comes from hearing, and hearing through the word of Christ" (Rom. 10:17). But we know from 2 Corinthians 4:4 that faith springs from "seeing the light of the gospel of the glory of Christ." Therefore we can say that seeing the glory of Christ is what happens in the heart when the hearing of the gospel is made effective by the Spirit. That is, when, through the gospel, the omnipotent, creative voice of God says, "Let light shine in the darkness of this heart," the gospel gives rise to faith. When hearing, by grace, produces seeing, it produces faith.

This is crucial because the glory of God is the ultimate reality. The glory of God is more ultimate than the Word of God. And so seeing is more ultimate than hearing. Nevertheless the glory of God does not come to us in a saving way except through the Word of God. Therefore, *seeing* the glory does not happen except through *hearing* the gospel. Word corresponds to hearing, and glory corresponds to seeing. Ultimately God has spoken in order to reveal his glory for the enjoyment of his people. Therefore we must hear what he says in order to see what he reveals. The Bible does not speak of hearing the glory of God, but seeing it. Hearing is the means. Seeing is the goal. The aim of all our hearing of God's truth is the seeing of God's glory.

The Aim of Seeing Is Savoring and Showing Christ

Yes, seeing divine glory is the goal of hearing divine truth. But *seeing* the glory of God is not our ultimate aim. Our ultimate aim is to glorify God by enjoying him forever. If seeing did not produce savoring, God would not be glorified by our seeing. Therefore the final goal *in our hearts* is the enjoyment of the glory of God, not just the seeing. And the final goal *in the universe* is the fullest possible display of the glory of God. That fullness comes to pass not only but mainly through the white-hot, joy-permeated worship of his people as they exult in the glory of his Son.

The reason I say "not only" is that the wrath of God against unbelief will also glorify his justice and wisdom. And the reason I say "but mainly" is that judgment is not God's highest design for the glory of his name; rather the highest design is "that the Gentiles might glorify God *for his mercy*" (Rom. 15:9). The revelation of the glory of his grace reflected in the joyful exultation of his people is God's highest and ultimate end in creation. "He chose us in Him before the foundation of the world . . . *to the praise of the glory of His grace*" (Eph. 1:4, 6 NASB).

Beholding Glory Means Becoming Enthralled

This will come to pass, and our hearts will be full of joy in it, if we fight to see the glory of God. Second Corinthians 3:18 gives the decisive word on the necessity of seeing for the sake of rejoicing in and reflecting the glory of God: "And we all, with unveiled face, *beholding the glory of the Lord*, are being transformed into the same image from one degree of glory to another. For this comes from the Lord who is the Spirit." By seeing the glory of Christ in the gospel we are changed. In what way? Not first externally, but first internally. What is this internal change that comes from "beholding the glory of the Lord"?

It is the awakening of joy in Christ himself, and all that God is for us in him. It is the awakening of a new taste for spiritual reality centering in Christ. It is the capacity for a new sweetness and a new enjoyment of the glory of God in the Word of God. Therefore, nothing is more important for us in life than to "behold the glory of the Lord." Satan, as Paul says four verses later (2 Cor. 4:4), uses all his devices to keep us from seeing "the light of the gospel of the glory of Christ." This is the most foundational strategy in the battle for joy—the strategic battle to see. In all the strategies commended in this book for how to fight for joy, this is always the aim. Directly or indirectly every strategy is a strategy to behold the glory of Christ and become enthralled with his beauty above all.

The Love of Christ in a Final Prayer

As Jesus came to his last night before the crucifixion, John, the beloved disciple, says, "Having loved his own who were in the world, he loved them to the end" (John 13:1). One of the demonstrations of that love was the great prayer that Jesus prayed for his disciples and for us who would believe on him through their word (John 17:20). And the climax of that prayer came with these words: "Father, I desire that they also, whom you have given me, may be with me where I am, *to see my glory* that you have given me because you loved me before the foundation of the world" (v. 24). Why would the most loving man who ever lived, at the most loving hour of his life, pray that we would be able to spend eternity *seeing his glory*?

The answer is not hard: This will satisfy our hearts and glorify his worth. That is what it means to be loved by Christ. He prays for what is eternally satisfying to us and eternally glorifying to him. Seeing his glory forever is the greatest gift he can give to us. Therefore praying and dying that we might have this gift is love. Resolving to fight with all our might that we might see what he died to show—that is a great honor to Christ. The rest of this book is an effort to help you do that. I am still learning myself. May the Lord give us the grace, more and more, to follow the lead of the apostle Paul and "look not to the things that are seen but to the things that are unseen" (2 Cor. 4:18). May this kind of looking enable us to see more of Christ than we would have ever seen if our looking stopped with what is seen.

What Does It Mean to See Christ with the Eyes of the Heart?

What then is this seeing with the eyes of the heart? It is a spiritual perception of the truth and beauty and worth of Christ for what they really are. To use the words of Jonathan Edwards, it is "a true sense of the divine excellency of the things revealed in the Word of God, and a conviction of the truth a reality of them thence arising."[6] The key word here is "sense." The person who sees with the eyes of the heart "does not merely rationally believe that God is glorious, but he has a *sense* of the gloriousness of God in his heart. There is not only a rational belief that God is holy, and that holiness is a good thing, but there is a sense of the loveliness of God's holiness."[7]

This "sense" or perception is different from physical perception, but not disconnected from it. When the gospel is heard and Christ is objectively portrayed in his perfections and his works, the physical perception of these things may lead to an embrace or rejection. But the spiritual perception leads only to an embrace. Indeed it may be so interwoven with the embrace that they are indistinguishable. Can we really distinguish between perceiving something as infinitely desirable from the awakening of desire for it? Is not the wakening of the desire for Christ the recognition of him as desirable?

The words of David in Psalm 34:8 seem to imply this: "Oh, *taste and see* that the LORD is good!" Which comes first: Tasting that the Lord is good, or seeing that the Lord is good? Or is the taste the sight? Listen to Thomas Binney's reflections on these words.

> There are some things, especially in the depths of the religious life, which can only be understood by being experienced, and which even then are incapable of being adequately embodied in words. "O taste and see that the Lord is good." The enjoyment must come before the illumination *or rather the enjoyment is the illumination.* There are things that must be loved before we can know them to be worthy of our love.[8]

That is the difference between physical perceiving and spiritual perceiving. Spiritual perceiving is the creation of a new taste in the soul. Before our conversion the honey of Christ tasted sour or bland and thus undesirable to our souls. Then, by grace, we were granted a new capacity for sweetness, and we tasted the honey of Christ for what it really is: sweet and desirable. This is the seeing that provides the enjoyment of Christ. The seeing and enjoying are inseparable. Indeed it appears that the enjoying is the seeing. Or as Jonathan Edwards says, the heart's seeing a person as lovely implies that the person is pleasant to the soul.

> There is a difference between having a rational judgment that honey is sweet, and having a sense of its sweetness. . . . So there is a difference between believing that a person is beautiful, and having a sense

of his beauty. The former may be obtained by hearsay, but the latter only by seeing the countenance. . . . When the heart is sensible of the beauty and amiableness of a thing, it necessarily feels pleasure in the apprehension. It is implied in a person's being heartily sensible of the loveliness of a thing, that the idea of it is sweet and pleasant to this soul.[9]

How Do Seeing and Enjoying Christ Relate to Knowing Him?

Together this spiritual seeing of Christ and enjoying him—or this spiritual sense of his beauty and corresponding pleasure in the soul—refer to what Paul calls "knowing" Christ. Paul prays in Ephesians 3:19 that we may *"know the love of Christ that surpasses knowledge."* And he says in Philippians 3:8, "I count everything as loss because of *the surpassing worth of knowing Christ Jesus my Lord."* This knowing is no mere intellectual knowledge. The devils have such knowledge and tremble (Jas. 2:19). This knowing "surpasses knowledge." This knowing includes tasting and seeing. It is the knowledge of honey that you have only when you put it on your tongue and taste that it is sweet. Therefore, knowing Christ in this way means seeing him for who he really is and enjoying him above all things.

Therefore the prophetic challenge, "Let us *know*; let us press on to *know* the LORD" (Hos. 6:3), is the same as the challenge of this book: let us fight to see; let us press on in the fight to see and enjoy the glory of Christ.

I also saw, moreover, that it was not my good frame of heart that made my righteousness better, nor yet my bad frame that made my righteousness worse, for my righteousness was Jesus Christ himself, "The same yesterday, today, and forever." Now did my chains fall off my legs indeed. I was loosed from my afflictions and irons; my temptations also fled away; so that from that time those dreadful scriptures of God [about the unforgivable sin] left off to trouble me; now went I also home rejoicing for the grace and love of God.

JOHN BUNYAN
Grace Abounding to the Chief of Sinners[1]

... looking to Jesus, the founder and perfecter of our faith, who for the joy that was set before him endured the cross, despising the shame, and is seated at the right hand of the throne of God.

HEBREWS 12:2

Rejoice not over me, O my enemy; when I fall, I shall rise; when I sit in darkness, the LORD will be a light to me. I will bear the indignation of the LORD because I have sinned against him, until he pleads my cause and executes judgment for me. He will bring me out to the light; I shall look upon his vindication.

MICAH 7:8-9

6

Fighting for Joy like a Justified Sinner

Learning the Secret of Gutsy Guilt

Nothing is more foundational for the joy of undeserving people than the cross of Jesus Christ. The fight for joy is a fight to grasp and marvel at what happened in the death of Christ—and what it reveals about our suffering Savior. If it were not for the death of Jesus in our place, the only possible joy would be the joy of delusion—like the joy on the *Titanic* just before it hit the iceberg. Without the cross, joy could be sustained only by denying (consciously or subconsciously) the inevitability of divine judgment. In fact, that's the kind of joy that drives most of the world—a joy that preserves the power of its pleasures by being oblivious to the peril just ahead. If the passengers were suddenly made aware that in a matter of hours most of them would drown in the icy ocean, all their merrymaking would cease. Their joy depends on their ignorance.

However, if the passengers knew that the ocean liner would sink, but that a great armada of utterly dependable ships and sailors was already on the way and would arrive and save everyone who followed their instructions, something very different would happen. To be sure, the lighthearted merrymaking would cease, and a great seriousness would spread over the *Titanic*; but there would be a different kind of joy—a deep sense of gratitude for the rescuers, and a deep sense of hope that, though much would be lost, lives would be saved. Some may panic in unbelief, doubting the promise of rescue. But others would rise in the strength of hope and do great acts of love in preparation for the coming destruction.

Titanic: We Are Corrupt and We Are Condemned

Jesus Christ came into the world as the divine Son of God in order to die for our sins and rescue us from the wrath of God, the burden of guilt, the condemnation of justice, the bondage of sin, the torment of hell, and the loss of all that is good—especially the loss of God. Our problem is not merely our own corruption but, more seriously, God's condemnation. To be sure, we are corrupt, or as the old theologians said, depraved. Paul's way of saying it is that "all . . . are *under sin.* . . . 'None is righteous, no, not one'" (Rom. 3:9-10).

This corruption is a massive obstacle to everlasting joy. We desire the wrong things, and we desire right things in the wrong way. And both are deadly—like eating pleasant poison. But our corruption is not our main obstacle to joy. God's wrath is greater. God is infinitely valuable, and we have offended him infinitely by valuing other things more. We have "exchanged the glory of . . . God" (Rom. 1:23). Or as Paul says in Romans 3:23, we all "fall short of the glory of God."

Therefore, God's holiness and justice will move him to settle accounts with us in his wrath. "Whoever does not obey the Son shall not see life, but *the wrath of God remains on him*" (John 3:36). "*Cursed* be everyone who does not abide by all things written in the Book of the Law, and do them" (Gal. 3:10). The consequence of this curse and wrath is eternal misery apart from the glory of God. "Those who do not obey the gospel of our Lord Jesus . . . will suffer the punishment of eternal destruction, away from the presence of the Lord and from the glory of his might" (2 Thess. 1:8-9). The iceberg just ahead is no happiness forever, only misery.

We are on a doomed *Titanic* because of our sin—all of us without exception. "Every mouth [is] stopped, and the whole world [is] held accountable to God" (Rom. 3:19). The sinful ship of our lives is headed for everlasting ruin because of God's righteousness and wrath. Without a Savior, that's the reality we must keep out of our minds in order to be happy on the *Titanic* of this world.

Jesus Christ Is a Great Savior from Everything That Destroys Joy

But we are not without a Savior. Jesus Christ has come. And he is a great Savior. Every need we have, he supplies. And his death on the cross is the price that purchases every gift that leads to deep and lasting joy.

Is there wrath and curse hanging over us?

> Christ redeemed us from the curse of the law by becoming a curse for us—for it is written, "Cursed is everyone who is hanged on a tree." (Gal. 3:13)

Is there condemnation against us in the courtroom of heaven?

> Who shall bring any charge against God's elect? It is God who justifies. Who is to condemn? Christ Jesus is the one who died. (Rom. 8:33-34)

Are there innumerable trespasses mounting up against us?

> In him we have redemption through his blood, the forgiveness of our trespasses, according to the riches of his grace. (Eph. 1:7)

Is righteousness required that we cannot produce?

> For our sake he made him to be sin who knew no sin, so that in him we might become the righteousness of God (2 Cor. 5:21). By the one man's obedience the many will be made righteous. (Rom. 5:19)

Are we cut off from eternal life?

> For God so loved the world, that he gave his only Son, that whoever believes in him should not perish but have eternal life. (John 3:16)

Are we trapped in the dominion of sin that ruins our lives?

> He himself bore our sins in his body on the tree, that we might die to sin and live to righteousness (1 Pet. 2:24). He died for all, that those

who live might no longer live for themselves but for him who for their sake died and was raised. (2 Cor. 5:15)

Will all the follies and failures of our past drag us down with irrevocable, destructive consequences?

We know that for those who love God all things work together for good, for those who are called according to his purpose. (Rom. 8:28)

Have we lost all the good things God planned for his children?

He who did not spare his own Son but gave him up for us all, how will he not also with him graciously give us all things? (Rom. 8:32)

Is there any hope that sinners like us could spend an all-satisfying eternity with God? Can I ever come home to God?

Christ also suffered once for sins, the righteous for the unrighteous, that he might bring us to God. (1 Pet. 3:18)

Oh, what a great salvation Jesus Christ accomplished when he died and rose again! All that, and more, Christ purchased by his death. Therefore, Christ crucified is the foundation of all honest and everlasting joy. No self-deception is necessary to enjoy it. Indeed all deception must cease in order to enjoy it to the full.

The Taste and Hope of Joy Sustained Christ in His Suffering

Christ himself connected joy and the cross in his own soul. Hebrews 12:2 tells us, "For the joy that was set before him [he] endured the cross." So in his own heart the unshakable hope of joy with the Father sustained him through his final suffering. Christ knew from experience the joy that he had with the Father before creation. He prayed the night before he died, "Father, glorify me in your own presence with the glory that I had with you before the world existed" (John 17:5).

But Jesus also knew this prayer depended on his obedience to the Father. He would have to complete the great work of salvation by deliberate death. Paul said that Jesus was "obedient to the point of death, even death on a cross," and "*therefore* God has highly exalted him and bestowed on him a name that is above every name" (Phil. 2:8-9). The word "therefore" means that his obedience unto death was the reason God exalted Christ and gave him the glory he had with the Father before creation. He had come to save sinners. When the price was paid, the work was decisively done. "It is finished," he cried (John 19:30). And God rewarded him with great glory.

Christ Died for His Joy and Ours

So in a sense Christ died for his own everlasting life and joy. He had done no sin and so did not need to be saved from guilt. He had none. But the Father had sent him to die, and not to do so would have been disobedient. And if he had been disobedient to God, neither his nor our eternal life would have been achieved. Therefore, the death of Jesus was the means by which he regained his place of glory with the Father and came into the fullness of his own everlasting joy. His joy was blood-bought at the price of his own obedient death.

The reason this matters to us is that Jesus planned for his joy to be our joy. He said in John 15:11, "These things I have spoken to you, *that my joy may be in you, and that your joy may be full.*" When Jesus bought his own joy at the price of his obedient death, he also bought ours. He said it again in John 17:13, "But now [Father] I am coming to you, and these things I speak in the world, that they may have *my joy fulfilled in themselves.*" The very joy that Jesus would have in the presence of the Father is the joy he died for us to have.

In the Parable of the Talents Jesus, the master, says to his faithful servant, "Well done, good and faithful servant. . . . *Enter into the joy of your master*" (Matt. 25:23). It is his joy first. Then he welcomes us into it. While he was on earth, the unwavering confidence that his joy would soon be made full sustained him in his suffering. And by his obedience he obtained everlasting joy for himself and for us.

The Fullness of His Joy and Ours Flows from His Glory

The joy he died to obtain for himself and give to us is joy in the glory of God. We know this because, after praying that his joy would be fulfilled in them (John 17:13), he prayed, "Father, I desire that they also, whom you have given me, may be with me where I am, *to see my glory that you have given me*" (v. 24). Because of his obedience, God elevated Jesus, the God-Man, to his right hand and acclaimed him as both God and Savior—triumphant Lion and sacrificed Lamb, omnipotent Lord and obedient Servant. Thus Christ regained the fullness of the divine glory that he had with God from the beginning. But now it was more fully displayed through his redeeming obedience and death. This glory from the Father was the ultimate ground of Jesus' joy.

And he prayed that we would be with him to see this glory. This would be our entrance into "the joy of the Master." This would be our joy fulfilled in his joy. The aim and achievement of the cross of Christ is the everlasting, ever-increasing[2] joy of his people as they see and savor the glory of Christ. That is what Jesus died to obtain for us—even while we were still sinners. Therefore, nothing is more foundational for the joy of undeserving people than the cross of Jesus Christ.

The Gospel Is Central in the Fight for Joy

Therefore, in the battle for joy we must take this truth and preach it to ourselves. The gospel of Christ crucified and risen is meant to be preached to the soul—both in corporate worship where we hear it week after week, and from hour to hour as we preach it to ourselves in the daily fight for joy. The message of the cross has a central and unique place in the fight for joy. Paul put the gospel in a class by itself when he said, "Far be it from me to boast except in the cross of our Lord Jesus Christ" (Gal. 6:14), and when he said, "I decided to know nothing among you except Jesus Christ and him crucified" (1 Cor. 2:2).

These are sweeping statements. No boast except in the cross! And no knowledge that is not a knowledge of Christ and him crucified! Every boast we make in any good thing must include the boast that, without the cross, we would have hell and not this good thing. Everything we know must include the knowledge that we do not know it rightly except in relation to Christ crucified.

Do Believers Need to Hear the Preaching of the Cross?

Therefore the cross must be central in the fight for joy. We must put ourselves under its preaching on the Lord's day, and we must preach it to ourselves all day every day. Don't neglect the corporate hearing of the word of the cross preached. I stress *preached* because I do believe that God has ordained that the word of the cross—and all things in relation to the cross—be preached and not just taught or discussed.

This may not mean much to some of you, since you may have had little experience of true preaching. That was J. I. Packer's experience, he said, until he heard Martyn Lloyd-Jones at Westminster Chapel in the school year of 1948-1949, when he was twenty-two years old. Packer heard Lloyd-Jones preach every Sunday evening. He said that he had "never heard such preaching." It came to him "with the force of electric shock, bringing to at least one of his listeners more of a sense of God than any other man." Packer said it was through this preaching that he learned about "the greatness of God and the greatness of the soul." "Listening to Martyn Lloyd-Jones," he said, "was like hearing a whole orchestra perform after a single piano."[3]

I don't mean that you must find a Martyn Lloyd-Jones to hear each Sunday in worship. There was only one Lloyd-Jones. The point is not personality; the point is depth and earnestness and a sense of the weight of glory. The point is heartfelt rigor in the unfolding of Scripture, which is heralded (not just discussed or analyzed) with a worshipful sense of exultation over the beauty of God's truth.

When Paul exhorts Timothy, "Preach the word" (2 Tim. 4:2), two things make me think he would encourage us to hear the Word preached in the setting of gathered worship. One is that the context of the passage relates to the church being "trained in righteousness" (2 Tim. 3:16), not mainly to evangelism among unbelievers. In other words, Paul means, "Preach the word to believers." The other point is that the word for "preach" here is a Greek word (*kēruxon*) that means "to herald." It was the work of one who made public proclamations for government officials before there was radio or television or print media. This kind of speech has a spirit of exultation and seriousness about it. It is part of worship. When it is done in the power of the Holy Spirit, it *is* worship. It is expository exultation. The preacher worships over the Word that he proclaims. There is Spirit-given truth, and there is Spirit-given passion. And the effect on God's people is to awaken aspects of joy in Christ that may not come any other way.

Please do not picture a fine, well-lit sanctuary with oak pews and a white pulpit. Don't even picture a flat multipurpose room with carpet and chairs and a keyboard. Picture a mud-walled room with a zinc roof, or a cave with torches, or a thatched roof on poles with no walls, or a living room with all the simple furniture removed, or a patch of grass under a tree. And don't picture thousands of hearers and the finest acoustics. Picture eight or twenty or forty worshipers. Even in small settings with small numbers, preaching can happen. The preacher will use his voice differently, but all the essentials of passion, and seriousness, and expository exultation can be there. They should be there. The word of the cross is the kind of news—incomparably good news—that calls for this kind of heralding, even for a dozen saints.

What If True Preaching Is Not Available to Me?

Surely the question will be raised: How shall I fight for joy with this weapon if I do not live in a place with this kind of worship gathering? What if the preachers do not believe the Bible? Or what if they do not preach the word of the cross but only human experiences? Or what if all the weightiness and seriousness is missing and the leaders seem bent on being mainly jocular? Or what if I am homebound and cannot get out to worship services? In answer to these questions, please do not take me to mean that hearing the word of the cross preached is the only arrow in your quiver. It is good. It is important. God brings churches into being with preaching as one of his purposes. Over the long haul, it hurts us not to have it.

But God is merciful and can supply our needs when we have no access to a church that preaches the word of the cross. He will meet you in your meditations on the Word. He will meet you in family worship. He will meet you in small groups where the Word is discussed and applied, even if no one there is called and gifted to preach. He will meet you through preaching on the radio or television or Internet or tapes and CDs. These are not the same as the living voice in the context of worship and community. But they are good, and God can make himself known powerfully through them.

Nevertheless, it is a biblical goal and norm for Christians to be a part of worship gatherings where the word of the cross is preached. God ordains this for our joy. Studying the Word is good. Meditation is good. Discussion is good. Analyzing and explaining is good. But preaching is also good, and God calls us to enjoy the blessing that comes to us when the word of the cross explodes in the heart of a godly preacher and overflows in exultation to the minds and hearts of a worshiping people. The fight for joy loses one of its weapons when it does not regularly hear the gospel preached. God can make it up to us in other ways. But preaching is one precious gift of God to the church. When it exults over "the word of the cross," it becomes "to us who are being saved . . . the power of God" (1 Cor. 1:18).

Fighting for Joy with the Bread and the Cup

Let's not overlook that eating the Lord's Supper with God's people is a kind of preaching that is also meant to feed the joy of Christ's people. "For as often as you eat this bread and drink the cup, you *proclaim* the Lord's death until he comes" (1 Cor. 11:26). The death and resurrection of Christ are being proclaimed in the act of serving and eating Communion. This proclamation is the means of our nourishment with the bread and cup.

Christ has appointed that we feast spiritually on the benefits of the cross as we eat the bread and drink the cup. "The cup of blessing that we bless, is it not a *participation* in the blood of Christ? The bread that we break, is it not a *participation* in the body of Christ?" (1 Cor. 10:16). We participate in the cup and the bread by feasting on what the blood and body of Christ obtained for us when he died, especially the forgiveness of sins, the gift of righteousness, and never-ending personal fellowship with Christ and his Father. This is why regular presence at the Lord's Table is a great weapon in the fight for joy.

Preaching for Joy, and Preaching for the Glory of God

Preaching the word of the cross is designed for our joy, because it's designed for the glory of God. Jonathan Edwards saw more clearly than most that preaching for the glory of God had implications for the role of preaching in the fight for joy. One of his great insights was that "God is glorified not only by his glory's being seen, but by its being rejoiced in."[4] He concluded, therefore, that the aim of preaching must be joy in the glory of God. So he described his preaching like this: "I should think myself in the way of my duty to raise the affections of my hearers as high as possibly I can, provided that they are affected with nothing but truth, and with affections that are not disagreeable to the nature of what they are affected with."[5] Truth and affections. Doctrine and joy. Both are essential. When the word of the cross is preached like this, a great blow is struck against the joylessness of God's people. And that is a blow for the glory of God.

Become a Preacher and Preach the Gospel to Yourself

But now we must go back to the other preaching that I mentioned. We should not only be preached to; we should become preachers and preach the word of the cross to ourselves every day. We must not rely only on being preached to, but must become good preachers to our own soul. The gospel is the power of God to lead us joyfully to final salvation, *if we preach it to ourselves*. Martyn Lloyd-Jones (1899-1981) emphasized this truth. He was the senior minister at Westminster Chapel in London from 1943 to 1968 and preached a series of messages that were published in 1964 as one of his most helpful and popular books, *Spiritual Depression: Its Causes and Cures*. I recommend it highly. He writes out of the conviction that

> the greatest need of the hour is a revived and joyful Church. . . .
> Nothing is more important . . . than that we should be delivered from
> a condition which gives other people looking at us, the impression
> that to be a Christian means to be unhappy, to be sad, to be morbid,
> and that the Christian is one who "scorns delights and lives laborious
> days." . . . Christian people too often seem to be perpetually in the
> doldrums and too often give this appearance of unhappiness and lack
> of freedom and of absence of joy. There is no question at all but that
> this is the main reason why large numbers of people have ceased to
> be interested in Christianity.[6]

His book is an exposition of Psalm 42, especially verse 5: "Why art thou cast down, O my soul? And why art thou disquieted in me? Hope thou in God: for I shall yet praise him for the help of his countenance" (KJV). Among the many things Lloyd-Jones sees in this verse is that the psalmist is preaching to himself. He applies this to us:

> Have you realized that most of your unhappiness in life is due to the fact that you are listening to yourself instead of talking to yourself? Take those thoughts that come to you the moment you wake up in the morning. You have not originated them but they are talking to you, they bring back the problems of yesterday, etc. Somebody is talking. Who is talking to you? Your self is talking to you. Now this man's treatment [in Psalm 42] was this: instead of allowing this self to talk to him, he starts talking to himself. "Why art thou cast down, O my soul?" he asks. His soul had been depressing him, crushing him. So he stands up and says, "Self, listen for a moment, I will speak to you."[7]

Do Not Surrender to the Victim Mentality, but Defy Yourself

This is a profound lesson. Far too many Christians are passive in their fight for joy. They tell me about their condition of joylessness, and I ask about the kinds of strategies they have pursued to defeat this enemy, and they give the impression that they are a helpless victim: "Joylessness is just there. What can I do?" Well, God does not mean for us to be passive. He means for us to fight the fight of faith—the fight for joy. And the central strategy is to preach the gospel to yourself. This is war. Satan is preaching for sure. If we remain passive, we surrender the field to him.

So Lloyd-Jones gets specific and gets tough:

> The main art in the matter of spiritual living is to know how to handle yourself. You have to take yourself in hand, you have to address yourself, preach to yourself, question yourself. . . . You must turn on yourself, upbraid yourself, condemn yourself, exhort yourself, and say to yourself: "Hope thou in God"—instead of muttering in this depressed, unhappy way, and then you must go on to remind yourself of God, Who God is, and . . . what God has done, and what God has pledged Himself to do. Then having done that, end on this great

note: defy yourself, and defy other people, and defy the devil and the whole world, and say with this man: "I shall yet praise Him for the help of His countenance, who is also the health of my countenance and my God."[8]

The word of the cross—the gospel of the glory of Christ—is the main source for truth about "Who God is," and "what God has done," and "what God has pledged Himself to do." These are the great discouragement slayers. They are all in the gospel. In the final analysis, it is the cross of Christ alone that can kill the joy-killers in our lives.

Of course, the "self" is not the only one who talks to us in our head. So does the devil, and so do other people as we replay their comments in our memories. Therefore, when Lloyd-Jones tells us to preach to ourselves, he knows we must be addressing all these joy-killing messages. That's why he talks about *defying* self, Satan, and other people. When we preach the gospel to ourselves, we are addressing every word of every enemy of every kind.

The Doctrine of Justification and the Fight for Joy

So let's consider a great example of this preaching that has helped me through many dark seasons. It comes from an unlikely place: the prophet Micah, who preached seven hundred years before Christ and gave one of the most practical applications in all the Bible of the great truth of justification by faith alone. This doctrine is at the heart of the gospel. It is the essence of the word of the cross. So before we consider Micah's application of the doctrine to his dark and miserable condition, let's clarify what justification is. We will come back to Micah shortly.

The doctrine of justification says that the remedy for my alienation from God is first a legal one, and only then a moral one. First, I have to be legally absolved of guilt and credited with a righteousness that I don't have. That is, I have to be declared righteous in the courtroom of heaven, where God sits as judge, and where I stand condemned by his law. That's what the word *justify* means: not *make* just, but *declare* just. We can see this in Luke 7:29 where the people "justified God" (RSV)! That is, they declared that he was just. They didn't *make* him just. The difference is that we are sinners and do not have a righteousness of our own. We should, but we don't. That's why we are guilty and destined for eternal punishment.

To make a way for us to be saved, God sent Christ to live a perfect divine-human life and die an obedient death. In this way Christ became both the substitute punishment for our sins (Matt. 26:28; 1 Cor. 15:3; 1 Pet. 3:18) and the substitute performer of our righteousness (Rom. 5:19; 10:4; 2 Cor. 5:21; Phil. 3:9). Therefore, in the courtroom of God, my guilt for sin is removed by Christ's blood ("In him we have redemption through his blood, the forgiveness of our trespasses" [Eph. 1:7]); and my title to heaven is provided by Christ's obedience ("By the one man's obedience the many will be made righteous" [Rom. 5:19]). I am declared just—freed from the punishment of sin and now possessing a title to heaven. This is what we mean by justification.

The Joy of Seeing That Justification Is by Faith Alone

And the capstone of its joy-producing glory is that justification is by faith alone apart from works of the law. Paul said, "We hold that one is justified by faith apart from works of the law" (Rom. 3:28). Then he contrasted two ways for sinners to try to get right with God. One is by working to deserve acceptance; the other is by trusting in the purely free act of grace that gives acceptance to those who will simply receive it as a precious gift. "To the one who works, his wages are not counted as a gift but as his due. And to the one who does not work but *believes in him who justifies the ungodly*, his faith is counted as righteousness" (Rom. 4:4-5).

For "the ungodly"—who know that they are riding the *Titanic* to destruction—the best news in all the world is the news that God will, by faith alone, count them as righteous because of Christ. This is the great ground of joy in the word of the cross: Justification is by *grace alone* (not mixed with our merit), through *faith alone* (not mixed with our works), on the basis of Christ *alone* (not mingling his righteousness with ours), to the glory of *God alone* (not ours).

Confusing Justification and Sanctification Will Kill Joy

Then, and only then, on the basis of this forgiveness and this declaration of righteousness, God gives us his Holy Spirit to transform us morally and progressively into the image of his Son. This progressive change is *not* justification but is based on justification. This change is what we call *sanctification*. "Now that you have been set free from sin and have become slaves of God, the fruit you get leads to sanctification and its end, eternal life" (Rom. 6:22). First the legal issue must be settled. In the courtroom of heaven, an ungodly sinner is declared righteous by faith alone! Christ's righteousness is imputed to him. He does not have a righteousness of his own when God accepts him (Phil. 3:9). His faith is all receiving. He has not yet become loving. Christ's faithful life of love, which perfectly fulfilled the law of God, is imputed to the ungodly. This is justification. This is the settling of the legal issue first.

When that is settled—and it is settled in the twinkling of an eye—then the moral progress goes forward (sanctification). Both are gifts, and both are bought by the blood of Christ. They are inseparable but different. Both are by faith alone. Justification is by faith alone because only faith receives the declaration that the ungodly is counted righteous. Sanctification is by faith alone because only faith receives the power to bear the fruit of love. It is crucial in the fight for joy that we not confuse or combine justification and sanctification. Confusing them will, in the end, undermine the gospel and turn justification by *faith* into justification by *performance*. If that happens, the great gospel weapon in the fight for joy will fall from our hands.

Become What You Are

One of the ways the Bible talks about our *action* in relation to our *standing* in Christ is to command us to become what we are. For example, using Old Testament ceremonial language Paul says, "Cleanse out the old leaven that you may be a new lump, as you really are unleavened" (1 Cor. 5:7). In other words, become what you are. You *are* unleavened (sinless in Christ); therefore *become* unleavened (sinless in practice).

Perfect sinlessness does not happen in this life, but we move toward it. Paul was clear on that: "Not that I have already obtained this or am already perfect, but I press on to make it my own, because Christ Jesus has made me his own" (Phil. 3:12). "I myself serve the law of God with my mind, but with my flesh I serve the law of sin" (Rom. 7:25). But the principle is clear: Fight for joy, not by doing things that establish your identity with God, but by becoming what your identity already is with God in Christ. Become what you are.

We are justified by grace through faith alone because of our union with Christ whose righteousness is counted as ours. Because of this union with Christ, we are already dead and raised and holy and light. The secret of rugged joy in the battle with sin is to fight to become what we are in Christ. You have already *died* with Christ (Rom. 6:5-6); therefore "consider yourselves dead to sin and alive to God in Christ Jesus" (Rom. 6:11). You have already been *made alive* together with Christ (Eph. 2:5); therefore, "seek the things that are above" (Col. 3:1). You are already *holy* in Christ (Col. 3:12); therefore "be holy in all your conduct" (1 Pet. 1:15). You *already* are the light of the world in Christ (Matt. 5:14); therefore, "let your light shine" (Matt. 5:16).

All of that is another way of saying, live as a justified sinner. Don't make peace with the sin in your life. If you make peace with sin and settle down with it as an accepted long-term partner, you show that you are not united with Christ. In union with Christ two things happen: his righteousness is imputed to us, and, because of that, a new impulse is given to become what we are. The great gospel weapon in the fight for joy is the rock-solid reality that we are counted righteous in Christ by faith alone. This imputed righteousness is because of his performance alone, not ours. By our behavior we gradually become what we are in him and because of him.

That gospel weapon is powerful only to the degree we keep the basis of our justification free from our own performances. God accepts us on the basis of Christ's righteousness, not ours. To be sure, our progressive sanctification—our all-too-slow growth in Christ-likeness—matters. It is the necessary evidence that our faith is real.[9] But, oh, what a difference it makes to be assured, in the discouraging darkness of our own imperfection, that we have a perfect righteous-ness—namely, Christ's.

John Bunyan: "Now Went I Also Home Rejoicing"

This was John Bunyan's experience. He tells his story to encourage us to rejoice in the doctrine of justification—that there is a perfect, objective, external righteousness imputed to us that is not our own but Christ's. Bunyan is the one who wrote *The Pilgrim's Progress*, which has sold more copies than any book besides the Bible. He was a pastor in the seventeenth century who spent over twelve years in prison because he refused to stop preaching the word of the cross. The greatest Puritan theologian and contemporary of Bunyan, John Owen, when asked by King Charles II why he went to hear an uneducated tinker preach, said, "May it please your Majesty, could I possess the tinker's ability for preaching, I would willingly relinquish all my learning."[10]

But Bunyan was not always so bold and full of gospel power. In his twenties there were terrible struggles.

> A whole flood of blasphemies, both against God, Christ, and the Scriptures were poured upon my spirit, to my great confusion and astonishment. . . . My heart was at times exceeding hard. If I would have given a thousand pounds for a tear, I could not shed one. . . . Oh, the desperateness of man's heart. . . . I feared that this wicked sin of mine might be that sin unpardonable. . . . Oh, no one knows the terrors of those days but myself.[11]

Then came the decisive moment of triumph over despair and joylessness. It was an awakening to the magnificent truth of the imputation of Christ's righteousness.

> One day as I was passing into the field . . . this sentence fell upon my soul. *Thy righteousness is in heaven.* And . . . I saw with the eyes of my soul Jesus Christ at God's right hand; there, I say, was my righteousness; so that wherever I was, or whatever I was doing, God could not say of me, he [lacks] my righteousness, for that was just before him. I also saw, moreover, that it was not my good frame of heart that made my righteousness better, nor yet my bad frame that made my righteousness worse, for my righteousness was Jesus Christ himself, "The same yesterday, today, and forever." Heb. 13:8. Now did my chains fall off my legs indeed. I was loosed from my afflictions and irons; my temptations also fled away; so that from

that time those dreadful scriptures of God [about the unforgivable sin] left off to trouble me; now went I also home rejoicing for the grace and love of God.[12]

He went home rejoicing. This is the effect of the word of the cross, when one sees, with the eyes of the heart, the glory of God's grace in justification. As he walked home from the field, Bunyan was breathing the same air as Martin Luther, who made the same discovery in a monastery. As the light dawned, Luther said:

> I began to understand [that] the righteousness of God is that by which the righteous lives by a gift of God, namely by faith. And this is the meaning: the righteousness of God is revealed by the gospel, namely, the passive righteousness with which [the] merciful God justifies us by faith. . . . Here I felt that I was altogether born again and had entered paradise itself through open gates.[13]

How Micah Fought for Joy When He Had Sinned

Bunyan and Luther describe the joy of discovering the truth of justification by faith alone. But the prophet Micah shows us how a person who *already believes* the doctrine can preach it into the face of the enemy (whether self or Satan or other people) and use it to fight for joy. So now we have finally returned to the example of Micah that I promised earlier. Even though he only knew the doctrine of justification in its Old Testament form, his application of it is a powerful illustration of how we can preach it to ourselves or to any enemy who tries to kill our joy with counsels of despair. This passage has proved to be a great help to me in many times of darkness.

Here is what Micah said:

> Rejoice not over me, O my enemy; when I fall, I shall rise; when I sit in darkness, the LORD will be a light to me. I will bear the indignation of the LORD because I have sinned against him, until he pleads my cause and executes judgment for me. He will bring me out to the light; I shall look upon his vindication. (Micah 7:8-9)

I like to call Micah's attitude *gutsy guilt*. On the one hand he is

guilty of real sin. In verse 9 he says, simply, "I have sinned against him."
Micah knows it and is not trying to hide it. He is sorry and broken and is
not trying to sweep anything under the rug. "I will bear the indignation
of the LORD." So not only is there real guilt, there is real divine indignation. God does not like what Micah did. He is angry. Micah does not
protest that this can't be—that God doesn't get angry at his children. He
does not short-circuit the discipline of his God by sentimental talk about
God's mercy. The mercy will have its place soon enough.

Micah is ashamed and accepts God's anger: "I sit in darkness." He
puts his hand on his mouth and accepts the sorrow and gloom that hang
over him. No quick fix here. There are many times in the Christian life
like this. It is foolish of us to make light of them, or trivialize them, or
try to deny that they exist. God is holy, and he disciplines the children
whom he loves. There is a fatherly anger that is no longer the wrath of
a judge (Heb. 12:5-11).

How Was Micah's Guilt Gutsy?

But I said that this text describes *gutsy* guilt. Astonishingly, in all his
contrition and gloom under God's anger, Micah gets in the face of
his enemy and says, "Rejoice not over me, O my enemy; when I fall,
I shall rise." The enemy is rubbing it in. The enemy is saying that the
sin of Micah cuts him off from his God. The enemy is lying and trying
to make Micah hopeless. This is a major battle against Micah's joy in
God. And Micah fights well—he preaches the gospel of justification by
faith. He gives us an example of how to fight for joy with the weapon
of the gospel.

He says, "When I sit in darkness, the LORD will be a light to me."
Remember, this darkness is the Lord's discipline. God's indignation
burns. And in the midst of the darkness imposed by God, Micah says,
"God will be my light." He counts on God's light in the darkness that
God himself has sent. That is gutsy. That is what we must learn to
do in our darkness—even the darkness we have brought on ourselves
because of our sin. Yes, I am under the gloom of failure. Yes, God
has put me here in his displeasure. But *no*, I am not abandoned, and
God is not against me. He is for me. Even in the darkness that he
imposes, he will sustain me. He will not let me go. Though he slay

me, he will save me. We must learn to preach to ourselves like this in our fight for joy.

Then, even more astonishingly, Micah says, "I will bear the indignation of the LORD because I have sinned against him, *until he pleads my cause and executes judgment for me.*" In the midst of his guilt, and in the gloom of its consequences, he knows that a limit has been set to the darkness. God will come. "And when he comes, he will come *pleading my cause.*" He will be my advocate, not the prosecuting attorney. The one who has thrown him in the jail of darkness will pay his bail and plead his case in court and make sure that he goes free to live in joy again.

He goes even further and says that when God comes to him in the darkness, he will "execute judgment" for him. Micah's enemies are saying that he has fallen and that this means God is *against* him. "Isn't it clear, Micah? You yourself admit that you sinned. You yourself say that God is angry. You yourself say that the darkness and gloom are from the Lord. There is only one reasonable explanation: God is executing judgment *against* you. You may have once called him Father, but no longer. Now he is Judge. You are guilty, and the judgment is falling—against you." That's what the enemy says.

Against all this "reasonable" accusation (from self, Satan, or others) Micah preaches the doctrine of justification by faith. If he had lived on this side of the cross of Christ, he would be making the ground of God's mercy explicit, namely, the righteousness of Jesus Christ. He says, "Watch out all you who speak thus. My God—my covenant God who declares me righteous by faith and not by works— is about to execute judgment *for* me. That means you, my enemies, will be the ones judged. Take heed, and learn from my rising hope and gutsy guilt the doctrine of justification by faith alone." If you do not learn this, your joys in this life will all be based on an illusion—that your ship is unsinkable.

Micah's words are an utterly crucial illustration of how to preach the gospel to ourselves when discouragement and darkness threaten to overwhelm us as Christians. Micah's way—the biblical way—is very different from the quick fix that tries to deny the seriousness of sin and the pain of God's discipline. We must not think that God only sends us to this painful school because of blatant sins. Paul accepted every calamity in life as from the disciplining hand of God. Even those that made him say, "We were so utterly burdened beyond our strength that we despaired of life itself"—even these he accepted as from God's sovereign hand. He explained that in all these things God's purpose was good, namely, "to make us rely not on ourselves but on God who raises the dead" (2 Cor. 1:8-9).

Gutsy Guilt Is the Opposite of Cheap Grace

In the fight for life-supporting, love-sustaining joy, we must learn to preach to ourselves with gutsy guilt. This is very different from "cheap grace." Do you remember Dietrich Bonhoeffer, the young German theo-logian? He was hanged on April 9, 1945, by a special order of Himmler at the concentration camp in Buchenwald. He wrote a little book that was read by many in the radical days of the late sixties when I was in college. It is called *The Cost of Discipleship*. I bought it when I was a senior in 1967. It cost me $1.45. I thank God when I look at my underlining in this book as a twenty-one-year-old student in search of a cause worth living for.

What Bonhoeffer attacks in this book is the opposite of what Micah did. People refuse to go with Micah into the darkness and bear God's reproach. Bonhoeffer calls such refusal "cheap grace." Here is the way he described it. We need to hear this, lest we confuse the fight for joy with cheap grace. The fight for joy is not cheap grace. It is Micah's gutsy guilt. It is the power of preaching justification by faith in the darkness of God's real indignation.

> Cheap grace is the preaching of forgiveness without requiring repentance, baptism without church discipline, Communion without confession, absolution without personal confession. Cheap grace is grace without discipleship, grace without the cross, grace without Jesus Christ, living and incarnate. . . . The only man who has the right to say that he is justified by grace alone is the man who has left all to follow Christ. . . . We . . . have gathered like eagles round the carcass of cheap grace, and there we have drunk of the poison which has killed the life of following Christ.[14]

Things have not improved since Bonhoeffer's day in the church of the West. Today cheap grace is common among evangelicals in the unpersecuted church. It is the wrong way to lean on grace in the pursuit of joy. There is another way to fight for joy—the way of Micah, the way of bold brokenness, the way of gutsy guilt.

In the battle for joy, the difference between Micah's gutsy guilt and "cheap grace" is that Micah takes sin so seriously. There was a reprehensible fall. There is real and terrible indignation from God. There is a time in awful darkness. There is brokenness, contrition, and remorse as we bear patiently the chastisement of our God. But in the ashes of our regret, the flame of boldness never goes out. It may flicker. But when self or Satan taunts us that we are finished, we lay hold on Micah's faith—indeed we lay hold on Christ and his righteousness—and say, "Rejoice not over me, O my enemy; when I fall, I shall rise; when I sit in darkness, the LORD will be a light to me. . . . He pleads my cause and executes judgment *for* me. He will bring me out to the light."

The Center of the Fight for Joy

Hearing the word of the cross, and preaching it to ourselves, is the central strategy for sinners in the fight for joy. Nothing works without this. Here is where we start. And here is where we stay. We never outgrow the gospel. Here we see the glory of Christ more clearly than anywhere else. Indeed the gospel *is* "the gospel of *the glory of Christ*, who is the image of God" (2 Cor. 4:4). If seeing Christ is the key to savoring Christ—and it is!—then here is where we must linger. The word of the cross is the revelation of the glory of Christ.

And here in the cross of Christ is where every enemy of joy is overcome: divine wrath, as Christ becomes a curse for us; real guilt, as he becomes forgiveness for us; lawbreaking, as he becomes righteousness for us; estrangement from God, as he becomes reconciliation for us; slavery to Satan, as he becomes redemption for us; bondage to sin, as he becomes liberation for us; pangs of conscience, as he becomes cleansing for us; death, as he becomes the resurrection for us; hell, as he becomes eternal life for us. And here I resist the desire to go on with dozens of ways that the cross defeats the enemies of our joy. Instead I send you to the place where I gathered fifty of them, *Fifty Reasons Why Jesus Came to Die.*[15]

Through the cross God purchased and secured every possible blessing that could ever be needed to make us happy forever. "He who did not spare his own Son but gave him up for us all, how will he not also with him graciously give us all things?" (Rom. 8:32). The answer to that question is not uncertain. God *will*—signed in blood—give us all things with Christ, because of the death of his Son. That is, he will give us all things that are truly good for us. We must preach this to ourselves every day, because Satan is preaching the opposite. What could stop our joy if we really believed this truth: Everything we need to be satisfied in God, the cross has made certain. It cannot fail.

The Cross, the Joy, the Sacrifice of Love, and the Glory of God

Jesus, in his obedient death, has become our righteousness with God. He has become, therefore, the ground of our unshakable joy. And therefore the ground of our most radical, risk-taking acts of love. When the famous five missionaries to Ecuador—Jim Elliot, Peter Fleming, Ed McCully, Nate Saint, Roger Youderian—made their last attempt in 1956 to take the love of God to the Waorani people, among their final preparations before they were killed on the river beach was to sing Edith Cherry's hymn, "We Rest on Thee." At the heart of this hymn is the verse with the heart of the gospel—the imputed righteousness of Christ:

> *Yea, in Thy Name, O Captain of salvation!*
> *In Thy dear Name, all other names above;*
> *Jesus our righteousness, our sure foundation,*
> *Our Prince of glory and our King of love.*[16]

Where do missionaries (who, like all of us, are sinners) get the courage to face the spears of those they love and not use the firearms in their hands, but rather die? They get it from the superior satisfaction that they have in Christ above all that this earth can offer. "He is no fool who gives what he cannot keep to gain what he cannot lose."[17] Yes, especially if what we cannot lose is the all-satisfying glory of Christ.

And underneath this superior satisfaction in Christ is the gospel of justification by faith alone. Christ was their righteousness. Christ was their sure foundation. Therefore their joy was invincible. And their love for people was greater than their love for life. Oh, that we might learn the secret of gutsy guilt and how to fight for joy like justified sinners. When the gospel of Christ has that effect, our joy will be full, and his glory will shine.

The Lord *revealed himself to Samuel at Shiloh by the word of the* Lord.

1 SAMUEL 3:21

More to be desired are [God's words] than gold,
even much fine gold;
sweeter also than honey
and drippings of the honeycomb.
Moreover, by them is your servant warned;
in keeping them there is great reward.

PSALM 19:10–11

The cross of Christ he gloried and rejoiced in; this his heart was set upon; and these were the effects of it—it crucified the world unto him, made it a dead and undesirable thing. The baits and pleasures of sin are taken all of them out of the world. . . . If the heart be filled with the cross of Christ, it casts death and undesirableness upon them all; it leaves no seeming beauty, no appearing pleasure or comeliness, in them.

JOHN OWEN
On Indwelling Sin in Believers[1]

7

The Worth of God's Word in the Fight for Joy

*Seeing the Measure of
This Mighty Weapon*

The fundamental reason that the Word of God is essential to joy in God is that God reveals *himself* mainly by his Word. And seeing this revelation of God is the foundation of our joy. As it was in the days of Samuel, so it is today: "The LORD *appeared* . . . at Shiloh, for the LORD *revealed himself* to Samuel at Shiloh *by the word of the LORD*" (1 Sam. 3:21). When it says, "The LORD *appeared*," it says something amazing. God was seen not with the eyes of the head, but with the eyes of the heart, for God is "the King of ages, immortal, *invisible*, the only God" (1 Tim. 1:17). And though it may seem strange, this *seeing* at Shiloh happened "*by the word* of the LORD." As the Word was heard, the Lord was seen. In the hearing was the seeing. The spiritual hearing of God's Word becomes the spiritual seeing of God's glory.

How Is God Seen Today?

So it is in the gospel today. Paul says that becoming a Christian means "seeing the light of the gospel of the glory of Christ" (2 Cor. 4:4). The gospel is news about the death and resurrection of Jesus (1 Cor. 15:1-4).

It is a word to be heard. And in this hearing there is something to be seen: "The light . . . of the glory of Christ." In the hearing is the seeing. The Lord opens the eyes of the heart to see the glory of Christ in the Word. God has chosen in this age to reveal himself to the world mainly through the incarnate Word, Jesus Christ, by means of the written Word, the Bible.[2]

The reason this is so crucial in the fight for joy is that God himself is the ultimate object of our enjoyment. But God "reveals himself . . . *by the word*." Oh, how precious is the Bible! Here is where we see God most clearly and most surely. The Holy Spirit opens our eyes and grants us to see the beauty of Christ (Matt. 16:17; Acts 16:14). If there were no Bible, there would be no lasting joy. Even those who yet have no Bible in their language depend on the Bible for the Christ-revealing, saving knowledge of God.

God can and does show himself in other ways, especially through the works of believers (Matt. 5:16; 1 Pet. 2:12; 1 Cor. 12:7). But none of them reveals God with the clarity and fullness of the Bible. All of them orbit around the sun of God's written Word. And if the central gravitational power of the sun is denied, all the planets fly into confusion.

To be sure, in the fight for joy we will not kneel forever over our Bibles. We will get up and walk with Jesus onto the Calvary road. And there, in the risks and the afflictions of love, we will see the Jesus of the Word in the manifestations of power. This too is part of our joy. Sometimes it will be extraordinary, miraculous power. More often it will be the supernatural grace of self-denying sacrifice, unwavering faith, and the conversion of sinners into lovers of Christ. In all this we will see the Lord and rejoice. But all these manifestations of Christ would be vague and blurry without the written Word to guide our understanding and guard our hearts. We need the Word of God not only to see God in the Word, but to see him rightly anywhere else.

Admitting the Sin of Reluctance to Read the Bible

A thousand interesting things compete for our attention to the Word of God. I confess that after fifty years of loving and reading and memorizing Scripture, I can be lured away from appointed times in the Word by something as insignificant as a new computer device. The illusory pleasure of newness can temporarily trump the far superior benefits of keeping my appointment with the Word of God.

This is evidence in me of what Paul calls indwelling sin (Rom. 7:17, 20, 23). It is part of the remaining corruption lingering after the death of the old self (Rom. 6:6). I am not proud of it. It grieves me. At times it frightens me. It is part of the reason I speak so much of the fight for joy. I know this sinful inclination must be fought to the death. It is this fight Paul has in mind when he says, "Put to death therefore what is earthly in you" (Col. 3:5). We will speak shortly about how the Word helps us do that. But first we must fight just to keep our appointments with the Word.

One of the ways we can fight against the inclinations that lure us from the Word of God to computers or television or any other substitute pleasure is to remind ourselves often of the immeasurable and superior benefits of the Word of God in our lives. We must put the evidence before us that reading, pondering, memorizing, and studying the Bible will yield more joy in this life and the next than all the things that lure us from it.

There are many different reasons why the Bible has this joy-producing effect. I don't want to minimize this diversity or belittle the range of benefits that the Bible has in our lives—more than any of us realizes. But I want to stress that ultimately, in and through all its benefits, the Bible leads us to superior and lasting joy because it leads us to Christ, especially to see his glory and enjoy his fellowship. All the varied benefits are beneficial finally because they show us and bring us more of Christ to enjoy.

Seeing the Worth of Scripture

In this chapter, then, consider with me just ten of these benefits, and as you read them, ask God to give you eyes to see the worth of Scripture and to waken in you an unyielding desire for the Word of God. This is a fight for joy, and the weapon in this chapter is a fresh sight of how the worth of God's Word surpasses all things on this earth.

1. The Word of God awakens and strengthens *faith*

The Holy Spirit does not awaken and strengthen faith apart from the Word of God. "Faith comes from hearing, and hearing through the word of Christ" (Rom. 10:17). The reason for this is that the Spirit has been sent into the world to glorify Christ. But Christ would not be glorified if the Spirit wakened faith in the absence of the revelation of the glory of Christ in the gospel.

"When the Spirit of truth comes," Jesus said, "he will glorify me" (John 16:13-14). If the Spirit brought us to faith in the absence of the proclamation of Christ in his Word, our faith would not be in Christ, and he would not be honored. Therefore the Spirit binds his faith-wakening ministry to the Christ-exalting Word. Which means that when we go to the Word of Christ, we put ourselves in the path of the Spirit's willingness to reveal Christ to us and strengthen our faith. And in this faith is the taste and the seed of all our joy. Therefore, the Word that wakens our faith works for our joy.

2. Through hearing the Word, God supplies the *Holy Spirit*

The Spirit of God produces both a subconscious influence bringing us to faith, and a conscious experience of power and personal fellowship that come through that very faith. This explains two things: (1) This is why the Bible can speak of the Spirit blowing where he wills and having merciful effects in our lives before we were able to choose them (John 3:6-8; 6:36, 44, 65). In other words, by his unconscious influence he works in us to enable us to hear and welcome the Word. And (2) this is also why the Bible speaks of the Spirit coming through our hearing the Word of God. In other words, conscious fellowship with the Spirit is given when we hear the Word of God with faith.

Thus Paul says in Galatians 3:5, "Does he who supplies the Spirit to you and works miracles among you do so by works of the law, or by hearing with faith?" The answer, of course, is "by hearing with faith." Notice the word *hearing*. It implies that words have been spoken. Paul has preached the Word of God. Now he reminds them: "Hearing that Word with faith was the means by which the Spirit was given to you." So the Spirit comes (unconsciously) *before* we trust him and thus enables us to believe in God's Word; and the Spirit comes (consciously) *in response to* our trusting him and gives us the conscious experience of his fellowship through God's Word—the experience Paul calls "the joy of the Holy Spirit." "You received the word . . . with the joy of the Holy Spirit" (1 Thess. 1:6).

This remains true even after we become Christians and have the

Holy Spirit in us. If we want more of the Spirit of God, we must hear more of the Word of God with faith. We must hear his promises, see their blood-bought certainty, value their goodness, and bank on them. That is the way God supplies more of his Spirit. The command in Ephesians 5:18-19, "Be filled with the Spirit, addressing one another in psalms and hymns and spiritual songs," is parallel with the command in Colossians 3:16, "Let the word of Christ dwell in you richly, teaching and admonishing one another in all wisdom, singing psalms and hymns and spiritual songs." Being filled with the Word of Christ and being filled with the Spirit of Christ are almost the same, because the Spirit comes with joy where the Word is embraced with faith.

In other words, not only does the first act of faith come by hearing, but all subsequent acts of faith come by hearing. And since God supplies his Spirit through this "hearing with faith," the fullness of the Spirit comes by the ongoing hearing of the Word of God. And when the Spirit comes, he comes to make much of Jesus. Which means he comes to ignite joy in our hearts over the glory of Jesus. Which means the Word of God is worth more than anything this world can offer.

3. The Word of God creates and sustains *life*

Jesus said, "I came that they may have life and have it abundantly" (John 10:10). To that end he taught many things, and then gave his life so that we might have life, eternal and abundant. We are born again into new life by the Word of God. "You have been *born again*, not of perishable seed but of imperishable, through the living and abiding word of God. . . . And this word is the good news that was preached to you" (1 Pet. 1:23-25). God makes the preaching of the gospel the occasion for creating new life in the soul of man. "The words that I have spoken to you," Jesus said, "are spirit and *life*" (John 6:63). Therefore when John had finished recording the words and works of Jesus in his Gospel he said, "These are written so that you may . . . have *life* in his name" (John 20:31). The words of John's Gospel—and all the Scriptures—lead to life.

Jesus said, "Man shall not *live* by bread alone, but by every *word* that comes from the mouth of God" (Matt. 4:4). Oh, how easily we are deceived into thinking that better life, or more life, comes from things that lure us from the Word. But, in fact, it is the Word itself that gives us life abundantly. The life we get from bread is fragile and short. The life we get from the Word is firm and lasts forever. That life is created and kept by the Word of God. And with that life comes the light of life, by which we see the glory of Christ. "With you is the fountain of *life*; in your light do we see *light*" (Ps. 36:9). Or as Jesus said, "Whoever follows me . . . will have the *light of life*" (John 8:12). In other words, the life that comes from the Word is a life of joy, because the Word brings us from the darkness of impending sorrow to the light of the glory of Christ.

4. The Word of God gives *hope*

In more ways than we can imagine the Word of God gives and strengthens our hope. We get a glimpse of how many ways the Bible gives hope when we hear Paul's astonishing assessment of the Old Testament alone: "Whatever was written in former days was written for our instruction, that through endurance and through the encouragement of the Scriptures we might have *hope*" (Rom. 15:4). Not just part of the Old Testament, but all of it—"whatever was written in former days"—was written with the divine design to give us hope.

One of the things this teaches us is that we have not begun to know all the ways it is possible to get hope. We have very small experience in life compared to God's wisdom. There are a thousand ways that God has designed to give us hope. Most of them we have not yet tasted or even conceived. Yet how often we murmur that the few proven ways we get hope are missing! We do not realize that there are ways to get hope that we have never thought of. How small-minded of us in our hopelessness to look at our closed Bible and say, "What I need is _____, and this is not in the Bible." How do we know we need _____ and not some utterly unexpected hope that the Bible will awaken in us when we read it in faith?

Indeed, we may lack hope because we think we need something we do not need. It may take the Word of God to show us what we really need, and then to give us the power to get it. In the end what we really need is Christ. He is the sum of all our hopes. Paul commends the Thessalonians for their "steadfastness of *hope in our Lord Jesus Christ*" (1 Thess. 1:3). He says that our "blessed *hope* [is] the appearing of the *glory of our great God and Savior Jesus Christ*" (Tit. 2:13). Therefore we are to "*hope in Christ*" (Eph. 1:12) and rejoice in the mystery of the gospel, which is "*Christ in you, the hope of glory*" (Col. 1:27).

Sometimes what we need from the Bible is not the fulfillment of our dream, but the swallowing up of our failed dream in the all-satisfying glory of Christ. We do not always know the path of deepest joy. But all Scripture is inspired by God to take us there. Therefore Scripture is worth more than all this world can offer.

5. The Word of God leads us to *freedom*

Jesus said, "You will know the truth, and the truth will set you free" (John 8:32). The truth of God's Word works freedom in many ways and brings joy in all of them. But Jesus signals his focus in verse 34: "Truly, truly, I say to you, everyone who commits *sin* is a slave to sin." The freedom he has in mind here is freedom from the enslaving, destructive effect of sin. The truth sets us free from this. So Jesus turns this truth into a prayer in John 17:17, "Sanctify them in the truth; your word is truth." *Sanctify* means to make holy, or free from sin.

This freedom is essential in the fight for joy for two reasons. One is that the *guilt* of sin would bring down the wrath of God on us if *the truth* of the gospel did not set us free from condemnation through the blood and righteousness of Christ. That's what we focused on in Chapter Six.

The other reason this freedom is essential in the fight for joy is that sin so defiles and corrupts our lives that we cannot see or savor what is best. Therefore, the corruption of sin is a great joy-killer. Jesus said, "Blessed are the pure in heart, for they shall see God" (Matt. 5:8). We devoted Chapter Five to the way that seeing God functions in the fight for joy. Here, suffice it to say that the impurity of sin so distorts our perception that we cannot see God as desirable. Therefore sin makes the greatest joys impossible.

Sin's Substitute Promises: Deceitful Pleasures

Of course, sin provides deceptive substitutes. The Bible calls them "deceitful desires" (Eph. 4:22), because they lie to us about the superiority of their outcomes. They call sweet sour, and sour sweet. They turn everything upside down. And those who believe them become more and more like them. "Their god is their belly, and they glory in their shame, with minds set on earthly things" (Phil. 3:19). Oh, how many people in our world glory in their shame and relish poisonous pleasures!

"Deceitful desires" can trick us into feeling that sinful thoughts and acts will be more satisfying than seeing God. This illusion is so strong it creates moral confusion, so that people find ways to justify sin as good, or, if not good, at least permissible. How many marriages have been destroyed by the self-justifying arguments that flow not from the truth of God's Word, but from "deceitful desires"!

Oh, how urgent the battle becomes when the "deceitful desires" are the strongest. Jesus uses his most violent language for the frontline battle against deceitful desires. "If your right eye causes you to sin, tear it out and throw it away. For it is better that you lose one of your members than that your whole body be thrown into hell" (Matt. 5:29). Jesus calls for violence against our own lust because he loves our true and lasting joy. Sexual desire is one of the most powerful deceivers about where that joy can be found. Even pastors by the thousand have been turned into fools who cannot tell their right hand from their left because of a woman's tenderness.

The Christian "Mean Streak" in Self-Control

Ed Welch has written powerfully about the "all-out war" demanded against deceitful desires:

> . . . there is a mean streak to authentic self-control. . . . Self-control is not for the timid. When we want to grow in it, not only do we nurture an exuberance for Jesus Christ, we also demand of ourselves a hatred for sin. . . . The only possible attitude toward out-of-control desire is a declaration of all-out war. . . . There is something about war that sharpens the senses . . . You hear a twig snap or the rustling of leaves and you are in attack mode. Someone coughs and you are ready to pull the trigger. Even after days of little or no sleep, war keeps us vigilant.[3]

Yes, there is a mean, violent streak in the true Christian life! But violence against whom, or what? Not other people! It's a violence against all the impulses in us that would be violent to other people. It's a violence against all the impulses in our own selves that would make peace with our own sin and settle in with a peacetime mentality. It's a violence against all lust in ourselves and all enslaving desires for food or caffeine or sugar or chocolate or alcohol or pornography or money or the praise of men and the approval of others or power or fame. It's a violence against the impulses in our own soul toward racism and sluggish indifference to injustice and poverty and abortion.

Christianity is not a settle-in-and-live-at-peace-with-this-world-the-way-it-is kind of religion. When Jesus said, "The truth will set you free" (John 8:32), he didn't mean without a battle. He meant that truth would win the war of liberation in the soul. Christianity is war. It is a declaration of all-out combat against our own sinful impulses. The apostle Peter said, "Beloved, I urge you as sojourners and exiles to abstain from the passions of the flesh, which *wage war* against your soul" (1 Pet. 2:11). To become a Christian is to wake up to the reality that our soul—the eternal joy of our soul—is at stake. Therefore, Christianity is mortal combat for true and lasting joy.

The Liberating Power of the Word Is the Power of Promised Joy

Jesus would set us free from the deadly illusions of worldly satisfaction. And he would do so by the truth of his Word. "You will know the truth, and the truth will set you free." So how does the truth of the Word set us free from deceitful desires, so that we can have deeper, stronger, sweeter, higher, longer joy than anything Satan or this world can offer?

Some Christians take the path of stoicism in the fight against sensuality. It doesn't work. It's not biblical. It is hopelessly weak and ineffective. And the reason it fails is that the power of sin comes from its promise of pleasure and is meant to be defeated by the blood-bought promise of superior pleasure in God, not by raw human willpower. Willpower religion, when it succeeds, gets glory for the will. It produces legalists, not lovers. Jonathan Edwards saw the powerlessness of this approach and said:

> We come with double forces against the wicked, to persuade them to a godly life. . . . The common argument is the profitableness of religion, but alas, the wicked man is not in pursuit of profit; 'tis pleasure he seeks. Now, then, we will fight with them with their own weapons.[4]

In other words, a passion for blood-bought, everlasting pleasure in God is the only power that can defeat the lusts of the age while producing lovers of God, not legalists who boast in their willpower.

This is how the truth of God's Word sets us free. It gives us the weapon with which we kill deceitful desires. Just as Jesus spoke of violence in the battle against desire, so does Paul: "*Put to death* therefore what is earthly in you . . . evil desire, and covetousness, which is idolatry" (Col. 3:5). And in another place he says, "If by the Spirit you *put to death* the deeds of the body, you will live" (Rom. 8:13). The fact that one text says put to death *desires* and another says put to death *deeds* simply shows that behind evil deeds are evil desires. It would do no good just to kill the deed and leave the desire. That is not the way of Jesus. Jesus' way is: put to death the deed by putting to death the desire. Strangle the deed by cutting off its air supply—namely, the deceit that it will bring us lasting joy.

Both Romans 8:13 and Colossians 3:5 say, "Kill!" This is mortal combat, and our lives—not to mention our joy—hang on it. Jesus and Paul agree: This is war. Christianity would look very different in many places if Christians pursued the joy of seeing God with this life-and-death seriousness and felt a deadly urgency in fighting the desires that deceive us and blind us to the all-satisfying glory of God.

How Do You Kill a Deceitful Desire?

How then does the truth of God's Word help us kill deceitful desires and set us free for solid joys? One key is to notice that Romans 8:13 says that the deceitful desires and deeds that threaten our life are to be killed "by the Spirit." How do you put to death a desire "by the Spirit"? First, by noticing that the one and only offensive weapon in Paul's description of "the armor of God" in Ephesians 6:11-18 (the weapon used for killing) is "the sword of the Spirit, which is the word of God." So when Romans 8:13 says that we should kill sinful deeds "by the Spirit," I take it to mean, "Experience the deceit-destroying power of the Spirit by believing in the Word of God concerning that deceitful desire." Even though we are mere humans and not God, we are to discharge (like a cannon) the power of the Spirit against sinful desires.

This deadly firepower (= the sword) is called "the word of God." I take it that our way of discharging this power is by believing this Word. This is confirmed by Galatians 3:5: "Does he who supplies the Spirit to you and works miracles among you do so by works of the law, or by hearing with faith?" In other words, we bring the power of the Spirit into vigorous, sin-killing action by *hearing with faith*. Hearing what? The Word of God. Therefore, the way we destroy deceitful, joy-killing desires that threaten to overwhelm us with destructive cravings is to hear and believe the Word of God when it says that he and his ways are more to be desired than all that sin can offer.

This is what Edwards meant when he said, "Now, then, we will fight with them with their own weapons." The power of sin is the promise of deceitful desires? Then we will match promise for promise! Go ahead, sin, put up your best promises! We will put God's promises against yours. Nothing—nothing in this world—can surpass in value and depth and height and durability the pleasure that God promises. "Blessed [happy!⁵] are the pure in heart, for they shall see God" (Matt. 5:8). "You give them drink from the river of your delights" (Ps. 36:8). "In your presence there is fullness of joy; at your right hand are pleasures forevermore" (Ps. 16:11). "You have put more joy in my heart than they have when their grain and wine abound" (Ps. 4:7). "Rejoice in that day, and leap for joy, for behold, your reward is great in heaven" (Luke 6:23). Nothing surpasses the joy God promises.

The fight for joy is the fight to see and believe Christ as more to be desired than the promises of sin. This faith and sight come by hearing, and hearing by the word of Christ. We look to the Word, we ponder, and we plead with God that the eyes of our hearts would be opened to see the superior glory and joy. This pleading is so important we will devote the whole of Chapter Nine to it. But suffice it to say for now that we are utterly dependent on the Spirit to make the promises of God more desirable to us than the promises of sin. And for that vital eye-opening, heart-changing work we pray every day.

How the Cross of Christ Kills Joy-Killing Sin

But let's be even more focused in how the truth sets us free from deceitful, joy-killing desires. Not only does the Word of God have promises perfectly suited to kill each deceitful desire,[6] it also has a central message designed to have special power in this battle. The central message is the gospel of Christ crucified. We spent all of Chapter Six on this. But I saved the witness of John Owen for this decisive place. Owen (1616-1683) was probably the greatest thinker and theologian among the Puritans in England. He combined deep biblical reflection with penetrating practical application.

One of his most famous works is but eighty-six pages long. It's called *Mortification of Sin in Believers*. "Mortify" means "kill" in seventeenth-century English. The whole book is an exposition of Romans 8:13 ("If by the Spirit you put to death [kill] the deeds of the body, you will live"). Owen put it like this: "Be killing sin or it will be killing you."[7]

My mother wrote in my Bible when I was fifteen years old—I still have the Bible—"This book will keep you from sin, or sin will keep you from this book." The point I am trying to make right now is that my mother's motto and Owen's motto, "Be killing sin or sin will be killing you," are virtually the same. The Word of God is the instrument for killing sin. The truth will set you free. For Owen the cross of Christ was the central message and sin-killing power of the Word of God. It was the central, liberating truth. To focus here, he said, is the main way to kill the sin that kills our joy.

> As to the object of your affections, in an especial manner, let it be the cross of Christ, which has exceeding efficacy towards the disappointment of the whole work of indwelling sin: "God forbid that I should glory, save in the cross of our Lord Jesus Christ, whereby the world is crucified unto me, and I unto the world" (Gal. 6:14). The cross of Christ he [Paul] gloried and rejoiced in; this his heart was set upon; and these were the effects of it—it crucified the world unto him, made it a dead and undesirable thing. *The baits and pleasures of sin are taken all of them out of the world.* . . . If the heart be filled with the cross of Christ, *it casts death and undesirableness upon them all; it leaves no seeming beauty, no appearing pleasure or comeliness, in them.* Again, says he, "It crucifies me to the world; makes my heart, my affections, *my desires, dead unto any of these things.*" It roots up corrupt lusts and affections, leaves no principle to go forth and make provision for the flesh, to fulfill the lusts thereof. *Labor, therefore, to fill your hearts with the cross of Christ . . . that there may be no room for sin.*[8]

This is the heart of the battle in the fight for joy. You will know the truth and the truth will set you free—free to see the surpassing glory of Christ, free from the blinding, joy-killing desires that make war on the soul. In the fight for joy, there is no replacement for the liberating power of truth—the truth of God's promises and the word of the cross, where all the promises were blood-bought by the death of Christ.

6. The Word of God is the key to *answered prayer*

Another benefit of the Word of God that wakens desire to read and ponder and memorize Scripture is the role it plays in answered prayer. Jesus said, "If you abide in me, and my words abide in you, ask whatever you wish, and it will be done for you" (John 15:7). The words of Jesus must abide in us if our prayers are to be effective.

The best way to see what it means for the words of Jesus to abide in us is to look at what Jesus says about abiding a few verses earlier. In verse 5 he says, "Whoever abides in me and I in him, he it is that bears much fruit." Notice the parallel. In verse 7 he says, "If you abide in me, and *my words* abide in you," and in verse 5 he says, "Whoever abides in me and *I* in him. . . ." In verse 5 *Jesus himself* abides in us when we abide in him. But in verse 7 *his words* abide in us when we abide in him. I think the point of this switch is to show us how Jesus abides in us, namely, by his words abiding in us.[9]

But this parallel also sheds light on what it means for the words of Jesus to abide in us. Letting the words of Jesus abide in us means letting Jesus himself abide in us, to us. It means that we welcome Jesus into our lives and make room for him to live, not as a silent guest with no opinions or commands, but as an authoritative guest whose words and priorities and principles and promises matter more to us than anything does.

What that means for letting the words of Jesus abide in us is that we do not just read or memorize or meditate or listen to the Bible the way we would ponder the wise sayings from ancient teachers. Jesus is alive today, but they aren't. He does not intend for our *thinking* about his words to replace *fellowship* with him through his words. He intends for musing on his words to *be* fellowship with him. We hear the words of Jesus as living words spoken by a living person. It is a spiritually intentional act of relating to a living person when you take his words into your mind. This is what it means for his words to abide in us.

How Does the Abiding Word of Christ Lead to
Effective Prayers?

The reason the abiding of Christ's words in us results in answered prayer is that it changes us into the kind of people who love what he loves, so that we ask for things according to his will. This is not absolute. It is progressive. The more we know the living Christ by communion with him in his Word, the more our desires become spiritual like his desires, instead of just worldly. This is what David meant when he said in Psalm 37:4, "Delight yourself in the LORD, and he will give you the desires of your heart." The desires of the heart cease to be merely natural desires when the heart delights above all else in the Lord. Delighting in the Lord—in the hallowing of his name and the seeking of his kingdom and the doing of his will—transforms all natural desires into God-related desires. That is what happens when the Word of Christ abides in us.

Another way of saying it is, if you want God to respond to your interests, you must be devoted to his interests. God is God. He does not run the world by hiring the consulting firm called Mankind. He lets us share in the running of the world through prayer to the degree that we live in fellowship with him and are gladly shaped by his heart and goals and purposes.

One evidence for this is 1 John 5:14, "This is the confidence that we have toward him, that *if we ask anything according to his will* he hears us." Prayer is not for gratifying our natural desires. It is for gratifying our desires when those desires have been so purified and so saturated with Christ and his Word that they coincide with his plans. This happens more and more as the Word of Christ abides in us.

The words of Jesus abiding in us prepare us for fruit-bearing prayer. "Whoever abides in me and I in him, he it is that bears much fruit" (John 15:5). If prayer is not for gratifying natural desires but for Christ-exalting fruit-bearing, the major challenge in praying is to become the kind of person who is not dominated by natural desires, but by spiritual fruit-bearing desires. The aim is to become what Paul calls a "spiritual person," as opposed to a merely "natural person" or carnal person (1 Cor. 2:14-15). The key to praying with power is to become the kind of persons who do not use God for our ends but are utterly devoted to being used for his ends.

This is why Jesus says, "If you abide in me, and my words abide in you, ask whatever you wish, and it will be done for you." The words of

Jesus abiding in us make us the kind of persons who are not dominated by merely natural desires, but are devoted to fruit-bearing for God's glory. If you ever longed for a life of deep and fruitful prayer, give yourself to the Word of God. Read it. Think about it. Memorize it. Be shaped by it.

> *When saturated by the Word,*
> *More surely will our prayers be heard.*

And since one of those daily prayers will be, "Satisfy us in the morning with your steadfast love, that we may rejoice and be glad all our days" (Ps. 90:14), the words of Jesus are more to be desired than all that this world can offer.

7. The Word of God is the source of *wisdom*

It is a great advantage to be wise. Wisdom is different from the mere knowledge of facts. Some very wise people have little formal education. And some very educated people, who know many facts, are not wise. Wisdom is the insight and sense of how to live in a way that accomplishes the goals for which we were made: the glory of God and the good of man. And since glorifying God involves delighting in God, and the good of man involves sharing our joy in God, therefore wisdom is the only path to deep and lasting joy.

It won't surprise us that this joy-producing wisdom comes through the Word of God. We just saw in the preceding section that Christ himself abides in us when his words abide in us, and Paul tells us that "in [him] are hidden all the treasures of *wisdom* and knowledge" (Col. 2:3). So by his Word he dwells in us, and with him come "all the treasures of wisdom." Paul says it more directly in Colossians 3:16, "Let the *word of Christ* dwell in you richly, teaching and admonishing one another *in all wisdom*." The Word of Christ brings "all wisdom" into our lives so that we can help each other know it and live in it.

One of the challenges I repeatedly hold out to the people of our church—especially the women—is that they make it one of their aims to age into a sage. I love the vision of older women full of seasoned spiritual fruit that comes only with long life and much affliction and deep meditation on the Word of God. So many younger women yearn for older women, who are deeply wise, to share the wisdom God has taught them over the years. The joy of giving and receiving this kind of gift is great. It is joy that comes by the Word of God. There is no better joy than what comes through wisdom. Therefore, the Word of God is more valuable than anything on earth.

8. The Word of God gives us crucial *warnings*

Psalm 19 celebrates the benefits of the Word of God as explicitly as any other Scripture. It comes to a climax like this: "More to be desired are they than gold, even much fine gold; sweeter also than honey and drippings of the honeycomb. Moreover, *by them is your servant warned;* in keeping them there is great reward" (vv. 10-11).

If we had perfect sight of what is wrong and right, and if we could know the future and the consequences of all behavior and all events, then perhaps we would need no warnings. But we are blind to many things and do not know the future, as God does. We need to be warned often that the step we are about to take is folly. Oh, how many joy-killing choices we are spared when we heed the warnings of the Bible! Mercifully God has given us a book that not only points us to the right path but sounds warnings when we are about to take the wrong one.

Warnings are humbling. They save our lives at the cost of our egos. My wife has saved my life several times. Once in Cambridge, England, where cars drive on the left side of the road, I was crossing a city street in front of our hotel. I made it to the middle of the street, and then my alertness failed me, and I looked to my right to see if cars were coming. All clear. Noël must have read my muscles, because in the split second when I was about to make a dash, she called out in a voice that clearly meant *stop*, "Johnny!" My body reacted instinctively to the warning as a car passed *from my left* perhaps three feet in front of me doing maybe thirty miles an hour. If she had not sounded the warning (firmly, with no frills), I do believe I would be either dead today or crippled.

I was given my life by a warning. The Bible is full of life-giving, joy-preserving warnings. How many people with venereal diseases would have been spared by heeding the warning, "Flee from sexual immorality" (1 Cor. 6:18)! How many people with lung cancer would have been spared by heeding the warning not to be enslaved by anything, including nicotine (1 Cor. 6:12)! How many people would not be in prison if they had heeded the warning, "You shall not murder," or, "You shall not steal," or, "You shall not bear false witness" (Ex. 20:13, 15, 16)! How many have ruined their lives by neglecting the crystal-clear warning, "Those who desire to be rich fall into temptation, into a snare, into many senseless and harmful desires that plunge people into ruin and destruction. . . . It is through this craving that some have wandered away from the faith and pierced themselves with many pangs" (1 Tim. 6:9-10)!

How merciful are the warnings of the Word of God! They are the source of untold joy for those who see in them the good heart of the Great Physician. He knows the prevention and the remedy for every sorrow. Does your desire go deeper and last longer than what the world can offer? Then go to the Word of God and get good warnings.

9. The Word of God enables us to *defeat the devil*

The devil is real and terrible. He is much stronger than we are, and he aims to deceive and destroy. Jesus said, "He was a murderer from the beginning, and has nothing to do with the truth, because there is no truth in him. When he lies, he speaks out of his own character, for he is a liar and the father of lies" (John 8:44). Yet he has been decisively defeated through the death and resurrection of Jesus. The Bible teaches that Christ took on himself human nature so "that through death he might destroy the one who has the power of death, that is, the devil" (Heb. 2:14). The destruction was decisive, though not final. Because of Christ's shed blood for our sins, the devil cannot destroy those who are in Christ. The reason is that his accusations are no longer valid. The only thing that could sentence us to eternal destruction is unforgiven sin. But the cross obtained complete forgiveness. Therefore, the devil can only kill us, but not damn us.

Yes, he has that much power. Jesus said to the church in Smyrna, "Do not fear what you are about to suffer. Behold, the devil is about to throw some of you into prison, that you may be tested, and for ten days you will have tribulation. *Be faithful unto death*, and I will give you the crown of life" (Rev. 2:10). Where is the victory in that? John tells us in Revelation 12:11: "And they have conquered [the devil] by the blood of the Lamb and by the word of their testimony, for they loved not their lives even unto death." By trusting Jesus' blood to cover all their sins, and by holding on to their faith even to death, they conquered the devil.

The devil is conquered wherever his design to devour faith is defeated. That defeat is by the cross of Christ and the Word of God. John, who knew the devil's workings so well, said in his first letter, "I write to you, young men, because you are strong, and the word of God abides in you, and you have overcome the evil one" (1 John 2:14). The Word of God is the power that overcomes the devil. So it was with Jesus in the wilderness. To every temptation thrown at him by the devil, he quoted Scripture (Matt. 4:4, 7, 10). If Jesus was himself the Word of God, and could command demons so that they obey him (Mark 1:27), and yet he depended on Scripture to deflect the temptations of the devil, so should we.

It's true, Paul says: "In all circumstances take up the *shield of faith*, with which you can extinguish all the flaming darts of the evil one" (Eph. 6:16). So *faith* is the great devil-defeater. "Resist him, firm *in your faith*" (1 Pet. 5:9). But faith in what? The Word of God. The promises of God. Therefore Paul instructs Timothy, "The Lord's servant must not be quarrelsome but . . . able to *teach* . . . *correcting* his opponents with gentleness. God may perhaps grant them repentance leading to a knowledge of *the truth*, and they may *escape from the snare of the devil*, after being captured by him to do his will" (2 Tim. 2:24-26). Teaching is the most common instrument that God uses to deliver "from the snare of the devil." Teaching what? "Knowledge of the truth"—the Word of God.

Therefore, if you would have power over the devil, and if you would escape the snare of his deceit and the destruction of your faith, then do what Jesus did and what all the triumphant saints have done: treasure up the Word of God, and wield it like a sword against your foe.

And though this world, with devils filled,
Should threaten to undo us,
We will not fear, for God hath willed
His truth to triumph through us.
The prince of darkness grim,
We tremble not for him;
His rage we can endure,
For lo! his doom is sure;
One little word shall fell him.[10]

When the powers of darkness are arrayed against you, and aim to destroy your joy forever, nothing is more precious than to have the Word of God ready for the battle. The fight for joy is not for the unarmed.

10. The Word of God is, therefore, the source of great and lasting *joy*
We have seen at least nine reasons why this is so. Now we see that
God, in the Bible, simply says it is so. The wise and godly man turns
away from the counsel of the wicked with all their promises of pleasure
and finds that "his *delight* is in the law of the LORD, and on his law he
meditates day and night. He is like a tree planted by streams of water
that yields its fruit in its season, and its leaf does not wither. In all that
he does, he prospers" (Ps. 1:2-3). The lovers of God's Word praise the
preciousness of the Bible and the pleasures it brings. They say that it
surpasses the most valuable earthly things, gold and silver; and they say
its taste on the tongue of the mind and heart is sweeter than honey, and
that its richness is like the finest food.

> The law of your mouth is better to me than thousands of gold and
> silver pieces. (Ps. 119:72)

> I rejoice at your word like one who finds great spoil. (Ps. 119:162)

> I love your commandments above gold, above fine gold.
> (Ps. 119:127)

> How sweet are your words to my taste, sweeter than honey to my
> mouth. (Ps. 119:103)

> I have not departed from the commandment of his lips; I have
> treasured the words of his mouth more than my portion of food.
> (Job 23:12)

> Your words were found, and I ate them, and your words became to
> me a joy and the delight of my heart, for I am called by your name,
> O LORD, God of hosts. (Jer. 15:16)

The great conclusion is: "Oh how I love your law! It is my meditation all the day" (Ps. 119:97). Which leads us to the question: If the
Word of God is this pleasant in itself, and if it is this crucial in the fight
for joy—if it is more valuable than anything on earth—how shall we
use it? That is the focus of the next chapter.

Oh how I love your law!
It is my meditation all the day.
PSALM 119:97

I have thought I am a creature of a day, passing through life as an arrow through the air. I am a spirit come from God and returning to God; just hovering over the great gulf, till a few moments hence I am no more seen. I drop into an unchangeable eternity! I want to know one thing, the way to heaven—how to land safe on that happy shore. God himself has condescended to teach the way: for this very end he came from heaven. He hath written it down in a book. O give me that book! At any price give me the Book of God! I have it. Here is knowledge enough for me. Let me be homo unius libri *[a man of one book].*

JOHN WESLEY
"Preface to Sermons on Several Occasions, 1746"[1]

How to Wield the Word in the Fight for Joy

Musing, Memorizing, and the Message of God

If the Bible, with the cross of Christ at its center, is more valuable than anything else on earth, then we should be serious about how we use it in the fight for joy. We should be like Wesley, quoted on the facing page, and like Charles Spurgeon, when he said, "It is blessed to eat into the very soul of the Bible until, at last, you come to talk in Scriptural language, and your spirit is flavored with the words of the Lord, so that your blood is Bibline and the very essence of the Bible flows from you."[2] So in this chapter my aim is to give practical counsel on how to do this. My prayer is that the preciousness of the Bible would become the measure of our passion for its place in our hearts.

The Paradox of Planning and Spontaneity

First, I would stress the importance of planning. I don't mean any elaborate, lifelong vision. I mean something as simple as, when you finish with this chapter, take three minutes to ask for God's help, and to consider your schedule, and to pick out a time to read your Bible, and then write it down somewhere so that you remember to do it. Many good things do not happen in our lives for the simple lack of planning.

Consultants get paid thousands of dollars to tell executives the obvious, because the obvious is neglected. It's the same with all of us. We fail to do what's best for us for lack of serious intention to do it. Another name for serious intention is planning. Most Christians neglect their Bibles not out of conscious disloyalty to Jesus, but because of failure to plan a time and place and method to read it.

The result is not spontaneity, but the same old rut. If your longing is to be spontaneous in the way you commune with God, then build discipline into your Bible reading and prayer. It sounds paradoxical. But it's no more so than the paradox of corn spontaneously growing in a Minnesota field because of the farmer's discipline of plowing and sowing and guarding the field. He doesn't make the corn grow. God does. But God uses his farming disciplines as part of the process. The rich fruit of spontaneity grows in the garden that is well tended by the discipline of schedule.

So I say again, plan a place and a time when you will read the Bible and think about it each day. There can always be more times during the day. There should be. But let there be one sacred time and place. Put it on your calendar. Treat it the same way you would an appointment with a partner or friend. If someone asks you to do something during that time, say, "I'm sorry, I already have an appointment then."

In General, Early Morning Is Best

I earnestly recommend that it be in the early morning, unless there are some extenuating circumstances.[3] Entering the day without a serious meeting with God, over his Word and in prayer, is like entering the battle without tending to your weapons. It's like taking a trip without filling the tires with air or the tank with gas. The human heart does not replenish itself with sleep. The body does, but not the heart. The spiritual air leaks from our tires, and the gas is consumed in the day. We replenish our hearts not with sleep, but with the Word of God and prayer. Thousands of saints have discovered through the centuries that starting the day by filling the mind with the Word of God will bring more joy and more love and more power than traveling on yesterday's gas.

Find a Place of Seclusion, or Make It by Rule

Pick a place of seclusion. If you try to read your Bible and pray where people are moving about, the powers of darkness will exploit that potential for distraction with all their might. Don't think it has to be comfy. In fact, comfy will probably put you to sleep. It needs to be secluded so that you are not distracted, and so that you can speak out loud and sing and cry. You will cry sooner or later—when you are wrestling for the soul of your teenager, or struggling to keep your marriage together, or laboring to kill the pride in your life. You need to be alone.

If your family situation or home does not have such a place, then create it, not by space, but by rule. That is, arrange that the children or the spouse or the roommates will not speak to you during the appointed time. One saintly mother with a large brood of children would use her apron to make a tent for her head and her Bible at the kitchen table, and the children were taught, when mother is in her tent, make no noise.

Plan How You Will Read Your Bible

Besides planning for the place and time, plan *how* you will read your Bible. There are many ways to read the Bible. Any is better than none. Coming to the appointed place and time with no plan for how to read the Bible usually results in a hit-and-miss approach that leaves you feeling weak, unreal, and discouraged.

For many years I have read through the Bible once each year following "The *Discipleship Journal* Bible Reading Plan."[4] The month is May as I write this chapter, and I have just read this morning sections from Mark, Galatians, Psalms, and 2 Samuel. The design is to read daily from two Old Testament and two New Testament books. I find this variety helpful. Others don't, and would rather use some other approach.[5] That's fine. The one great benefit of "The *Discipleship Journal* Bible Reading Plan" is that it gives you assignments for only twenty-five days out of the month. This means that any failures to keep up can be overcome each month in the makeup days. This is a wonderful dose of realism for the average sinful reader (including me). And if you are already up-to-date at the end of twenty-five days, then you have five or six days to do special memory work or to read some other part of the Bible that you have been missing.

How George Müller Fought for Joy

One of the greatest witnesses I know of to the power of regular disciplined reading of the Bible for the sake of love-producing joy is George

Müller (1805-1898), who is famous for founding orphanages in Bristol, England, and for depending on God for meeting all his needs. He asked the very question this book is asking, and he gave the same answer:

> In what way shall we attain to this settled happiness of soul? How shall we learn to enjoy God? How shall we obtain such an all-sufficient soul-satisfying portion in him as shall enable us to let go the things of this world as vain and worthless in comparison? I answer, This happiness is to be obtained through the study of the Holy Scriptures. God has therein revealed Himself unto us in the face of Jesus Christ.[6]

That's what we have seen so far in this book: happiness in God comes from seeing God revealed to us in the face of Jesus Christ through the Scriptures. Müller says, "In them . . . we become acquainted with the character of God. Our eyes are divinely opened to see what a lovely Being God is! And this good, gracious, loving, heavenly Father is ours—our portion for time and for eternity."[7] Knowing God is the key to being happy in God.

> The more we know of God, the happier we are. . . . When we became a little acquainted with God . . . our true happiness . . . commenced; and the more we become acquainted with him, the more truly happy we become. What will make us so exceedingly happy in heaven? It will be the fuller knowledge of God.[8]

Therefore the most crucial means of fighting for joy in God is to immerse oneself in the Scriptures where we see God in Christ most clearly. When he was seventy-one years old, Müller spoke to younger believers:

> Now . . . I would give a few hints to my younger fellow-believers as to the way in which to keep up spiritual enjoyment. It is absolutely needful . . . we should read regularly through the Scriptures, consecutively, and not pick out here and there a chapter. If we do, we remain spiritual dwarfs. I tell you so affectionately. For the first four years after my conversion I made no progress, because I neglected the Bible. But when I regularly read on through the whole with reference to my own heart and soul, I directly made progress. Then my peace and joy continued more and more. Now I have been doing this for 47 years. I have read through the whole Bible about 100 times and I always find it fresh when I begin again. Thus my peace and joy have increased more and more.[9]

He would live and read his Bible for another twenty-one years. But he never changed his strategy for satisfaction in God. When he was seventy-six, he wrote the same thing he had learned for over fifty years: "I saw more clearly than ever, that the first great and primary business to which I ought to attend every day was, to have my soul happy in the Lord."[10] And the means stayed the same:

> I saw that the most important thing I had to do was to give myself to the reading of the word of God, and to meditation on it. . . . What is the food of the inner man? Not prayer, but the word of God; and . . . not the simple reading of the word of God, so that it only passes through our minds, just as water runs through a pipe, but considering what we read, pondering over it, and applying it to our hearts.[11]

The Indispensable Strategy of Bible Memorization

How shall we use the Word of God to fight for joy? The first answer I have given is to read it with plan and regularity. The next answer I give is to memorize verses and paragraphs and chapters and even whole books of the Bible. The older you get, the harder it is. I am fifty-eight as I write this, and I still invest significant time in memorizing Scripture, but it is much harder now than it used to be. It takes far more repetition to make the words stick to this aging brain.

But I would not give it up any more than a miser would give up his stash of gold. I feel the same way Dallas Willard does when he says:

> Bible memorization is absolutely fundamental to spiritual formation. If I had to choose between all the disciplines of the spiritual life, I would choose Bible memorization, because it is a fundamental way of filling our mind with what it needs. This book of the law shall not depart out of your mouth. That's where you need it! How does it get in your mouth? Memorization.[12]

The joy-producing effects of memorizing Scripture and having it in my head and heart are incalculable. The world and its God-ignoring, all-embracing secularism is pervasive. It invades my mind every day. What hope is there to have a mind filled with Christ except to have a mind filled with his Word? I know of no alternative.

The Word brings joy directly and indirectly. *Directly* by simply showing us the beauty of Christ and his ways and all the good things he has promised to be for us forever. *Indirectly* by weaning us off the toxic pleasures of the world by means of the superior pleasures of Christ, so that, in purity of heart, we can see the beauty of Christ more clearly. We discussed how this happens in the previous chapter.

How Memory Helps Us Make War

But now observe that memorization suits both these paths of joy. It offers us all day the immediate beauty of Christ in his Word, and it offers us all day the weapons by which we cut the nerve of sin's sweet deception. Memorization corresponds to both paths of joy. First, the direct joy of tasting beauty: "More to be desired are [God's words] than gold, even much fine gold; sweeter also than honey and drippings of the honeycomb" (Ps. 19:10). Second, the indirect joy through purity: "I have stored up your word in my heart, that I might not sin against you" (Ps. 119:11).

When you memorize the Word of God, it's there *directly* giving joy to you and (if you speak it) to others, and it's there *indirectly* serving your joy by transforming your mind. How shall we obey the command, "Be transformed by the renewal of your mind" (Rom. 12:2) if we neglect to saturate our minds with the thoughts of God? Ask yourself: Of all the spiritually minded people you have known—those who seem to walk most consistently with God and are in tune with God's Spirit— do they not all overflow with Scripture? Are they not like John Bunyan? Prick them, and they bleed Bible.[13] This is no coincidence. Memorizing Scripture is one of the surest routes to going deep with God and walking in communion with him. Which means walking in joy.

One of the greatest scenes in *The Pilgrim's Progress* is when Christian recalls in the dungeon of Doubting-Castle that he has a key to the door. Very significant is not only what the key is, but where it is:

> "What a fool I have been, to lie like this in a stinking dungeon, when I could have just as well walked free. In my chest pocket I have a key called Promise that will, I am thoroughly persuaded, open any lock in Doubting-Castle." "Then," said Hopeful, "that is good news. My good brother, do immediately take it out of your chest pocket and try it." Then Christian took the key from his chest and began to try the lock of the dungeon door; and as he turned the key, the bolt

unlocked and the door flew open with ease, so that Christian and Hopeful immediately came out.[14]

Three times Bunyan says that the key out of Doubting-Castle was in Christian's "*chest* pocket" or simply his "chest." I take this to mean that Christian had hidden God's promise in his heart by memorization and that it was now accessible in prison for precisely this reason. This is how the promises sustained and strengthened Bunyan. He was filled with Scripture. Everything he wrote was saturated with Bible. He pored over his English Bible, which he had most of the time. This is why he could say of his writings, "I have not for these things fished in other men's waters; my Bible and concordance are my only library in my writings."[15]

A Radical Call to Major Memorization

Let me be very practical and challenge you to do something you perhaps have never done. If you are not a memorizer at all, shift up to memorizing a Bible verse a week.[16] If you only memorize single verses, shift up to memorizing some paragraphs or chapters (like Psalm 1 or Psalm 23 or Romans 8). And if you have ventured to memorize chapters, shift up to memorize a whole book or part of a book. Few things have a greater effect on the way we see God and the world than to memorize extended portions of Scripture.

Andrew Davis, the pastor of First Baptist Church in Durham, North Carolina, has written a very helpful little book called *An Approach to the Extended Memorization of Scripture.*[17] It inspired me in 2001 to tackle the memorizing of Romans 1—8. By God's grace, I made it. Oh, how sweet and how terrible to live so intimately with the greatest truth in the world!

Since then my focus has been on memorizing significant paragraphs and chapters of the Bible rather than whole books. All Bible memory is valuable, whether of verses, chapters, or books. But don't shrink back from the effort to memorize extended portions of Scripture. My own conviction is that a hundred—I dare say a thousand—problems will be solved in your life by memorizing Scripture this way *before* the problems ever come. This is impossible to prove, but I commend it to you for your consideration.

How Do You Memorize a Whole Book?

I will borrow Andrew Davis's method and simply give it to you as he gives it in his booklet. It's the method I use.

> *Sample daily procedure*: The following is an example of how someone could go about memorizing Ephesians at the rate of one verse per day:
>
> 1) *Day one*: Read Ephesians 1:1 out loud ten times, looking at each word as if photographing it with your eyes. **Be sure to include the verse number.**[18] Then cover the page and recite it ten times. You're done for the day.
>
> 2) *Day two*: **Yesterday's verse first!!** Recite yesterday's verse, Ephesians 1:1 ten times, being sure to include the verse number. Look in the Bible if you need to, just to refresh your memory. Now, do your **new verse**. Read Ephesians 1:2 out loud ten times, looking at each word as if photographing it with your eyes. **Be sure to include the verse number.** Then cover the page and recite it ten times. You're done for the day.
>
> 3) *Day three*: **Yesterday's verse first!!** Recite yesterday's verse, Ephesians 1:2 ten times, being sure to include the verse number. Again, you should look in the Bible if you need to, just to refresh your memory. **Old verses next, altogether:** Recite Ephesians 1:1-2 together once, being sure to include the verse numbers. Now, do your **new verse**. Read Ephesians 1:3 out loud ten times, looking at each word as if photographing it with your eyes. **Be sure to include the verse number.** Then cover the page and recite it ten times. You're done for the day.
>
> 4) *Day four*: **Yesterday's verse first!!** Recite yesterday's verse, Ephesians 1:3 ten times, being sure to include the verse number. Again, you should look in the Bible if you need to, just to refresh your memory. **Old verses next, altogether:** Recite Ephesians 1:1-3 together once, being sure to include the verse numbers. Now, do your **new verse**. Read Ephesians 1:4 out loud ten times, looking at each word as if photographing it with your eyes. **Be sure to include the verse number.** Then cover the page and recite it ten times. You're done for the day.
>
> This cycle would continue through the entire book. Obviously, the **"old verses altogether"** stage will soon swell to take the most time of all. That's exactly the way it should be. The entire book of Ephesians can be read at a reasonable rate in less than fifteen minutes. Therefore, the **"old verses altogether"** stage of your review should not take longer than that on any given day. Do it with the Bible ready at hand, in case you draw a blank or get stuck . . . there's no shame in looking, and it actually helps to nail down troublesome verses so they will never be trouble again.

Why So Much Emphasis on Memorization?

I spend this much time on Bible memory because I believe in the power of the indwelling Word of God to solve a thousand problems before they happen, and to heal a thousand wounds after they happen, and to kill a thousand sins in the moment of temptation, and to sweeten a thousand days with the "drippings of the honeycomb." I am jealous for you, my readers, that you would "let the word of Christ dwell in you richly" (Col. 3:16). This is the path to solid joy and all the service of love that it sustains. Christ will be seen as the fortune he is when we treasure his Word more than money, and when the joy it wakens overflows with sacrificial love (2 Cor. 8:2).

The Word of God, a Pad of Paper, a Day Away

Another suggestion I would make is that you plan to take periodic retreats with nothing but the Word of God and a pad of paper and pen (and perhaps a hymnal). This may be for a Saturday morning, or a weekend, or for several days. The aim is to free yourself from the press and hurry of the world, in order to see more of Christ, because of the unique focus of those hours. Some of the richest times with God I ever spent have been the extended hours alone simply to read long stretches of the Bible and pray. I recall one very powerful time that stands out from years ago when I was out of town by myself and decided in my lonely apartment to spend the morning reading the Gospel of Mark at one sitting, praying as I read.

Wesley Duewel, in his book *Let God Guide You Daily*, describes what it is like for him to seek God in a retreat of solitude: "I have at times read as many as fifty chapters from God's Word before I was completely alone with God. But on some of those occasions I received such unexpected guidance that my life has been greatly benefited."[19] When I read this, I had to ask, as I am sure you do: Have I ever read fifty chapters of the Bible in one day? What blessings and joys might await those who are hungry enough to take a day for such a thing?

There Are Eyes in Pencils and in Pens

I mentioned that you might want to take a pad and pen on such a retreat. In fact I would say, always keep a pad and pen nearby when you read the Bible. I have often counseled people who tell me that they don't see anything when they read the Bible, "Go home and this time, write the text, instead of just reading it. If anything stands out as helpful, make a mark and write down your ideas about it. Keep writing till you are done with that insight. Then keep reading and writing the text till you see something else to write about, or until you are out of time."

The main value in this is that writing forces us to slow down and see what we are reading. Some of us have very bad habits of passive reading that certain types of formal education have bred into us, by forcing us to read quickly when we ought to be reading slowly—thinking as we go. Writing is a way of slowing us down and opening our eyes to see what we do not otherwise see. This struck me so forcefully one day that I paused and wrote:

> I know not how the light is shed,
> Nor understand this lens.
> I only know that there are eyes
> In pencils and in pens.

Learning to Muse over the Word of God

This suggestion that you write what you read, and that you take notes, is moving us toward what is usually called meditation. Memorizing and reading slowly with pen in hand are ways of making meditation possible. And meditation is crucial in the fight for joy. God commanded Joshua that a leader must be ever musing on the Word of God: "This Book of the Law shall not depart from your mouth, but you shall *meditate on it day and night*" (Josh. 1:8). The scroll was rare and precious. Joshua did not have a "pocket scroll" to carry around. This means that God made memory and meditation part of what it took to lead his people. The same is true today.

This was not a burden to the saints of old: "Oh how I love your law! It is my *meditation* all the day. . . . I have more understanding than all my teachers, for your testimonies are my *meditation*" (Ps. 119:97, 99). "His delight is in the law of the LORD, and on his law he *meditates day and night*" (Ps. 1:2). "My eyes are awake before the watches of the night, that I may *meditate* on your promise" (Ps. 119:148). "I remember the days of old; I *meditate* on all that you have done; I *ponder* the work of your hands" (Ps. 143:5). "On the glorious splendor of your majesty, and on your wondrous works, I will *meditate*" (Ps. 145:5).

Now what does this meditation involve? The word *meditation* in Hebrew means basically to speak or to mutter. When this is done in the heart, it is called musing or meditation. So meditating on the Word of God day and night means to speak to yourself the Word of God day and night and to speak to yourself about it—to mull it over, to ask questions about it and answer them from the Scripture itself, to ask yourself how this might apply to you and others, and to ponder its implications for life and church and culture and missions.

One simple way to do this is to memorize a verse or two and then say them to yourself once, emphasizing the first word. Then say them to yourself again, emphasizing the second word. Then say them a third time, emphasizing the third word. And so on, over and over again, until you have meditated on the reason why each word is there. Then you can start asking relational questions. If *this* word is used, why is *that* word used? The possibilities of musing and pondering and meditating are endless. And always we pray as we ponder, asking for God's help and light.

Reading Serious Books about the Bible and Thinking

I would add here that many of us have made the mistake of thinking that the only kind of meditation that will give rise to joy is the kind that comes easy and involves little hard thinking. Since reading hard books or thinking complex thoughts is usually not accompanied with pleasure for most people, we assume that they are not the path to pleasure. That is a mistake—at least it will prove to be a mistake for many people.

Of course, not all people should read the "great books" of Christian history. Thousands of Christians will not be able to read at all and will do all their meditation from orally received words. Many more will have the kinds of work that keep them laboring from sunup till sundown, and reading will be a luxury for rare snatched hours. Others will live in places and be so poor that there is no access to any books, and perhaps only fragments of the Bible. So please don't take me to mean that everyone must be a reader of great books in order to fight for joy successfully.

However, for thousands of people who read this book, and millions of others like you, I would challenge you to throw off the notion that weighty books of doctrine are joy-squelching, while light devotional books are joy-producing. It's true that the joy of serious reading and the thinking that goes with it (sometimes called study) may not be as immediate as the joy of singing in church, or seeing a sunset, or talking with a friend, or hearing a preacher with lots of stories. But the payload for joy may be greater. Raking is easier than digging, but you only get leaves. If you dig you may get diamonds.

I have the profound sense that many people who complain of not being able to rejoice in God treat the knowledge of God as something that ought to be easy to get. They are passive. They expect spiritual things to happen to them from out of nowhere. They don't grasp the pattern of the Bible expressed in Proverbs 2:1-6.

> If you *receive* my words and *treasure up* my commandments with you, *making your ear attentive* to wisdom and *inclining your heart* to understanding; yes, if you *call out* for insight and *raise your voice* for understanding, if you *seek* it like silver and *search* for it as for hidden treasures, then you will understand the fear of the LORD and find the knowledge of God. For the LORD gives wisdom; from his mouth come knowledge and understanding.

Look at all those aggressive words: "receive . . . treasure up . . . make your ear attentive . . . incline your heart . . . call out . . . raise your voice . . . seek . . . search"—*if* you do these, then knowledge of God will be yours. Not because you can make it happen. The giving of the knowledge is still in the hands of God: "For the LORD *gives* wisdom." No, the pursuit of the knowledge of God is not because you can make it happen, but because God freely chooses to bless seeking with finding. The pattern is seen in 2 Timothy 2:7 where Paul says, "*Think* over what I say, for the Lord will *give* you understanding in everything." You think. The Lord gives. Our thinking does not replace his giving. And his giving does not replace our thinking.

Does Hard Thinking Create Cold Hearts?

It is a tragedy that hard thinking has come to be associated with cold hearts. This has not been the experience of the greatest Christian minds. Delight and study have gone hand in hand. "Great are the works of the LORD, *studied* by all who *delight* in them" (Ps. 111:2). The wise English Puritan Thomas Goodwin (1600-1680) saw this pattern in the Bible and pleaded with his readers:

> Endeavour to preserve and keep up lively, holy, and spiritual affec-
> tions in thy heart, and suffer them not to cool. . . . For such as your
> affections such must your thoughts be; . . . Indeed, thoughts and
> affections are . . . the mutual causes of each other: "Whilst I mused,
> the fire burned" (Psalm 39:3); so that thoughts are the bellows that
> kindle and inflame affections; and then if they are inflamed, they
> cause thoughts to boil.[20]

Almost all the impulses in American publishing and church life
today communicate that fire in the bones will come *not* by doctrine
and thinking, but by quick nuggets, accessible stories, light devotional
books, and music. C. S. Lewis had a totally different experience, and
mine is the same as his.

> For my own part, I tend to find the doctrinal books often more help-
> ful in devotion than the devotional books, and I rather suspect that
> the same experience may await many others. I believe that many who
> find that "nothing happens" when they sit down, or kneel down, to
> a book of devotion, would find that the heart sings unbidden while
> they are working their way through a tough bit of theology with a
> pipe in their teeth and a pencil in their hand.[21]

Amen! (Well, with the exception of the pipe!) Of course, there are
very bad theology books, just as there are very bad devotional books.
Both will dry up your joy in a minute. But one should not stop eating
fruit because the last time he tried it was a lemon. Most of the sweet,
rich fruit of Christian doctrine is old. Augustine, John Calvin, Martin
Luther, the Puritans, Jonathan Edwards, Charles Hodge. Read the old
books. It is a great mistake to think that the great books of old are too
hard to understand. C. S. Lewis is right to point out that the greatness
of the old writer is this: "The great man, just because of his greatness,
is much more intelligible than his modern commentator."[22]

The newer the doctrinal books are, the more prevalent is the sad
separation between scholarship and manifest passion for Christ. Most
evangelicals have bought into the need for apparent indifference in writing about massively important things. It is very sad. Wayne Grudem's
Systematic Theology[23] is a happy exception, and I recommend it to the
average reader as one place where the heart may "sing unbidden" while

working through a tough bit of theology. There are others. And you will not have to pick so carefully if you search among the Puritans.[24]

Why So Much Talk about Human Authors?

Of course, someone may ask: Why are you talking about human authors in a chapter on the role of the Word of *God* in the fight for joy? The answer is that God has appointed for us to be helped in our understanding and enjoyment of Scripture by human teachers—living and dead. Clearly he has ordained that there be elders who are "able to teach" (1 Tim. 3:2). What they teach is the Word of God. Therefore God wills that we read and memorize and meditate on the Word of God if we have access to it. But he also wills that we be taught by faithful elders or pastors. Some of these write down their teachings. This is why we have books.

One way to think about Christian books by dead authors is that they are the ministry of the Body of Christ across the centuries, and not just across the miles. We are meant to learn the meaning of the Scriptures from Christian teachers out of the pulpit and out of the past. None of us is so free from sin or bias or blindness that we can see the infallible Scriptures infallibly. We need help. We need correction. We need guidance and encouragement. Oh, the wonders that others have seen in the Bible that we have not seen! What a folly and what a blow to joy if we neglect these books! Many of the greatest God-given helpers in our quest for joy are dead. But God has preserved their helpfulness in books.

> The best way to guard a true interpretation of Scripture, the Reformers insisted, was neither to naively embrace the infallibility of tradition, or the infallibility of the individual, but to recognize the *communal* interpretation of Scripture. The best way to ensure faithfulness to the text is to read it together, not only with the churches of our own time and place, but with the wider "communion of saints" down through the age.[25]

What If You Read Slowly Like Me?

These older works are like reading the Bible through the mind and heart of great knowers and lovers of God. Don't let long books like John Calvin's *Institutes* daunt you. To be sure, finishing a great book is not as important as growing by it. But finishing it is not as hard as you might think.

Suppose you read slowly as I do—maybe about the same speed that you speak—200 words a minute. If you read fifteen minutes a day for one year (say just before supper or just before bed), you will read 5,475 minutes in the year. Multiply that by 200 words a minute, and you get 1,095,000 words that you would read in a year. Now an average serious book might have about 360 words per page. So you would have read 3,041 pages in one year. That's ten very substantial books. All in fifteen minutes a day.

Or, to be specific, my copy of Calvin's *Institutes* has 1,521 pages in two volumes, with an average of 400 words per page, which is 608,400 words. That means that even if you took a day off each week, you could read this great biblical vision of God and man in less than nine months (about thirty-three weeks) at fifteen minutes a day. The point is: the words and ways of God will abide in you more deeply and more powerfully if you give yourself to some serious reading of great books that are saturated with Scripture. It certainly does not have to be John Calvin—or my favorite, Jonathan Edwards—but not to read any of the great old books when you have access to them may be owing to nothing better than what Lewis calls "chronological snobbery."[26]

Being with Bible-Saturated People, Living and Dead

In the fight for joy I would also add this tactic in the overall strategy of using the Word of God: expose yourself to Bible-saturated people, both the living and the dead. Their lives and their words are a great help to our joy. The *living* are the church that you are a part of. The *dead* are the Body of Christ whose Word-saturated lives reach us through their biographies.

God wills that we strengthen each other's hands in the fight for joy. Paul said, "We work with you for your joy" (2 Cor. 1:24). Hebrews tells us: "Take care, brothers, lest there be in any of you an evil, unbelieving heart, leading you to fall away from the living God. *But exhort one another every day*, as long as it is called 'today,' that none of you may be hardened by the deceitfulness of sin" (3:12-13). And Proverbs says, "Whoever walks with the wise becomes wise" (Prov. 13:20). We are not meant to fight for joy alone. Christian joy is a community project.

Just as God ordained that there be teachers, living and dead, so he ordained that the whole Body of Christ speak the Word of God to each other every day in the fight for joy. "Exhort one another every day." Specifically, "Let us consider how to stir up one another to love and good works, not neglecting to meet together, as is the habit of some, but encouraging one another, and all the more as you see the Day drawing near" (Heb. 10:24-25). All of us should feel the calling to exhort others with the Word of God. But that's not my point here. My point here is that you should make sure this is *done to you*. Put yourself in some kind of fellowship, small enough so that this one-another ministry is happening. One of my first questions in dealing with a joyless saint is, "Are you in a small group of believers who care for each other and pray for each other and 'consider how to stir one another up to love'"? Usually the answer is no.

The Word of God Is a Community Treasure

As much as I stress Bible reading, and Bible memorization, and Bible meditation, and reading great books on Bible doctrine, all of that could sound very individualistic. It suits my American bent. But the Word of God is meant to be a community treasure and a community event. It should be alive in the fellowship of believers. This is probably the normal form that the gift of prophecy should take today: anointed, Spirit-guided speaking and application of Scripture in timely ways for each person's need. That is what we need from each other in the fight for joy. Don't rest until you have sought out, or called together, a group of believers where this is happening.

Let me be very specific in regard to church membership in the fight for joy. I know it is possible to be a member of a church—that is, to have your name on an official roll—and not be connected to other believers in a way that stirs up spiritual life and joy and obedience. Indeed it is possible to be a member of a local church and not even be a believer. Nevertheless I believe it is the will of Christ for all of his people to be responsible members of Christ-exalting, Bible-believing local churches. This may be impossible in some locations. God knows that and will supply what we need if the normal means of grace are lacking. But in ordinary circumstances Christians should be responsible *members* of a local church.

When the New Testament uses the word *member* to refer to a Christian in relation to a local body of believers, it uses the word first metaphorically. That is, we are members of a local body of believers the way hands and feet are members of the human body. "As the body is one and has many members, and all the members of the body, though many, are one body, so it is with Christ. . . . If the foot should say, 'Because I am not a hand, I do not belong to the body,' that would not make it any less a part of the body" (1 Cor. 12:12, 15). This is a picture not of the universal body of Christ, but of the local expression of that body in a specific place. We know this for several reasons.

One reason is that when Paul refers to the universal body of Christ, he says the "head" is Christ himself. "He is the head of the body, the church" (Col. 1:18; 2:19; Eph. 5:23). But when Paul refers to the local body of believers, he uses the term "head" as just another member, like hand or foot: "The eye cannot say to the hand, 'I have no need of you,' nor again *the head* to the feet, 'I have no need of you'" (1 Cor. 12:21). Another reason we know that the picture of "membership" in 1 Corinthians 12 is membership in a *local body* of believers, and not just membership in the universal body of Christ, is that it speaks of close relationships of care and responsibility that go with this membership: "God has so composed the body . . . that there may be no division in the body, but that the *members may have the same care for one another*" (1 Cor. 12:24-25). This kind of mutual care is not possible in the universal body of Christ, but only in local expressions of that body.

Therefore, it is clear that the apostle Paul moves beyond the metaphorical use of *member* (hand and foot and head and eye) to the real, personal, responsible membership in a local church. Membership moves from the metaphorical connectedness to real, concrete organizational connectedness that creates the expectation of both care and accountability. This is why Paul can take church discipline so seriously and even speak of the rare cases when a member is put out of the church. "For what have I to do with judging outsiders? Is it not those inside the church whom you are to judge? God judges those outside. 'Purge the evil person from among you'" (1 Cor. 5:12-13). Such a formal *removal* would not be possible if there were no formal membership.

I stress this biblical perspective on church membership because we live in a day when people shun responsibility and accountability. We are very individualistic and resistant to others holding us to any standard that might cross our immediate desires. But God loves us and does not call us to what is bad for us. Church membership is a gift of grace.

Like all relationships (marriage, parenting, employment, teams, citizenship), it has its pain. But, more than most of us realize, it has its life-sustaining, faith-strengthening, joy-preserving effect according to God's plan and mercy. The Christ-displaying, corporate ministry of the Word of God comes to us in church membership in ways that we cannot predict. I urge you not to cut yourself off from this blessing by staying on the edges of Christ's church.

One of the things that gives this corporate ministry of the Word such power is that the Word comes incarnated in real persons. We are not reading pages—we are hearing living persons. Paul pointed to the power of this personal ministry when he said, "So, being affectionately desirous of you, we were ready to share with you not only the gospel of God *but also our own selves,* because you had become very dear to us" (1 Thess. 2:8). When the Word of God, tailored to our need, comes to us in a person who gives us his very self, there is a great triumph of love that almost always leads to joy.

Christian Biography and the Fight for Joy

And even the dead can live in this way. The entire eleventh chapter of Hebrews can be included in the reference to Abel: "And through his faith, though he died, he still speaks" (v. 4). In answer to how we "stir one another up to love," the book of Hebrews answers: through the lives of the living and the dead. "Remember your leaders, those who spoke to you the word of God. Consider the outcome of their way of life, and imitate their faith" (Heb. 13:7). A Christian life, whether past or pres-ent, is a demonstration of the truth of God's Word and a display of God's grace. Therefore, since the fight for joy is a fight to see and savor all that God is for us, we would be poor warriors not to seek Christian fellowship and read Christian biography.

The Inspiration of Edwards's Fight for Joy

My friendship with Jonathan Edwards has grown over the years, though Edwards has been dead since 1758. What I have learned from his words and his works is incalculable. I thank God for him with all my heart. I wrote my tribute to him in *God's Passion for His Glory: Living the Vision of Jonathan Edwards.*[27] His own battle for joy has been a great inspiration and guidance to my own. For example, he wrote seventy resolutions when he was a young man. Three of them have remained with me over the years in my own fight for joy. Number 22 says: "*Resolved*, To endeavor to obtain for myself as much happiness, in the other world, as I possibly can, with all the power, might, vigor, and vehemence, yea violence, I am capable of, or can bring myself to exert, in any way that can be thought of." You can see that he grasped the warfare of joy early on. As a means to that end he said in number 28: "*Resolved*, To study the Scriptures so steadily, constantly and frequently, so that I may find, and plainly perceive myself to grow in the knowledge of the same." He was preeminently biblical, for all his philosophical powers. And that has helped to keep me riveted on the Word of God. And to put a passion behind this Word-soaked quest for eternal joy, he gave these simple but inspiring words in resolution number 6: "*Resolved*, To live with all my might, while I do live."[28]

When you read Christian biography you get to see a person fight for joy over a lifetime. This is tremendously helpful. It gives guidance in the warfare. It gives inspiration because of triumphs of grace. It gives humility and hope because of failures and recoveries. And sometimes there are glimpses of what is possible in relation to God that set a reader to praying and longing as never before. For example, Edwards recalled his experience from the time he was thirty-four:

> Once, as I rid out into the woods for my health, *anno* [year] 1737; and having lit [dismounted] from my horse in a retired place, as my manner commonly has been, to walk for divine contemplation and prayer, I had a view that for me was extraordinary, of the glory of the Son of God, as Mediator between God and man, and his wonderful, great, full, pure and sweet grace and love, and meek and gentle condescension. This grace that appeared so calm and sweet, appeared also great above the heavens. The person of Christ appeared ineffably excellent, with an excellency great enough to swallow up all thought and conception—which continued, as near as I can judge, about an hour; which kept me the greater part of the time in a flood of tears, and weeping aloud. I felt an ardency of soul to be, what I know not otherwise how to express, emptied and annihilated; to lie in the dust, and to be full of Christ alone; to love him with a holy and pure love; to trust in him; to live upon him; to serve and follow

him; and to be perfectly sanctified and made pure, with a divine and heavenly purity. I have several other times had views very much of the same nature, and which have had the same effects.[29]

This story freed me in my twenties from the foolish notion that great theology and serious doctrine keep a person from weeping for joy. Ever since then I have rejected the notion that the rigorous effort to *know* more of God must cause one to *feel* less of God.

For the sake of your joy in Christ read Christian biography. It will take you out of yourself and put you in another time and another skin, so that you see Jesus with eyes more full of wonder than your own. Find some Bible-saturated, Christ-exalting, God-centered saints from centuries gone by and learn from them how to fight for joy.

Luther's Strange Helper in Understanding and Enjoying Scripture

The topic of biography gives me a chance to mention one more tactic in how to use the Word of God in the fight for joy. Martin Luther (1483-1546), the great German Reformer, taught me the essential role of suffering in seeing the fullness of Christ in the Scriptures and knowing the fullness of joy.

Luther noticed in Psalm 119 that the writer not only prayed and meditated over the Word of God in order to understand it—he also suffered in order to understand it. The psalmist says, "Before I was *afflicted* I went astray, but now I keep your word. . . . It is good for me that I was afflicted, that I might learn your statutes" (Ps. 119:67, 71). An indispensable key to understanding the Scriptures is suffering in the path of righteousness. It is sure that we will all be given this key: "Through many tribulations we must enter the kingdom of God" (Acts 14:22). For some, the Word comes with the key attached: "You received the word in much affliction, with the joy of the Holy Spirit" (1 Thess. 1:6). That's the way it was for Luther.

He proved the value of trials over and over again in his own experience.

> For as soon as God's Word becomes known through you, the devil will afflict you, will make a real doctor [teacher of doctrine] of you, and will teach you by his temptations to seek and to love God's

Word. For I myself . . . owe my papists [Roman Catholic adversaries] many thanks for so beating, pressing, and frightening me through the devil's raging, that they have turned me into a fairly good theologian, driving me to a goal I should never have reached.[30]

Suffering was woven into life for Luther. Emotionally and spiritually he underwent the most oppressive struggles. For example, in a letter to Melanchthon on August 2, 1527, he writes:

For more than a week I have been thrown back and forth in death and Hell; my whole body feels beaten, my limbs are still trembling. I almost lost Christ completely, driven about on the waves and storms of despair and blasphemy against God. But because of the intercession of the faithful, God began to take mercy on me and tore my soul from the depths of Hell.[31]

These were the trials that opened his eyes to the meaning of Scripture. These experiences were as much a part of his exegetical labors as was his Greek lexicon. Seeing such things in the lives of the saints has caused me to think twice before I begrudge the trials of my ministry. How often I am tempted to think that the pressures and conflicts and frustrations are simply distractions from the business of ministry and Bible study. Luther (along with Psalm 119:67, 71) teaches us to see it all another way. The stresses of life, the interruptions, the disappointments, the conflicts, the physical ailments, the losses—all of these may well be the very lenses through which we see the meaning of God's Word as never before. Paradoxically, the pain of life may open us to the Word that becomes the pathway to joy.

There is more that could be said about how to use the Word of God to fight for joy. Indeed, more will be said in the following chapters. For now, in closing, remember this: The Bible is the Word of a living Person, Jesus Christ, who is our God and Savior. Therefore, read and meditate and memorize with a view to seeing him in the words that he records and the works he recounts. He is as near as your own breathing and is infinitely merciful and mighty.

Satisfy us in the morning with your steadfast love,
that we may rejoice and be glad all our days.

PSALM 90:14

Until now you have asked nothing in my name. Ask, and you
will receive, that your joy may be full.

JOHN 16:24

I pray, O God, that I may know You and love You, so that I
may rejoice in You. And if I cannot do so fully in this life may I
progress gradually until it comes to fullness. Let the knowledge
of You grow in me here, and there [in heaven] be made complete;
let Your love grow in me here and there be made complete, so
that here my joy may be great in hope, and there be complete
in reality. Lord, by Your Son You command, or rather, counsel
us to ask and You promise that we shall receive so that our "joy may
be complete." I ask, Lord, as You counsel through our admirable
counsellor. May I receive what You promise through Your truth
so that my "joy may be complete." God of truth, I ask that I may
receive so that my "joy may be complete." Until then let my mind
meditate on it, let my tongue speak of it, let my heart love it, let
my mouth preach it. Let my soul hunger for it, let my flesh thirst
for it, my whole being desire it, until I enter into the "joy of the
Lord," who is God, Three in One, "blessed forever. Amen."

ANSELM
Proslogion[1]

9

The Focus of Prayer in the Fight for Joy

*Desiring All Else Only Because
We Desire God*

What do you do when you don't desire the Word of God? Or when you read it and don't see anything that gives you joy? Or when your joy is weak and disintegrates before the allurements of the world? What do you do if you are not satisfied in the God of the Bible, but prefer the pleasures of the world? Did Paul or the psalmists or the celebrated saints of history ever struggle with this? Yes, they did. And we should take heart. We all struggle with seasons of lukewarmness and spiritual numbness of heart. There are times in the lives of the most godly people when spiritual hunger becomes weak, and darkness threatens to consume the light, and everything but the vaguely remembered taste of joy evaporates.

Martin Luther's Misery

For example, on the outside, to many, Martin Luther looked invulnerable. But those close to him knew the affliction. He wrote to Melanchthon from Wartburg Castle on July 13, 1521, while he was supposedly working feverishly on the translation of the New Testament:

> I sit here at ease, hardened and unfeeling—alas! Praying little, grieving little for the Church of God, burning rather in the fierce fires of my

untamed flesh. It comes to this: I *should* be afire in the spirit; in reality I am afire in the flesh, with lust, laziness, idleness, sleepiness. It is perhaps because you have all ceased praying for me that God has turned away from me. . . . For the last eight days I have written nothing, nor prayed nor studied, partly from self-indulgence, partly from another vexatious handicap [constipation and piles (hemorrhoids), we find out in another place]. . . . I really cannot stand it any longer; . . . Pray for me, I beg you, for in my seclusion here I am submerged in sins.[2]

The spiritual sight of saints is not uniformly clear. Clouds set in, and when the glory of Christ is obscured, the fires of affection may smolder. We will say more about this in Chapter Twelve. Suffice it to say now that these need not be wasted seasons in the life of faith. God has his wise and holy purposes for bringing his loved ones to the brink of despair (see 2 Cor. 1:8-10).

But to go to the valley of darkness, or stay there, is never our aim. The biblical command is, "Rejoice in the Lord." And even when the Bible commands, "Be wretched and mourn and weep. Let your laughter be turned to mourning and your joy to gloom" (Jas. 4:9)—even then, the aim is not to stay there. The next verse says, "Humble yourselves before the Lord, and *he will exalt you*." "For godly grief produces a repentance that leads to salvation without regret, whereas worldly grief produces death" (2 Cor. 7:10). The goal of brokenhearted repentance is the blessing of humble, Christ-exalting joy.

How then do we fight for joy when our desires languish and we may have no inclination for the Word of God? The answer we are focusing on in this chapter is prayer. The key to joy in God is God's omnipotent, transforming grace, bought by his Son, applied by his Spirit, wakened by the Word, and laid hold of by faith through prayer.

Prayer: "The Offering Up of Our Desires unto God"

How shall we define prayer so that we know what we are talking about? B. B. Warfield recounts a story about D. L. Moody, the nineteenth-century evangelist, making a visit to Britain and learning about the value of the Westminster Catechism in relation to prayer. He was staying with a Scottish friend in London.

A young man had come to speak to Mr. Moody about religious things. He was in difficulty about a number of points, among the rest about prayer and natural laws. "What is prayer?," he said, "I can't tell what you mean by it!" They were in the hall of a large London house. Before Moody could answer, a child's voice was heard singing on the stairs. It was that of a little girl of nine or ten, the daughter of their host. She came running down the stairs and paused as she saw strangers sitting in the hall. "Come here, Jenny," her father said, "and tell this gentleman 'What is prayer.'" Jenny did not know what had been going on, but she quite understood that she was now called upon to say her Catechism. So she drew herself up, and folded her hands in front of her, like a good little girl who was going to "say her questions," and she said in her clear childish voice: "Prayer is an offering up of our desires unto God for things agreeable to his will, in the name of Christ, with confession of our sins and thankful acknowledgement of his mercies." "Ah! That's the Catechism!" Moody said, "thank God for that Catechism."[3]

The central definition of prayer in the Westminster Catechism is "an offering up of our desires unto God." Therefore prayer is the revealer of the heart. What a person prays for shows the spiritual condition of his heart. If we do not pray for spiritual things (like the glory of Christ, and the hallowing of God's name, and the salvation of sinners, and the holiness of our hearts, and the advance of the gospel, and contrition for sin, and the fullness of the Spirit, and the coming of the kingdom, and the joy of knowing Christ), then probably it is because we do not desire these things. Which is a devastating indictment of our hearts.

This is why J. I. Packer said, "I believe that prayer is the measure of the man, spiritually, in a way that nothing else is, so that how we pray is as important a question as we can ever face."[4] How we pray reveals the desires of our hearts. And the desires of our hearts reveal what our treasure is. And if our treasure is not Christ, we will perish. "Whoever loves father or mother more than me," Jesus said, "is not worthy of me, and whoever loves son or daughter more than me is not worthy of me" (Matt. 10:37).

The Fight for Joy: Worshipful, Loving, Serious, and Dangerous

Therefore, the fight for joy with the weapon of prayer is very serious. Ultimately the glory of God is at stake. This is true because God is most glorified in us when we are most satisfied in him. It is true also because the joy of the Lord is our strength (Neh. 8:10) in the cause of mercy and justice and missions. For when the light of Christ shines in these ways, people see our good works and give glory to our Father in heaven (Matt. 5:16). Being more satisfied in God than in prosperity or the praise of man makes you willing to be persecuted for the sake of Christ. So it was said of the early Christians, "You *joyfully* accepted the plundering of your property, since you knew that you yourselves had a better possession and an abiding one" (Heb. 10:34). That is what joy in God (not earthly security) produces. Therefore praying for such liberating joy in God is one of the most worshipful and loving things a person can do. And it is very dangerous.[5]

Praying for joy is not the emotional pampering of joyless people. It is preparation for sacrifice. What's at stake in the fight for joy is the radiance of the worth of Jesus made visible for the world to see in sacrifices of love flowing from the joy of blood-bought, soul-satisfied, Christ-exalting people. When Paul said to the Corinthians, "We work with you for your joy" (2 Cor. 1:24), he was not saying, "We pamper you." He was saying, "We prepare you for radical, Christ-exalting sacrifices of love."

What Joy Did in Macedonia

You can see this as clear as day in 2 Corinthians 8:1-4. Paul celebrated what happened to the Christians in Macedonia so that the Corinthians would seek the same thing—namely, the grace of God, which led to joy in God, which led to love. This is a pattern we see over and over again.

> We want you to know, brothers, about *the grace of God* that has been given among the churches of Macedonia, for in a severe test of affliction, *their abundance of joy* and their extreme poverty have *overflowed in a wealth of generosity* on their part. For they gave according to their means, as I can testify, and beyond their means, of their own accord, begging us earnestly for the favor of taking part in the relief of the saints. (2 Cor. 8:1-4)

First, there was the power of *grace*. And Paul makes clear that this power is available for the Corinthians, not just the Macedonians: "God is able to make *all grace* abound to you, so that having all sufficiency in all things at all times, you may abound in every good work" (2 Cor. 9:8). Then, rising in the heart because of grace, there was "abundance of joy." This was not because of circumstances or prosperity. It was "in a severe test of affliction," and it was out of "extreme poverty." This is not a health, wealth, and prosperity gospel. The joy they had was in Christ, not things. Then, after grace gave rise to abundant joy in Christ, love overflowed. This joy "overflowed in a wealth of generosity" for the poor. And this was not constrained, but free and lavish.

This is serious and dangerous. If you believe that joy is peripheral, and what matters is generosity for the relief of the poor, whether you feel like it or not, you are against the Word of God.[6] In this same context Paul says, with devastating clarity, "Each one must give as he has made up his mind, not reluctantly or under compulsion, for God loves a cheerful giver" (2 Cor. 9:7). God does not delight in reluctant, disinclined obedience. And we do not feel loved when we are served begrudgingly. Therefore, to labor for a person's joy in Christ is not pampering. It is preparing him for the most dangerous deeds of love.

Praying for Joy and Praying for All Else for the Sake of Joy

Therefore, we want to follow such persons. So we ask, how did the early Christians pray for joy? First, we may assume that they prayed the prayers of the only Bible that they had, namely, the Old Testament. Thus they would have prayed: "Satisfy us in the morning with your steadfast love, that we may rejoice and be glad all our days" (Ps. 90:14). "Let me hear joy and gladness; let the bones that you have broken rejoice" (Ps. 51:8). "Restore to me the joy of your salvation, and uphold me with a willing spirit" (Ps. 51:12). "Make us glad for as many days as you have afflicted us" (Ps. 90:15). "Will you not revive us again, that your people may rejoice in you?" (Ps. 85:6). Don't miss how radical these prayers are. They assume that we are unable to make ourselves satisfied in God. And they assume that God has the right to do it, is able to do it, and does it in answer to prayer.

Second, the early Christians prayed for joy in accord with the example of the apostles. Paul prayed, "May the God of hope fill you *with all joy* and peace in believing" (Rom. 15:13), and "May you be strengthened with all power, according to his glorious might, for all endurance and patience *with joy*" (Col. 1:11). So the early church looked not only to the Old Testament, but to the emerging New Testament for their mandate to fight for joy by prayer.

Third, they took Jesus at his word when he said, "Until now you have asked nothing in my name. Ask, and you will receive, *that your joy may be full*" (John 16:24). So they did all their asking in the name of Jesus with a view to having full joy in him. Every prayer was based on his blood-bought grace. When every prayer was attended with the words, "In Jesus' name, amen," it was not empty, worn-out Christian jargon for them.

Paul explained why: "For all the promises of God find their Yes in him. That is why it is through him that we utter our Amen to God for his glory" (2 Cor. 1:20). In other words, because Christ died in our place, all of God's wrath is averted from us, and only mercy comes to us from heaven (Rom. 5:9; 8:32). That is the ground of all our prayers. They were bought for us by the blood of Christ. Praying in Jesus' name means we believe that and lay claim to answers only because of Christ's righteousness, not ours.

In All Prayer for His Gifts We Are Praying for More of God

So in obedience to Christ the early church prayed in Jesus' name, *and* they prayed with the aim Jesus told them to: "that your joy may be full." Every prayer, no matter what it was for, was a prayer for the fullness of joy in Christ. They knew that Christ was not calling the church to exploit God's mercy for material gain. Prayer was for glorifying God and magnifying his Son. "Whatever you ask in my name," Jesus said, "this I will do, *that the Father may be glorified in the Son*" (John 14:13). The early church knew that in the very act of praying, a person might make a lackey out of God by not desiring God but only his gifts. "You ask and do not receive," James said, "because you ask wrongly, to spend it on your passions" (Jas. 4:3). It is not wrong to want God's gifts and ask for them. Most prayers in the Bible are for the gifts of God. But ultimately every gift should be desired because it shows us and brings us more of him.

Augustine put it like this in one of his prayers: "He loves thee too little, who loves anything together with thee, which he loves not for thy sake."[7] Every Christ-exalting prayer for the gifts of God is at root a prayer for the glory of Christ. Christ is exalted when he is desired above God's gifts. "Because your steadfast love is better than life, my lips will praise you" (Ps. 63:3). If his love is better than life, it must be better than all that life can give.

How else can we explain the words of Habakkuk 3:17-18, "Though the fig tree should not blossom, nor fruit be on the vines, the produce of the olive fail and the fields yield no food, the flock be cut off from the fold and there be no herd in the stalls, yet I will rejoice in the LORD; I will take joy in the God of my salvation"? When this world totally fails, the ground for joy remains: God. Therefore, surely every prayer for life and health and home and family and job and ministry in this world is secondary. And the great purpose of prayer is to ask that—in and through all his gifts—God would be our joy.

Watching the Early Church Pray for Everything for Joy

It is amazing to see this truth in action in the New Testament. Walk with me for a few minutes among the prayers of the early Christians, and you will see what they prayed for and how all of it was part of the fight for joy in God.

1. The early Christians called on God to exalt his name in the world

"Pray then like this: 'Our Father in heaven, hallowed be your name'" (Matt. 6:9). This is a prayer for joy in two ways. First, to see God's name honored is the greatest joy of all who love God. Therefore to pray that his name be honored is to pray for what we desire more than anything. Second, since God is most glorified in us when we are most satisfied in him, a prayer for his name to be hallowed (glorified) is a prayer that we and millions of others would be more satisfied in him than anything. The psalmists link the joy we have in God with the praise we bring his name. "I will *be glad and exult in you*; I will sing praise to your name, O Most High" (Ps. 9:2).

2. The early Christians called on God to extend his kingdom in the world

"Your kingdom come, your will be done, on earth as it is in heaven" (Matt. 6:10). At the arrival of God's kingdom in the fullness of its glory, "he will wipe away every tear from their eyes, and death shall be no more, *neither shall there be mourning nor crying nor pain anymore*" (Rev. 21:4). Therefore, to pray for this kingdom to come is to pray for the greatest possible joy to fill the creation.

But not only far in the future. The spiritual triumph of God's kingdom in the soul and in the church and here and there in the world today is defined explicitly by the apostle Paul as "righteousness and peace and joy." "The kingdom of God is not a matter of eating and drinking but of righteousness and peace and *joy* in the Holy Spirit" (Rom. 14:17). Therefore, to pray for God's rule in someone's life (including your own) is to pray for joy.

3. The early Christians called on God for the fullness of the Holy Spirit

"If you then, who are evil, know how to give good gifts to your children, how much more will the heavenly Father give the Holy Spirit to those who ask him!" (Luke 11:13; see also Eph. 3:19). The uniform experience of the early church was that the fullness of the Holy Spirit resulted in joyful boldness in witness (Acts 4:31) and joyful freedom in worship (Eph. 5:18-19). This is because "the fruit of the Holy Spirit is . . . *joy* . . ." (Gal. 5:22).

4. The early Christians called on God to save unbelievers

"Brothers, my heart's desire and prayer to God for them is that they may be saved" (Rom. 10:1). This was a prayer for joy in two senses. First, to be saved is to find the greatest treasure in the universe and joyfully count everything else as secondary. "The kingdom of heaven is like treasure hidden in a field, which a man found and covered up. Then *in his joy* he goes and sells all that he has and buys that field" (Matt. 13:44). Second, when a sinner repents, there is "*more joy* in heaven than over ninety-nine righteous persons who need no repentance" (Luke 15:7).

Therefore, all who have the heart of heaven rejoice with those who rejoice—especially the angels and God himself.

5. The early Christians called on God for healing

"Is anyone among you suffering? Let him pray. Is anyone cheerful? Let him sing praise. Is anyone among you sick? Let him call for the elders of the church, and let them pray over him, anointing him with oil in the name of the Lord. And the prayer of faith will save the one who is sick, and the Lord will raise him up. And if he has committed sins, he will be forgiven" (Jas. 5:13-15). We see what happened in Samaria when Philip healed people there: "Many who were paralyzed or lame were healed. So there was much *joy* in that city" (Acts 8:7-8).

6. The early Christians called on God for strategic wisdom

"If any of you lacks wisdom, let him ask God, who gives to all men generously without reproach, and it will be given him" (Jas. 1:5; see also Col. 1:9). In daily life, to live wisely is to achieve the God-centered goals for which we were created, including the glory of God in the gladness of our worship. Thus Paul describes the effect of being taught "in all wisdom"—namely, "singing psalms and hymns and spiritual songs, with thankfulness in your hearts to God" (Col. 3:16).

7. The early Christians called on God for unity and harmony in the ranks

Jesus modeled this prayer for them: "I do not ask for these only, but also for those who will believe in me through their word, that they may all be one, just as you, Father, are in me, and I in you, that they also may be in us, so that the world may believe that you have sent me" (John 17:20-21). When Paul thought on this kind of unity, he said to the Philippians, "*Complete my joy* by being of the same mind, having the same love, being in full accord and of one mind" (Phil. 2:2). The unity of God's people is a great joy to those who desire "that the world may believe" God has sent Jesus Christ.

8. The early Christians called on God to help them know him better

"[We have not ceased to pray for you to be] increasing in the knowledge of God" (Col. 1:10; see also Eph. 1:17). Spiritually (not just intellectually) knowing God is the foundation of all joy. That's why Jesus said the pure in heart are blessed (happy)—because they see God (Matt. 5:8).

9. The early Christians called on God to help them comprehend the love of Christ

"I bow my knees before the Father . . . that you may have strength to comprehend with all the saints what is the breadth and length and height and depth and to know the love of Christ that surpasses knowledge" (Eph. 3:14, 18). The difference between whether or not the love of Christ gives joy to the soul is whether we are able to comprehend some measure of the incomprehensible. As long as the love of Christ remains an idea, it does not move our hearts. But to pray for the power to comprehend is to pray for the awakening of joy.

10. The early Christians called on God for a deeper sense of assured hope

"I do not cease to give thanks for you, remembering you in my prayers . . . that you may know what is the hope to which he has called you" (Eph. 1:16, 18). It is the universal experience of man and the explicit witness of the apostles that joy flows from hope: "May the God of *hope* fill you with all *joy* and peace in believing" (Rom. 15:13). "We rejoice in hope of the glory of God" (Rom. 5:2). "Rejoice in hope" (Rom. 12:12).

11. The early Christians called on God for strength and endurance

"[We have not ceased to pray for you to be] strengthened with all power, according to his glorious might, for all *endurance* and patience *with joy*" (Col. 1:11; see also Eph. 3:16). It's not surprising that strength and endurance should be linked with joy because Nehemiah 8:10 already taught that "the joy of the LORD is your strength."

12. The early Christians called on God for their faith to be preserved

First Jesus gave an example of this kind of prayer as he prayed for Peter just before his three denials: "I have prayed for you that your faith may not fail. And when you have turned again, strengthen your brothers" (Luke 22:32). Jesus also instructs the disciples to pray for persevering faith: "Stay awake at all times, praying that you may have strength to escape all these things that are going to take place, and to stand before the Son of Man" (Luke 21:36). Then Paul makes plain that as he prays and works for the faith of the churches, he is explicitly working for their joy. "I will remain and continue with you all, for your progress and joy in the faith" (Phil. 1:25). "Not that we lord it over your faith, but we work with you for your joy, for you stand firm in your faith" (2 Cor. 1:24).

13. The early Christians called on God that they might not fall into temptation

"Lead us not into temptation" (Matt. 6:13). "Watch and pray that you may not enter into temptation" (Matt. 26:41). What is temptation? It is always, in one way or another, the deception that something is more to be desired than God and his ways. Therefore, the prayer for deliverance is that we would not fall for that deception but always taste and know that God and his ways are to be desired above all others.

14. The early Christians called on God to complete their resolves and enable them to do good works

"To this end we always pray for you, that our God may . . . fulfill every resolve for good and every work of faith by his power" (2 Thess. 1:11). "[We have not ceased to pray for you that you will] walk in a manner worthy of the Lord, fully pleasing to him, bearing fruit in every good work" (Col. 1:10). We know from experience and from the words of Jesus in Acts 20:35 that "it is more blessed to give than to receive." Therefore, when we pray for the enabling to give like this, we are praying for a great and joyful blessedness.

15. The early Christians called on God for forgiveness for their sins

"Forgive us our debts, as we also have forgiven our debtors" (Matt. 6:12). This is a plea for the ongoing application and enjoyment of the great verdict rendered over us in Jesus Christ: *justified!* This standing in Christ that assures us of God's favor is the foundation of all our joys.

16. The early Christians called on God for protection from the evil one

"Deliver us from evil" (Matt. 6:13). The devil is the great deceiver, and the aim of all his deception, as with temptation, is that we desire anything—even good, safe, wholesome things—above God. He offers a thousand substitutes and threatens us with a thousand miseries in this world. When we pray for deliverance from him, we mean: never let us be attracted by the substitutes, and never let us infer from our miseries that God is not our all-satisfying Friend.

Everything the early church prayed for was part of their fight for joy in God. If this were not true, prayer would have been mercenary. They would have been making God into a genie and prayer into Aladdin's lamp. But when Jesus said, "Ask, and you will receive, that your joy may be full" (John 16:24), he meant, "In all your asking look for the fullness of joy in me. In this way all your asking will glorify me." So let us fight for joy by asking for it earnestly from God, and let us fight for joy by asking for everything else with this one great goal: in and through all his gifts to see more and taste more of Christ.

Prayer and Meditation Are as Inseparable as God's Word and Spirit

It may seem strange, in this chapter and the next, to put so much emphasis on prayer after two chapters on the utterly indispensable role of *the Word of God*. The reason is that prayer and meditation are inseparable in the fight for joy. This inseparability is rooted in God's design to make the Spirit of God and the Word of God inseparable. His purpose for our lives is that the work of his Spirit happen through his Word, and that the work of his Word happen through his Spirit. The Spirit and the Word are inseparable in wakening and sustaining joy, from the first act of regeneration to the final act of glorification. God works by the Spirit through his Word to glorify his Son and satisfy his people.

Prayer and meditation correspond to God's Spirit and God's Word. *Prayer* is our response to God in reliance on his Spirit; and *meditation* is our response to God in reliance on his Word.

In *prayer* we praise the perfections of God through his Spirit, we thank God for what he has done by his Spirit, we confess our failures to trust the promise of his Spirit, and we ask for the help of his Spirit—all in Jesus' name. Prayer is the human expression of treasuring and trusting the Spirit of God.

In *meditation*, as the counterpart to prayer, we hear and ponder and prize the Word of God. Meditation means reading the Bible and chewing on it to get the sweetness and the nourishment from it that God designs to give. It should involve memorizing the Word so that you can chew on it and be strengthened by it day and night. The essence of meditation is to think your way into the very mind of the inspired writers who were granted by inspiration to think the thoughts of God (cf. 2 Tim. 3:16-17; 2 Pet. 1:21). Think and mull and ponder and chew until you see God the way they see God—namely, as precious and valuable and beautiful and desirable. This is how the Word serves joy.

Thus, even as the Spirit and the Word are inseparable in our lives, so prayer and meditation are inseparable. The fight for joy always involves both. Prayer without meditation on the Word of God will disintegrate into humanistic spirituality. It will simply reflect our own fallen ideas and feelings—not God's. And meditation, without the humility of desperate prayer, will create proud legalism or hopeless despair.

Without prayer we will try to fulfill the Word in our own strength and think we are succeeding and so become proud Pharisees; or we will realize we are not succeeding and will give up in despair. Those are the only alternatives for those who try to live the Word of God without the Spirit of God—that is, those who try to separate the discipline of meditation from the dependence of prayer.

The Spirit Wakens Joy Where the Word Exalts Christ

There is a crucial, Christ-exalting reason why the Spirit creates and sustains God-centered joy only through the Word of God. The reason is this: the Spirit binds his saving, joy-producing work to the Christ-centered Word of God so that Jesus Christ will be glorified through the joy that the Spirit inspires. The Spirit has been given, Jesus said, to glorify the Son of God (John 16:14). Therefore, he works through the Word that exalts the Son. And therefore prayer, which seeks for his work, is inseparable from meditation, which savors his Word.

Let me illustrate. In Luke 2:10-11 we hear a word from God to the shepherds: "Fear not, for behold, I bring you good news of a great joy that will be for all the people. For unto you is born this day in the city of David a Savior, who is Christ the Lord." Now what was the aim of this word? The aim was, at least, to produce joy. "We bring you good news of *a great joy.*" In other words, the truth about Jesus—that he is a Savior and Messiah and Lord, and that he was born in the prophesied city of David—all this truth was meant to inspire great joy. And when it did, who got the glory? Jesus did. Why? Because the Spirit used *news about him* to inspire the joy. He is Savior, Christ, Lord.

But suppose the shepherds were out in the fields keeping watch over their flocks by night, and suddenly the Holy Spirit came upon them, unidentified, and filled them with great joy but used no news at all to do it. No word. No revelation. Only the Spirit-created feeling of joy—like a euphoria that you might feel when you take a drug. Who, then, would be glorified for that? There is no word about Christ, and the Spirit remains incognito. The answer is, nobody would be glorified for this joy, except maybe the shepherds, for seeming so resilient against the cold winter's night.

How would it glorify Christ if the Spirit created in us all kinds of good feelings with no reference to Jesus and his cross and resurrection? It wouldn't. So the way the Spirit inspires and sustains joy in our lives is by humbly and quietly enabling us to see the beauty of Christ *in the Word.* Then our joy consciously arises from the truth about Christ, and he is glorified, but the Spirit remains the behind-the-scenes power that opened the eyes of our hearts. Thus we pray earnestly for the indispensable work of the Spirit, but we look earnestly to the indispensable Word of God.

How This Works in My Experience

Very practically what this means for the fight for joy is that every day we must not just go to the Word, but pray over the Word—indeed before we even get to the Word, lest he fail to come. I close this chapter with the way this works in my own experience.

Almost every day I pray early in the morning that God would give me desires for him and his Word, because the desires I ought to have are absent or weak. In fact, I follow the acronym myself that I have given to many people to help them fight for joy. The acronym is I O U S. It is very limited and focused. It's not all we should pray for. But this book (and most of my life) is about the fight for joy. And that is what I O U S focuses on. Here's the way I pray over the Word in my fight for joy.

I—(*Incline!*) The first thing my soul needs is an *inclination toward God* and his Word. Without that, nothing else will happen of any value in my life. I must *want* to know God and read his Word and draw near to him. Where does that "want to" come from? It comes from God. So Psalm 119:36 teaches us to pray, "*Incline my heart* to your testimonies, and not to selfish gain!" Very simply we ask God to take our hearts, which are more inclined to breakfast and the newspaper, and change that inclination. We are asking that God create desires that are not there.

O—(*Open!*) Next I need to have *the eyes of my heart opened* so that when my inclination leads me to the Word, I see what is really there, and not just my own ideas. Who opens the eyes of the heart? God does. So Psalm 119:18 teaches us to pray, "*Open my eyes*, that I may behold wondrous things out of your law." So many times we read the Bible and see nothing wonderful. Its reading does not produce joy. So what can we do? We can cry to God: "Open the eyes of my heart, O Lord, to see what it says about you as *wonderful.*"

U—(*Unite!*) Then I am concerned that my heart is badly fragmented. Parts of it are inclined, and parts of it are not. Parts see wonder, and parts say, "That's not so wonderful." What I long for is a united heart where all the parts say a joyful *Yes!* to what God reveals in his Word. Where does that wholeness and unity come from? It comes from God. So Psalm 86:11 teaches us to pray, "Unite my heart to fear your name." Don't stumble over the word *fear* when you thought we were seeking *joy*. The fear of the Lord is a joyful experience when you renounce all sin. A thunderstorm can be a trembling joy when you know you can't be destroyed by lightning. "O Lord, let your ear be attentive to . . . the prayer of your servants who *delight to fear your name*" (Neh. 1:11). "His *delight* shall be in the *fear of the* LORD" (Isa. 11:3). Therefore pray that God would *unite* your heart to joyfully fear the Lord.

S—(*Satisfy!*) What I really want from all this engagement with the Word of God and the work of his Spirit in answer to my prayers is *for my heart to be satisfied with God* and not with the world. Where does that satisfaction come from? It comes from God. So

Psalm 90:14 teaches us to pray, "*Satisfy us* in the morning with your steadfast love, that we may rejoice and be glad all our days."

I O U S Admits God Is Our Only Hope for Joy

This acronym has served me well for years. This is frontline warfare for me. I know the agonizing experience of Robert Robinson's hymn "Come, Thou Fount of Every Blessing." What makes this hymn so relevant for me is that it acknowledges God's absolute right to bind my heart to himself, and then it turns that right into a prayer.

> *O to grace how great a debtor*
> *Daily I'm constrained to be!*
> Let Thy goodness, like a fetter,
> Bind my wandering heart to Thee.
> *Prone to wander, Lord, I feel it,*
> *Prone to leave the God I love;*
> *Here's my heart, O take and seal it,*
> *Seal it for Thy courts above.*[8]

"Let Thy goodness, like a fetter, bind my wandering heart to Thee." A "fetter" is a chain. I pray this—oh, how I pray this with all my wandering heart—"Grant me, O God, to see the surpassing value of your goodness so that it binds me, as with a chain, to you." It's the same prayer that George Croly prayed in his well-known hymn, "Spirit of God, Descend upon My Heart."

> *Spirit of God, descend upon my heart;*
> *Wean it from earth; through all its pulses move;*
> *Stoop to my weakness, mighty as Thou art,*
> *And make me love Thee as I ought to love.*[9]

I have heard people object to that last line. They say love should be free, not forced. True. But there are two kinds of forcing. One is against our will. The other is by changing our will. The first results in coerced action. The second results in free action. My own suspicion is that those who object to this prayer have never seriously confronted their own hardness of heart. They have not taken seriously enough the biblical diagnosis of our condition found in the word *cannot* in Romans 8:7-8: "The mind that is set on the flesh . . . does not submit to God's law; indeed, it *cannot*. Those who are in the flesh *cannot* please God." And I wonder, have those who object to this hymn ever come to terms with why the psalmist prays so urgently and repeatedly, "Incline my heart" (Ps. 119: 36, 112; 141:4)? For my part, the only hope I have to love God as I ought is that he would overcome all my disinclination and bind my heart to himself in love. That is the grace I must have to be a Christian and to live in joy.

Hence I pray to God repeatedly: Incline my heart! Open the eyes of my heart! Unite my heart! Satisfy my heart! Prayer is, therefore, not only the measure of our hearts, revealing what we really desire; it is also the indispensable remedy for our hearts when we do not desire God the way we ought.

Rejoice always, pray without ceasing.

1 THESSALONIANS 5:16-17

When Daniel knew that the document had been signed, he went to his house where he had windows in his upper chamber open toward Jerusalem. He got down on his knees three times a day and prayed and gave thanks before his God, as he had done previously.

DANIEL 6:10

My practice had been, at least for ten years previously, as an habitual thing, to give myself to prayer, after having dressed myself in the morning. Now . . . the first thing I did, after having asked in a few words the Lord's blessing upon His precious word, was, to begin to meditate on the word of God, searching, as it were, into every verse, to get blessing out of it. . . . The result I have found to be almost invariably this, that after a very few minutes my soul has been led to confession, or to thanksgiving, or to intercession, or to supplication; so that, though I did not, as it were, give myself to prayer, but to meditation, yet it turned almost immediately more or less into prayer. When thus I have been for awhile making confession, or intercession, or supplication, or have given thanks, I go on to the next words or verse, turning all, as I go on, into prayer for myself or others, as the Word may lead to it.

GEORGE MÜLLER
A Narrative of Some of the Lord's Dealings with George Müller[1]

10

The Practice of Prayer in the Fight for Joy

*Morning, Noon, and Evening
without Ceasing*

To be as practically helpful as possible, I would like to look at the question, How then do we pray for joy? By "how" I mean the nitty-gritty questions of when, and where, and what wording? I hope that these thoughts will feel like empowering encouragements rather than confining prescriptions.

The Source of the Fruit-Bearing Life of Love

Let's begin by considering the simple words of 1 Thessalonians 5:17, "Pray without ceasing." The words might seem to dangle in a string of commands. But there is a flow of thought here that makes this admonition relevant to the fight for joy—and the love that flows from it. It is a flow of thought much like the flow we saw in the previous chapter from 2 Corinthians 8:1-3, and like the flow of thought in Psalm 1, where delighting in the law of the Lord day and night makes you like a tree that bears nourishing fruit even in drought. Here is the relevant context:

> And we urge you, brothers, admonish the idle, encourage the faint-hearted, help the weak, be patient with them all. See that no one

repays anyone evil for evil, but always seek to do good to one another and to everyone. Rejoice always, pray without ceasing, give thanks in all circumstances; for this is the will of God in Christ Jesus for you. (1 Thess. 5:14-18)

Admonishing, encouraging, helping, being patient, not repaying evil for evil, seeking to do good to all—this is a fruit-bearing life. He is telling us to be like trees planted by streams of water that bring forth fruit. This is the effect of delighting in the Word of God in Psalm 1:3. Look at all these needy people draining you. The "idle" are provoking you; the "fainthearted" are leaning on you; the "weak" are depleting you. But you are called to encourage and help and be patient and not return evil for evil. In other words, you are called to have spiritual resources that can be durable and fruitful and nourishing when others are idle and fainthearted and weak and mean-spirited.

How? Where do we get the resources to love like that? Verse 16 answers, "Rejoice always." That corresponds to "delight" in Psalm 1. Presumably, this rejoicing is not primarily based on circumstances, but on God and his promises, because the people around us are idle and fainthearted and weak and antagonistic. This would make an ordinary person angry, sullen, and discouraged. But we are supposed to have our roots planted somewhere other than circumstance. The roots of our lives are supposed to be drawing up the nutriments of joy from a source that cannot be depleted—the river of God and his Word. The one who delights in the Lord is "like a tree planted by streams of water."

What then is the key to this rejoicing, or this delight, which sustains the life of fruit-bearing love? Verse 17 says, "Pray without ceasing." And verse 18 says, "Give thanks in all circumstances." So the answer seems to be that continual prayer and thanksgiving is a key to joy in God that makes a person durable and fruitful in relation to all kinds of people.[2] Therefore one biblical key to maintaining joy in God and his Word is to pray without ceasing.

What Does "Pray without Ceasing" Mean?

If we are going to be fruit-bearing people, and not wither under the pressures of idle, fainthearted, weak, and hurtful people, then we must fight, as 1 Thessalonians 5:16 says, to "rejoice always" or to "delight . . . in the word of the LORD . . . day and night" (Ps. 1:2). And to do that, as verse 17 says, we need to "pray without ceasing." Which leads to the question of what that means.

Praying without ceasing means at least three things. First, it means that there is a spirit of dependence that should permeate all we do. This is the very spirit and essence of prayer. So, even when we are not speaking consciously to God, there is a deep, abiding dependence on him that is woven into the heart of faith. In that sense, we "pray" or have the spirit of prayer continuously.

Second—and I think this is what Paul has in mind most immediately—praying without ceasing means praying repeatedly and often. I base this on the use of the word "without ceasing" (*adialeiptōs*) in Romans 1:9, where Paul says, "For God is my witness, whom I serve with my spirit in the gospel of his Son, that *without ceasing* [*adialeiptos*] I mention you.*" Now we can be sure that Paul did not mention the Romans every minute of his waking life, or even every minute of his prayers. He prayed about many other things. But he mentioned them over and over, and often. So "without ceasing" doesn't mean that, verbally or mentally, we have to be speaking prayers every minute of the day in the fight for joy. It means we should pray over and over, and often. Our default mental state should be: "O God, help . . ."

Third, praying without ceasing means not giving up on prayer. Don't ever come to a point in your life where you cease to pray at all. Don't abandon the God of hope and say, "There's no use praying." Jesus is very jealous for us to learn this lesson. One of his parables is introduced by the words, "And he told them a parable to the effect that they ought always to pray *and not lose heart*" (Luke 18:1). He knew our experience in prayer would tempt us to quit altogether. So he, along with the apostle Paul, says, Never lose heart. Go on praying. Don't cease.

So from the context of 1 Thessalonians 5, I say that the key to "rejoice always" is to "pray without ceasing." Lean on God all the time for the miracle of joy in your life. Never give up looking to him for help. Come to him repeatedly during the day and often. Make your default mental state a Godward longing for all that you need, especially for spiritual desires.

Ceaseless Prayer and Persistent Discipline

In Chapter Eight we made the case that continual communion with God in his Word is important. The upright man of Psalm 1 meditates on the law of the Lord "day and night." We might have said "meditates without ceasing." But then we made the case that this continual, spontaneous communion with God by his Word depends in part on plan and discipline. In other words, if there are no set and disciplined times of Bible reading and meditation and memorization, the spontaneity and continual communion will dry up. The plants of spontaneous communion grow in the well-tended garden of disciplined Bible-reading and memorization.

So it is with prayer. We are told to pray "without ceasing." We may do it anywhere, anytime. It is the air we breathe. But that will cease to be the case if there are no disciplined times set aside for prayer and a plan to keep them. If you want to have a vital hour-by-hour, spontaneous walk with God, you must also have disciplined regular meetings with God for prayer. A husband who says he never has special times alone with his wife because the daily air is charged with intimacy will not long breathe that air. The plants of ceaseless prayer grow in the garden of persistent discipline.

Daniel's Defiant Discipline in Prayer

The prophet Daniel is a good example. He had a remarkable relationship with God, especially when it was critically needed. But what did that continual relationship grow out of? It was the disciplined regularity of his prayer life. Darius, the king, issued a decree that no one should pray to any god but only to the king himself (Dan. 6:7-9). The penalty for disobedience would be death.

What did Daniel do? He reveals to us the discipline from which his spiritual power flowed. According to Daniel 6:10, "When Daniel knew that the document had been signed, he went to his house where he had windows in his upper chamber open toward Jerusalem. He got down on his knees three times a day and prayed and gave thanks before his God, *as he had done previously.*" Daniel's daily custom was to pray in the same place three times a day.

The point is not that three times a day is the ideal number. Others have prayed more often: "Seven times a day I praise you for your righteous rules" (Ps. 119:164). The point is this: If we hope to fight for joy day and night by praying without ceasing, we will need to develop disciplined times of prayer.[3]

How Important Is Early-Morning Prayer?

The example of Jesus and the testimony of lovers of Christ throughout the centuries points us to early-morning prayer as decisively important. "And rising very early in the morning, while it was still dark, [Jesus] departed and went out to a desolate place, and there he prayed" (Mark 1:35). I commend the early morning as one crucial time for a disciplined, regular meeting with God over the Word and prayer.

First, it signals to our conscience that this is of first importance in the day. That witness from our action to our conscience has a joyful effect on the Christian mind. Second, early-morning prayer strikes the first blow in the battle of the day, instead of waiting till we are besieged from all sides. Third, what we do daily and do early shapes the spirit of our minds and brings us into a disposition of humility and trust that will bear better fruit than anxiety or self-reliance. Fourth, since beginning the day with the Word of God is crucial (as we saw in Chapter Eight), therefore prayer is equally crucial since the Word will not open its best wonders to us without prayer: "Open my eyes, that I may behold wondrous things out of your law" (Ps. 119:18). Fifth, it is uncanny how Satan can use even good things to squeeze prayer out of our schedule if we miss the early-morning hour. I have seen it again and again. If I say to myself, "I will give some time to prayer later," it generally does not happen.

William Law (1686-1761), who is famous mainly for his classic *A Serious Call to a Devout and Holy Life*, argues vigorously for "daily early prayer in the morning." "His own day, which began at 5 a.m., was carefully planned to allow time for reading, writing, and works of charity, as well as prayer."[4] His main argument is that the discipline of early rising for prayer and the Word cultivated and demonstrated a spiritual condition that glorified Christ and gratified the soul.

> If our blessed Lord used to pray early before day; if He spent whole nights in prayer; if the devout Anna was day and night in the temple; if St. Paul and Silas at midnight sang praises unto God; if the primitive Christians, for several hundred years, besides their hours

of prayers in the daytime, met publicly in the churches at midnight, to join in psalms and prayers; is it not certain that these practices showed the state of their heart? Are they not so many plain proofs of the whole turn of their minds?[5]

Law was persuaded that "sleep is . . . a dull, stupid state of existence" and that "prayer is the nearest approach to God, and the highest enjoyment of Him that we are capable of in this life."[6] Therefore, his book overflows with the benefits of early-morning prayer.

> If you were to rise early every morning as an instance of self-denial, as a method of renouncing indulgence, as a means of redeeming your time and fitting your spirit for prayer, you would find mighty advantages from it. This method, though it seems such a small circumstance of life, would in all probability be a means of great piety. It would keep it constantly in your head that softness and idleness were to be avoided, that self-denial was a part of Christianity. It would teach you to exercise power over yourself, and make you able by degrees to renounce other pleasures and tempers that war against the soul. . . .
>
> But, above all, one certain benefit from this method you will be sure of having; it will best fit and prepare you for the reception of the Holy Spirit. When you thus begin the day in the spirit of religion, renouncing sleep, because you are to renounce softness and redeem your time; this disposition, as it puts your heart into a good state so it will procure the assistance of the Holy Spirit; what is so planted and watered will certainly have an increase from God. You will then speak from your heart, your soul will be awake, your prayers will refresh you like meat and drink, you will feel what you say, and begin to know what saints and holy men have meant by fervors of devotion.[7]

Planned Meetings with God Later in the Day

I do not want to give the impression that the early-morning hour is the only time for regular, planned meetings with God in prayer. The fight for joy is too relentless for that. Daniel kept his appointments with God three times a day. I would commend a longer time in focused prayer and meditation early in the morning, perhaps an hour (the length will vary with your situation in life), and then two or three other short times later in the day, roughly corresponding to lunch, dinner, and bedtime. These may be no more than a few minutes. What matters more than the length is the intensity of the focus.

In these later times of prayer, I am not referring to the thoughts directed Godward as you walk back to work from the cafeteria or as you run to the car. These are good. They are part of praying without ceasing. Rather I am referring to a few minutes of very focused stillness and solitude, with the Bible open in front of you—or the memory serving up some nourishing text on the tongue of your soul. The aim is to call to mind a few verses and to pray that God would now satisfy your heart in him for the next part of the day and free you from sinful desires, so that you exalt Christ and love people. In this way each segment of the day (and then the night before you go to bed) is consciously dedicated to God by an act of consecration in focused prayer. It is amazing how just a few minutes over the Word at midday and mid-evening can bring spiritual clarity and power and peaceful joy to the next few hours, even in the midst of much pressure.

Plan the Time before It Comes

I have assumed that these times of prayer, especially the early-morning time, have their own special place and time. I urge you to plan for this. Think ahead what the time will be. Win that victory the night before, not in the morning. Decide the evening before when the alarm will call you from sleep to prayer.

The discipline to rise early is not as difficult as the discipline of going to bed. This did not used to be so. Before electricity and radio and television and the Internet, going to bed soon after dark was not so difficult. There wasn't much to do. Today the strongest allurements to stay up and be entertained are against us. Therefore, the battle against weariness, which makes us drowsy as soon as we open our Bible in the morning, has to be fought in the evening, not just in the morning. When you have decided when the alarm will call you to prayer, then decide when you must go to bed so that you are not exhausted when the alarm goes off. If you need caffeine to keep you awake in the morning, I will leave that with your conscience. Maybe that's why God created it.

Staying awake to pray is certainly a better use of caffeine than staying awake for almost anything else.

Think Creatively about the Place Where You Pray

In the evening decide beforehand not only when but *where* you will pray and read when you get up in the morning. There needs to be a measure of privacy so that you are not distracted and are able to read and sing and cry. If complete seclusion is not possible, create the best situation you can, explaining to spouse or children or roommates that when you are in that chair at that hour you would like to be undisturbed.

I would suggest that you think creatively about the place of prayer. I have often wondered why Christians build houses with a room designated for play (called a den) and for food (called a kitchen) and for sleep (called a bedroom) and for cleaning (called a bathroom) and for clothes (called a closet), but do not build a room for the solitude of prayer and meditation. But if we gave thought to this, could we not find or create such a space? The reason we don't do it is mainly that nobody thinks of it. But now I have caused you to think of it. Where could you create such a space? Is there a space under the stairs that could have a kneeling mat and a prayer bench and a light?

In 1975, when we bought our first home, I built a prayer bench with a place for my elbows in a kneeling posture, and a place for my Bible to lie, and a shelf underneath for the Bible or other books and a notepad. It has been with me ever since in three different houses. For the last twenty-one years we have lived in the same house, and there has a been a nook in my study, created by positioning filing cabinets to block it off from the rest of the space. There the prayer bench welcomes me every morning and several times during the day. God alone knows the tears and songs that have mingled there. I urge you to think creatively. Seriously consider building a place of prayer, even if it is just the rearrangement of furniture or the cleaning out of an unused storage space.

Going Outside May Be Best of All

Of course, living in a cold climate, as I do, I don't naturally think of praying and meditating out of doors. But surely that is a good idea for some. George Müller, the nineteenth-century pastor and lover of orphans in Bristol, England, has been a great help to me in the counsel he has given about the fight for joy through prayer and meditation. He is unabashed in saying that the fight for joy is paramount:

> According to my judgement the most important point to be attended to is this: above all things see to it that your souls are happy in the Lord. Other things may press upon you, the Lord's work may even have urgent claims upon your attention, but I deliberately repeat, it is of supreme and paramount importance that you should seek above all things to have your souls truly happy in God Himself! Day by day seek to make this the most important business of your life.[8]

Müller discovered that walking early in the morning with a New Testament in hand was an excellent way of fighting for joy.

> I find it very beneficial to my health to walk thus for meditation before breakfast, and am now so in the habit of using the time for that purpose, that when I get into the open air, I generally take out a New Testament of good sized type which I carry with me for that purpose. . . . I find it very profitable, not only to my body, but also to my soul.[9]

Whether outdoors or indoors, places are not sacred intrinsically. But we make them sacred by what we do there. In the battle for joy, small places indoors or open spaces outdoors can become powerfully strategic.

Plan Your Method of Prayer

When a place and time are settled, move toward settling a method of prayer that will intensify your fight for joy. I don't mean anything like a straitjacket that hinders spontaneity. I mean simple, planned structures that keep us from mental wandering and rambling and empty phrases and worldly desires.

The Great Benefits of Praying the Word of God

The main method of prayer in the fight for joy is to pray the Word of God. That is, to read or recite the Word and turn it into prayer as you go. Most people (certainly including me) do not have the power of mind to look at nothing and yet offer up to God significant spiritual desires for any length of time. I suspect this has always been the case. To pray for longer than a few minutes in a God-centered, Christ-exalting way requires the help of God's Spirit, and the Spirit loves to help by the Word he inspired.

This difficulty of focusing the mind and staying on track accounts, in part, for the fact that so many of the Psalms, even though they are prayers, are permeated with the history of redemption that had been recorded in Scripture (e.g., Ps. 77; 99; 103:6-8; 104; 105; 106). It also accounts for why the glimpse we get into the prayers of the early church reveals that they were, at least sometimes, built out of Scripture.

> They lifted their voices together to God and said, "Sovereign Lord, who made the heaven and the earth and the sea and everything in them, who through the mouth of our father David, your servant, said by the Holy Spirit, 'Why did the Gentiles rage, and the peoples plot in vain? The kings of the earth set themselves, and the rulers were gathered together, against the Lord and against his Anointed.' . . . Lord, look upon their threats and grant to your servants to continue to speak your word with all boldness." (Acts 4:24-26, 29)

George Müller's Discovery about the Word and Prayer

It was a great encouragement to me over twenty years ago to read the testimony of George Müller, that he leaned heavily on the Word in order to keep his focus while praying. It took him ten years of faltering prayer before he learned this lesson. Perhaps his story can spare you such a struggle. Müller wrote this in May 1841 when he was thirty-five years old. He had been converted when he was twenty.

> The difference then between my former practice and my present one is this. Formerly, when I rose, I began to pray as soon as possible. . . . But what was the result? I often spent a quarter of an hour, or half an hour, or even an hour on my knees, before being conscious to myself of having derived comfort, encouragement, humbling of soul, &c.; and often, after having suffered much from wandering of mind for the first ten minutes, or a quarter of an hour,

or even half an hour, I only then began *really to pray*. I scarcely ever suffer now in this way.

My practice had been, at least for ten years previously, as an habitual thing, to give myself to prayer, after having dressed myself in the morning. *Now* . . . the first thing I did, after having asked in a few words the Lord's blessing upon His precious word, was, to begin to meditate on the word of God, searching, as it were, into every verse, to get blessing out of it. . . . The result I have found to be almost invariably this, that after a very few minutes my soul has been led to confession, or to thanksgiving, or to intercession, or to supplication; so that, though I did not, as it were, give myself to *prayer*, but to *meditation*, yet it turned almost immediately more or less into prayer. When thus I have been for awhile making confession, or intercession, or supplication, or have given thanks, I go on to the next words or verse, turning all, as I go on, into prayer for myself or others, as the Word may lead to it.[10]

This is the central method of prayer that I believe most earnest Christians have discovered: "to meditate on the word of God . . . turning all, as I go, into prayer." Someone may ask, "How can I spend an hour in prayer? I'm done asking for what I need in five or ten minutes." I answer: Take a passage of Scripture, and start reading it slowly. After each sentence, pause and go back and turn what you read into prayer. In this way you can pray as long as you can read. You may pray all day.

Do You Pray the Way an Unbeliever Would?

There are more benefits to praying over the Word in this way than the fact that it helps us stay focused. It also has the effect of shaping our minds and hearts, so that we desire what the Word encourages us to desire, and not just what we desire by nature. That is why the prayers of Bible-saturated people sound so different. Most people, before their prayers are soaked in Scripture, simply bring their natural desires to God. In other words, they pray the way an unbeliever would pray who is convinced that God might give him what he wants: health, a better job, safe journeys, a prosperous portfolio, successful children, plenty of food, a happy marriage, a car that works, a comfortable retirement, etc. None of these is evil. They're just natural. You don't have to be born again to want any of these. Desiring them—even from God—is no evidence of saving faith. So if these are all you pray for, there is a deep problem. Your desires have not yet been changed to put the glory of Christ at the center.

But when you saturate your mind with the Christ-exalting Word of God and turn it into prayer, your desires and your prayers become spiritual. That is, they are shaped by the Holy Spirit into God-centered, Christ-exalting prayers. The glory of Christ, and the name of God, and the spiritual well-being of people, and the delight you have in knowing Jesus—these become your dominant concerns and your constant requests. You still pray for health and marriage and job and journeys, but now what you want to happen is that, in all these, Christ will be exalted. This changes the pattern and passion of your prayers. Your prayer for a journey is not merely that it be safe, but that all along the way your joy would be in God and that he would shine through you. Your prayer for your job is not merely that it be stable and peaceful and prosperous, but that it truly serves the needs of society and that in all your labor and all your relationships your joy in Christ and your love for people would make a name for Jesus.[11]

What Does It Mean to Pray in the Holy Spirit?

Another advantage of praying the Word of God is that this is part of what it means to "pray in the Holy Spirit," and praying in the Spirit is how we "keep ourselves in the love of God." I get these two phrases from the book of Jude. There the brother of the Lord Jesus commands us, "Beloved, build yourselves up in your most holy faith; *pray in the Holy Spirit*; keep yourselves in the love of God" (vv. 20-21). Literally, the first two commands are participles and tell us *how* to keep ourselves in the love of God: "Beloved, [by] building yourselves up in your most holy faith, [and by] praying in the Holy Spirit, keep yourselves in the love of God."

Don't think that keeping yourself in the love of God hangs decisively on us. The book of Jude begins and ends with the opposite truth. It begins with the words, "To those who are called, beloved in God the Father and *kept for* Jesus Christ" (v. 1). Here Christians are identified with three words: called, loved, and *kept*. And the keeping is done by God, not us.

Then the book of Jude ends with the words, "Now to him who is able to *keep* you from stumbling and to present you blameless before the presence of his glory with great joy" (v. 24). Again it is God who is keeping. Therefore when Jude says that by "praying in the Holy Spirit" we are to keep ourselves in the love of God, we know he means that prayer is one of God's instruments for keeping us in his love. Beware of the cynical mind-set that says, "If God is the decisive keeper of my soul (vv. 1, 24), then I don't need to 'keep myself in the love of God'" (v. 21). That would be like saying, since God is the decisive giver of life, then I don't need to breathe.[12]

Praying the Word and Praying in the Spirit

Now how does praying the Word of God the way Müller suggests relate to praying in the Holy Spirit? The best brief statement I have found of what it means to pray in the Holy Spirit goes like this: It means "so to pray that the Holy Spirit is the *moving* and *guiding* power."[13] In other words, when you pray in the Holy Spirit, the Spirit of God is "moving" you to pray. That is, his power motivates, enables, and energizes your prayer. And when you pray in the Holy Spirit, the Spirit of God is "guiding" how you pray and what you pray for. So to pray in the Holy Spirit is to be moved and guided by the Holy Spirit. We pray by his *power* and according to his *direction*.

These two—the Spirit's power and direction—correspond to two ways that the Word of God functions in our prayer. The *power* of the Spirit is offered in the promises of God's Word, and we experience it by *faith* in the promise. The *direction* of the Spirit is embodied in the wisdom of God's Word, and we experience it by *being saturated* with that wisdom. So if we would "pray in the Holy Spirit" we should, like Müller, pray the Word of God, trusting the promises and absorbing the wisdom.

Staying in the Love of God Is Joy Unspeakable

So when we follow Mueller's advice and turn the Scriptures into prayer as we read, we will be helped to "pray in the Holy Spirit." The Scriptures will awaken faith in the Spirit's power to help us pray (Rom. 8:26), and the Scriptures will shape our minds to pray in the direction of the Spirit's will. When Christ's words dwell in us richly, he abides in us powerfully (Col. 3:16; Eph. 5:18). And when we thus "pray in the Holy Spirit," we will, as Jude says, "keep yourselves in the love of God" (v. 21). And as our precious position in the love of God becomes more and more real to us,[14] we will rejoice with joy unspeakable. Therefore, praying the Word of God is a crucial strategy in the fight for joy.

Something Fixed and Something Free

William Law adds this counsel to increase the benefit of our regular times of prayer: "At all stated hours of prayer it will be a great benefit to you to have something fixed and something at liberty in your devotions."[15] He means more than having the fixed Word of God as your guide in meditation and prayer. He means that in the fight for joy, it helps to have a focused center to your praying, and it helps to have some written, Bible-saturated prayers to keep you from sinking to a low level of man-centered craving.

Centering on God with the Lord's Prayer

I have found over several decades that the first three petitions of the Lord's prayer help me keep God at the center of my desires in prayer: "Our Father in heaven, hallowed be your name. Your kingdom come, your will be done, on earth as it is in heaven" (Matt. 6:9-10). According to Jesus' instruction the first burden we should bring to God in prayer is that the name of God be "hallowed." In the Lord's prayer we are asking that God would do whatever he must do so that his name is revered and esteemed and cherished in the world.[16] We are asking that his spiritual kingdom come in the hearts of people, and that the in-breaking of his final, glorious kingdom move toward consummation. We are asking that world events, and the progress of missions, would move quickly toward the time when all those who are left on earth would do the will of God the way the angels do it in heaven.

If these three petitions become the lodestar in the constellation of our prayers, all other requests will have their proper place. These three will shine in and through them all, so that every request, even for daily bread, is really a concrete way of asking that God's name and will and kingdom take the supreme place in our hearts and in history.

Helping Us Be Sober and Serious before God in Prayer

In the modern, developed world, our minds are permeated with superficial entertainment. Coming to God in prayer with reverence and awe is not natural. Feeling the utter seriousness of the fight for joy in God is foreign to us. We need help. William Law suggests that we regularly use some fixed form such as the following when we come to God with requests.

> O Savior of the world, God of God, Light of Light, Thou that art The Brightness of Thy Father's glory, and the express Image of his person; Thou that art the Alpha and Omega, the Beginning and End of all things; Thou that hast destroyed the power of the devil, that hast overcome death; Thou that art entered into the Holy of Holies, that sittest at the right hand of the Father, that art high above all thrones and principalities, that makest intercession for all the world; Thou that art the judge of the quick and the dead; Thou that wilt speedily come down in Thy Father's glory to reward all men according to their works, be Thou my light and my peace, etc.[17]

The point of such a formal beginning to prayer—which is full of descriptions of Jesus—Law says, is that these descriptions "are not only proper acts of adoration, but will, if they are repeated with attention, fill our hearts with the highest fervors of true devotion."[18]

It may be that some of you are naturally inclined and able to tell the Lord Jesus how great and wonderful he is as you begin your prayers. But most of us are prone to bluster into the throne room of heaven—as into a hardware store with a broken piece of plumbing—rather than with joyful wonder that we are admitted here only by the blood of Christ and that we come to the greatest Being in the universe. Therefore, it is helpful that some "fixed form"—at least from time to time—remind us that adoration is a fitting approach.

The other form that William Law suggests as a beginning to our plea for help is the following—as a way of wakening our hope of being heard with mercy.

> O Holy Jesus, Son of the most high God, Thou that wert scourged at a pillar, stretched and nailed upon a cross for the sins of the world, unite me to Thy cross, and fill my soul with Thy holy, humble, and

suffering spirit. O Fountain of Mercy, Thou that didst save the thief upon the cross, save me from the guilt of a sinful life; Thou that didst cast seven devils out of Mary Magdalene, cast out of my heart all evil thoughts and wicked tempers. O Giver of Life, Thou that didst raise Lazarus from the dead, raise up my soul from the death and darkness of sin. Thou that didst give to Thy Apostles power over unclean spirits, give me power over mine own heart. Thou that didst appear unto Thy disciples when the doors were shut, do Thou appear to me in the secret apartment of my heart. Thou that didst cleanse the lepers, heal the sick, and give sight to the blind, cleanse my heart, heal the disorders of my soul, and fill me with heavenly light.[19]

The point here is that often when we come to pray, our minds are filled with ordinary earthly things and the potential and power of what the world can do for us, if we try harder. The poet William Wordsworth describes our unfitness for Nature's gifts the way I would describe our unfitness for God's gifts as we come to pray.

The world is too much with us; late and soon,
Getting and spending, we lay waste our powers;
Little we see in Nature that is ours;
We have given our hearts away, a sordid boon![20]

We do not naturally or easily shift from the mind-set of "getting and spending" into a mind-set that sees Jesus as more desirable than the "sordid boon" of this world. We need—at least sometimes—"something fixed" to remind us, from Christ's own life and death, that surely he will hear our cries for help and become our all-satisfying treasure.[21]

When we look at the "sordid boon" that the world offers, the fight for joy is to see that it will not satisfy. Prayer is an essential strategy in seeing the world this way. We must ask God "without ceasing" that our eyes be open to the insufficiency of worldly pleasures, even the innocent ones. And we must plead that the taste buds of our souls be ever alive to the beauty of Christ.

Fasting, the Humble Handmaiden of Prayer

Two additional strategies in the fight for faith can intensify the earnestness of this kind of praying. The first is fasting. I won't say much here, because I have written an entire book on fasting called *A Hunger for God: Desiring God through Fasting and Prayer*.[22] But the essence of fasting is so relevant in the fight for joy, I should at least mention it. Jesus said, "When you fast, anoint your head and wash your face, that your fasting may not be seen by others but by your Father who is in secret. And your Father who sees in secret will reward you" (Matt. 6:17-18). The reward is ultimately God himself. Therefore fasting is an expression of hunger for God.

In another place Jesus referred to himself as a bridegroom and his disciples as the wedding guests and said, "Can the wedding guests mourn as long as the bridegroom is with them? The days will come when the bridegroom is taken away from them, and then they will fast" (Matt. 9:15). We live in the days when the Bridegroom has been taken away (between the first and second coming of Christ). The meaning of fasting in these days is that we long to have the Bridegroom back.

So in both these texts the point of fasting is to express longing for Christ and all that God is for us in him. Fasting is the hungry hand-maid of prayer. Like prayer she both reveals and remedies. She reveals the measure of food's mastery over us—or television or computers or whatever we submit to again and again to conceal the weakness of our hunger for God. And she remedies by intensifying the earnestness of our prayer and saying with our whole body what prayer says with the heart: I long to be satisfied in God alone!

Is eating then evil? No. Paul said that false teachers will arise who "forbid marriage and require abstinence from foods that God created to be received with thanksgiving by those who believe and know the truth" (1 Tim. 4:3). How then do the goodness of eating and the goodness of fasting fit together? I will try to answer with some brief excerpts from *A Hunger for God*.

> Bread magnifies Christ in two ways: by being eaten with gratitude for his goodness, and by being forfeited out of hunger for God himself. When we eat, we taste the emblem of our heavenly food—the Bread of Life. And when we fast we say, "I love the Reality above the emblem." In the heart of the saint both eating and fasting are worship. Both magnify Christ. Both send the heart—grateful and yearning—to the Giver. Each has its appointed place and each has

its danger. The danger of eating is that we fall in love with the gift; the danger of fasting is that we belittle the gift and glory in our willpower. . . .

My aim and my prayer in writing this book is that it might awaken a hunger for the supremacy of God in all things for the joy of all peoples. Fasting proves the presence, and fans the flame, of that hunger. It is an intensifier of spiritual desire. It is a faithful enemy of fatal bondage to innocent things. It is the physical exclamation point at the end of the sentence: "This much, O God, I long for you and for the manifestation of your glory in the world!" . . .

If you don't feel strong desires for the manifestation of the glory of God, it is not because you have drunk deeply and are satisfied. It is because you have nibbled so long at the table of the world. Your soul is stuffed with small things, and there is no room for the great.[23] God did not create you for this. There is an appetite for God. And it can be awakened. I invite you to turn from the dulling effects of food and the dangers of idolatry, and to say with some simple fast: "This much, O God, I want you."[24]

As with many difficult things in life, fasting is meant to help us in the fight for joy. William Law put it like this:

Although these abstinences give some pain to the body, yet they so lessen the power of bodily appetites and passions, and so increase our taste of spiritual joys, that even these severities of religion, when practiced with discretion, add much to the comfortable enjoyment of our lives.[25]

When My Prayers Are Answered by the Prayers of Others

I will mention one more strategy for intensifying the power of prayer in the fight for joy—namely, the importance of having other people pray with you and for you. After telling us to call for the elders to pray for us when we are sick, James says, "Therefore, confess your sins to one another and pray for one another, that you may be healed. The prayer of a righteous person has great power as it is working" (Jas. 5:16). The implication here for the fight for joy is that we should involve other Christians in our fight. We should confess to them our struggles, and we should ask them to pray that we would be "healed" from our half-hearted love for Jesus.

God has his reasons why the prayers of others might lift my darkness when my own prayers didn't. But be careful here. Don't assume that all your praying was in vain. It may be that your own praying was used by God to make you willing to seek the prayers of others. It may be that your prayers were answered in the blessing that came in answer to their prayers. One of God's reasons for calling us to corporate prayer is given in 2 Corinthians 1:11. Paul asks for prayer for himself and gives his reason: "You also must help us by prayer, so that many will give thanks on our behalf for the blessing granted us through the prayers of many." When people are involved in each other's lives, more thanksgiving rises to God when any of them is blessed.

In other words, everything I have written in these chapters about praying for joy will be multiplied in its effectiveness when we think of it corporately. The fight for joy is a battle to be fought alongside comrades. We do not fight alone. To be a Christian is to be a part of the Body of Christ. We are meant to help each other fight for joy. This was the apostle's life: "We work with you for your joy" (2 Cor. 1:24). And prayer for each other[26] is at the heart of this camaraderie.

For everything created by God is good, and nothing is to be rejected if it is received with thanksgiving, for it is made holy by the word of God and prayer.

1 TIMOTHY 4:4-5

The heavens declare the glory of God,
and the sky above proclaims his handiwork.

PSALM 19:1

I was standing today in the dark toolshed. The sun was shining outside and through the crack at the top of the door there came a sunbeam. From where I stood that beam of light, with the specks of dust floating in it, was the most striking thing in the place. Everything else was almost pitch-black. I was seeing the beam, not seeing things by it. Then I moved so that the beam fell on my eyes. Instantly the whole previous picture vanished. I saw no toolshed, and (above all) no beam. Instead I saw, framed in the irregular cranny at the top of the door, green leaves moving on the branches of a tree outside and beyond that, 90 odd million miles away, the sun. Looking along the beam, and looking at the beam are very different experiences.

C. S. LEWIS
"Meditation in a Toolshed"
God in the Dock[1]

11

How to Wield the World in the Fight for Joy

*Using All Five Senses to See the
Glory of God*

In this chapter we wrestle with the relationship between physical causes and spiritual effects. If that sounds vague, consider some examples: Can physical sounds (like music or thunder) cause spiritual effects (like joy in Christ or fear of God)? Can deep ravines produce reverence for Christ? Can a sizzling steak produce satisfaction in Jesus? Everybody knows that music and thunder can cause joy and fear. But can they cause spiritual joy and spiritual fear? Can cliffs and food waken the joy of faith?

Usually the word *spiritual* in the New Testament refers to something or someone that is brought forth by the Holy Spirit, controlled by the Holy Spirit, and directed to the goals of the Holy Spirit, especially the adoration of Christ. But music and thunder and ravines and steak are not the Holy Spirit. They are natural parts of the material creation. What is the relationship between them and spiritual joy?

Or to ask the question another way: In the fight for joy in God can we use physical means? The answer is not easy. That's why I said we would "wrestle" in this chapter. Not all joy exalts Christ. Joy exalts what we rejoice in. If we rejoice in revenge, then we exalt the value of revenge. If we rejoice in pornography, we exalt the value of pornography. Those are clearly sinful. But what about innocent pleasures? If we rejoice in a beautiful sunrise, what do we exalt? The sunrise? Or the Creator of the sunrise? Or both? And what makes the difference in our hearts and minds?

Many unbelievers are deeply moved to rejoice in the beauty of a sunrise. They do not have the Holy Spirit and do not adore Christ. What is the difference between their joy and spiritual joy? Is the experience the same and only our knowledge different? Or is the joy itself different? If so, how?

Is Patience a Fruit of the Spirit or of Sleep?

I take up this question because our everyday experience, as well as the Bible itself, demands it. We know from experience that our spiritual and physical life are intertwined. Losing sleep increases our impatience and irritability, but the Bible says that *love* is "patient . . . it is not irritable" (1 Cor. 13:4-5), and it calls love and patience fruits of the Spirit (Gal. 5:22). So are love and patience fruits of the Spirit, or are they the fruit of sleep?

Even in the Lord's work no one would deny that a rush of adrenaline may accompany some great challenge and give wakefulness and energy for some God-ordained task. But the apostle Paul says, "I toil, struggling with all his energy that *he* powerfully works within me" (Col. 1:29). What is the difference between Paul's physical adrenaline and the powerful energy he feels from Christ? Are they totally separate? Or does Christ somehow work through adrenaline?

The World of Sight and Sound

To grasp the scope of this issue, think of your five senses and the countless sensations they bring and how these affect your emotions and your spiritual life. You have the sense of *sight*, and you see the sky with its clouds and its shades of blue and its horizons of red and orange and its nighttime of moon and stars. You see the earth with its thousands of species of birds and land animals and fish and trees and plants, and its varied terrains of deserts, fields, mountains, plains, forests, hills, canyons, and ravines with rivers. And you see human beings, male and female, short and tall, thin and heavy, with countless hues of skin, no two alike. And you see all that man can make:

paintings, sculptures, dramas, movies, machines, buildings, roads, computers, planes, clothing, electrical generators, nuclear plants, artificial hearts, microwave ovens, cell phones, air conditioning, antibiotics, universities, and governments.

And you have a sense of *hearing*. You hear the sounds of animals: the bird singing, the cat meowing, the dog barking, the snake hissing, the mosquito humming, the frog croaking, the horse neighing and clip-clopping, the pig oinking, the cow mooing, and the rooster crowing. And you hear the sounds of inanimate nature: the ocean waves crashing, the dead tree falling, the landslide plunging, the frozen lake cracking, the volcano exploding, the stream rippling, the thunder rumbling, the rain pounding. And you hear the sounds of man: talking, laughing, whistling, humming, clapping, crying, groaning, screaming, stomping, singing, playing on a hundred instruments, pounding nails, revving engines, operating machines, scraping old houses, thumping along with crutches, cooking sizzling hamburgers on a grill, tearing open an envelope, slamming a door, spanking a child, breaking a dish, and mowing the lawn.

The World of Taste, Smell, and Touch

And you have a sense of *taste*. You taste hundreds of foods and drinks: sour lemons, sweet honey, sharp cheese, tart grapefruit, salty chips, hot salsa, tangy punch, and countless unique flavors of bananas, milk, nuts, bread, fish, steak, lettuce, chocolate, coffee, green peppers, onions, vanilla ice cream, red Jell-O, and a range of medicines you would rather swallow than taste.

And you have a sense of *smell*. You smell roses, honeysuckle, apple blossoms, lilacs, bread baking, bacon sizzling, toast browning, pizza warming, coffee percolating, clove spice, spilled garbage, raw sewage, paper factories, hog farms, favorite perfumes, newly mown grass, gasoline fumes, pine forests, old books, and cinnamon rolls.

And you have the sense of *touch* and inner sensations. You feel cozy heat curled by a fire, warm flannel sheets on a cold night, a cool breeze on a sunny day, the silk edge of an old blanket, a dog's fur and soft tummy, a foot rub, a shoulder massage, sexual stimulation, the resistance of weightlifting, the pounding of jogging, the dive into a cold mountain lake, the hammer landing on your thumb, the ache in your lower back, the migraine headache, the nausea of seasickness, the kiss of a lover.

Physical Sensations and the Sweetness of God

Any one of these five senses, or any combination of them, can give you emotions. And some of these emotions feel virtually the same as the spiritual emotions we are commanded to have in the Bible: joy (Phil. 4:4), delight (Ps. 37:4), gladness (Ps. 67:4), hope (Ps. 42:5), fear (Luke 12:5), grief (Rom. 12:15), desire (1 Pet. 2:2), tenderheartedness (Eph. 4:32), gratitude (Eph. 5:20), etc.

Not only do our senses produce emotions, but the proper or improper use of our bodies can have a huge effect on the way we experience spiritual reality. Rejoicing in the Lord is different when you have nausea from when you are well and singing in a worship service. Proper eating and exercising and sleeping have a marked effect on the mind and its ability to process natural beauty and biblical truth.

So the question must be faced: How do we use the created world around us, including our own bodies, to help us fight for joy in God? In God, I say! Not in nature. Not in music. Not in health. Not in food or drink. Not in natural beauty. How can all these good gifts serve joy in God, and not usurp the supreme affections of our hearts?

Our situation as physical creatures is precarious. The question we are asking is not peripheral. It addresses the dangerous condition we are in. We are surrounded by innocent things that are ready to become idols. Innocent sensations are one second away from becoming substitutes for the sweetness of God. Should we use mood music and dim lighting and smoke and incense to create an atmosphere that conduces to good feelings and "spiritual" openness? You can feel the dangers of manipulation lurking just below the surface.

But no one escapes the problem. Everybody uses physical means. We all choose some kind of lighting. We all choose some kind of atmosphere, no matter how stark. We all use some kind of music, even if only voice. We all make choices about how we sleep and exercise and eat. And presumably we are not acting like atheists when we make these choices; we believe they have something to do with God. There is no way around the issue. We must all come to terms with how our physical, sensory lives relate to our spiritual joy in God.

Joy without Brains?

As much as we are sure that our joy in God is more than chemicals and electronic impulses in the brain, we are also sure that, in this present age, we experience this spiritual joy only in connection to a physical body. And the interplay between the two is mysterious. There is, in some strange way, an overlapping of spiritual joy and psychological emotion and physiological event. They are not identical. We know this because God has strong spiritual emotions, like anger (Ps. 80:4) and joy (Zeph. 3:17), but he has no physical body. So there are spiritual emotions that exist independently of physical bodies. And presumably, redeemed people will have strong emotions of adoration and satisfaction at God's right hand after they die and before their bodies are raised from the dead (see Phil. 1:23; Rev. 6:10). So we believe that joy in Christ is not identical with physical brain waves but has an existence above material reality.

In spite of the theoretical popularity of naturalistic evolution, which says all there is in the universe is matter and energy, almost nobody will approve if you put their sense of justice in the same category as a dog's bark. So even those who have no conscious belief in God intuitively operate on the assumption that their emotion of love and their sense of justice are more than electrochemical events in the brain.[2]

Nevertheless, these supra-physical things are linked with our physical brains. And so it is that our joy in God and its physical expression in the brain are inseparable in this mortal life. Spiritual emotions (which are more than physical) can have physical effects, and physical conditions can have spiritual effects.

The Spiritual Orchestra and the Physical Piano

C. S. Lewis thought deeply about this issue and wrote about it in a sermon called "Transposition." His argument is that the spiritual life of emotion is higher and richer than the material life of physical sensation in the way a symphony orchestra is richer than a piano. When the music of spiritual joy plays in the soul, it gets "transposed" into physical sensations. But since the spiritual "orchestra" is richer and more varied than the physical "piano," the same piano keys have to be used for sounds that in the orchestra are played with different instruments. As physical people with souls, we always experience spiritual emotions at both levels: the orchestra and the piano.

There are at least four reasons why Lewis's analysis is helpful. One is that it explains the fact that introspection can never find spiritual joy in God, but only its residue of physical sensation. The reason is that the moment we turn from focusing on God to focusing on the emotion itself, the emotion is no longer what it was. It leaves its trace only in the physical sensation, not in the spiritual reality. The reality of spiritual joy depends moment by moment on the steadfast seeing of the glory of God.[3]

Second, Lewis's analysis helps explain why the physical sensations we find when we look behind the spiritual emotions of ecstasy and terror seem to be identical. In other words, the physical trembling and the queasy stomach seem to be the same for terror and ecstasy when we analyze them by introspection. Lewis explains that this is what we would expect when an orchestra of emotion is transposed down onto a simpler instrument: very different spiritual emotions must play on the same piano key.

If a good man looks into the face of his fiancée and feels the pleasure of a warm love somewhere—he can't tell if it's in his head or chest, or even more visceral—and then he turns from looking at his lover to find the pleasure—wherever it is—what he will probably find is a physical sensation indistinguishable from lust. The orchestra of love uses the same physical note on the piano that lust uses to play her music, but everyone knows that love and lust are not identical emotions.

But if they are the same at one level—playing on the same piano key of the body—why then do we experience the spiritual emotions so differently when they are actually happening—even differently in our bodies? For we do indeed experience lust and love, or terror and ecstasy, as physically different. We experience terror as unpleasant and do not want to repeat it, but we experience ecstasy as pleasant and would like to have it again.

Spiritual Emotion Enters and Transforms
Physical Sensation

Lewis answers that in the transposition from the higher to the lower, the spiritual emotion actually enters into the physical sensation so that the sensation becomes part of the higher emotion.

> The very same sensation does not merely accompany, nor merely signify, diverse and opposite emotions, but becomes part of them. The emotion descends bodily, as it were, into the sensation and digests, transforms, transubstantiates it, so that the same thrill along the nerves *is* delight or *is* agony.[4]

This is extremely important. It leads to the third reason why Lewis's analysis is helpful: It answers the materialist-skeptic who looks at the brain waves for "delight" and for "agony" and argues that there can be no reality to the so-called spiritual difference, since both are registered in the brain with the same electrochemical reactions. So he concludes that there is no such thing as spiritual emotions, but only physical sensations. Tragically, that is what millions of modern people claim to believe. But Lewis's analysis shows that this mistake is exactly what we would expect if "transposition" is true. The person who approaches it only "from below" can only hear the piano.

> The brutal man never can by analysis find anything but lust in love . . . physiology never can find anything in thought except twitchings of the gray matter. . . . [The materialist] is therefore, as regards the matter in hand, in the position of an animal. You will have noticed that most dogs cannot understand *pointing*. You point to a bit of food on the floor: the dog, instead of looking at the floor, sniffs at your finger. A finger is a finger to him, and that is all. . . . As long as this deliberate refusal to understand things from above, even where such understanding is possible, continues, it is idle to talk of any final victory over materialism. The critique of every experience from below . . . will always have the same plausibility. There will always be evidence, and every month fresh evidence, to show that religion is only psychological, justice only self protection, politics only economics, love only lust, and thought itself only cerebral biochemistry.[5]

Fourth, Lewis's analysis helps us understand how to use the world of physical sensation for spiritual purposes. From his contrast between the spiritual orchestra of emotion and the physical piano of sensation we are reminded not to equate spiritual emotion and physical sensation. They are not identical. That is a crucial truth to keep in mind. On the other hand, Lewis also reminds us that spiritual emotions, like joy in God, are only experienced in connection with physical sensations. They are not identical, but they are almost always inseparable. In this earthly life, we are never disembodied souls with only spiritual emotions. We are complex spiritual-physical beings who experience joy in Christ as something more, but almost never less, than physical sensation. I say "almost" to leave open the exceptional possibility that, contrary to his usual way of working, God can do miracles in the midst of suffering, such as ecstasy in the midst of flames, while burning at the stake.

Moreover, Lewis reminds us to be amazed that the higher can actually transform the lower. Spiritual emotions, which are more than physical, can have chemical effects, and not just the reverse. It is true that chemicals can affect emotions. But too seldom do we pray and plan for the spiritual to have chemical effects. As legitimate as sedatives and anti-depressants may be in times of clear chemical imbalance, we should not overlook the truth that spiritual reality may also transform the physical and not just vice versa.

Being Intentional in How We Use the Physical for the Sake of Joy in God

But our main question in this chapter is how the lower can affect the higher. That is, how can the physical world of sensation properly assist our joy in Christ? What Lewis has shown us is that God has created us in such a way that there is a correspondence in this life between spiritual emotion and physical experience. God ordained that the brain and the soul intersect and correspond. They are not identical. The physical events in the brain and the spiritual events in the soul do not correspond one to one. But they are interwoven in a way that encourages us to take steps so that the influence flows in both directions for the glory of Christ.

That would mean, for example, that on the one hand we seek by prayer and meditation on God's Word to waken joy in Christ so that it has a healing, strengthening effect on the body. And it would mean, on the other hand, that we use the physical world, including our own bodies, so that, according to the laws of God's creation, joy in Christ will be more intense and more constant. In other words, Lewis has helped us see that there are some legitimate steps we can take at the physical, sensory level in order to properly increase our joy in God.

I say this in spite of the danger mentioned earlier that we run the risk of manipulation (mood music, smoke, and dim lighting) to create "spiritual" emotions, which turn out not to be spiritual at all. There is no running from the responsibility of using physical reality wisely for spiritual ends. Our physical lives will affect our spiritual lives whether we plan it or not. Better to think it through and be intentional.

The Bible Itself Says: See God in the World

Far more important than the wisdom of Lewis is the biblical wisdom of God. The Bible gives us good evidence that we should indeed be intentional about touching our joy in God with physical means. We have already seen in Chapter Five that *seeing* the glory of God is the essential and proper basis of our joy in God. We argued from 2 Corinthians 4:4 that the most central and controlling means of seeing God is by means of hearing the gospel. "The god of this world [Satan] has blinded the minds of the unbelievers, to keep them from seeing *the light of the gospel of the glory of Christ*, who is the image of God." The deepest foundation of our joy, as justified sinners, is that Christ died for our sins and thus revealed the smiling face of God for all who believe. That's the way it is with all the Scriptures: they enable us to see, in them and through them, the glory of God. "The LORD revealed *himself* . . . by *the word of the LORD*" (1 Sam. 3:21). God himself stands forth to be spiritually seen and enjoyed "by the word of the LORD."

But the Bible tells us of other means of seeing the glory of God, and therefore other means of wakening and intensifying our joy in him. For example, Psalm 19:1-4:

> *The heavens declare the glory of God*, and the sky above proclaims his handiwork. Day to day pours out speech, and night to night reveals knowledge. There is no speech, nor are there words, whose

voice is not heard. Their measuring line goes out through all the earth, and their words to the end of the world.

If seeing the glory of God is a proper spiritual cause of our joy in him, then our physical gaze at the heavens—the sun and moon and stars and clouds and sunrises and sunsets and thunderstorms—is a proper means of helping us rejoice in God. So here we have a clear biblical warrant for using the physical world ("the heavens"), by means of the physical organ of sight, to pursue a spiritual effect, namely, seeing the glory of God and experiencing our joy in it.

Other scriptures make explicit the connection between the physically visible work of God and joy. For example, Psalm 92:4, "For you, O LORD, have made me glad by your work; at the works of your hands I sing for joy." I assume that this joy is not idolatrous—that is, I assume it does not terminate on the works themselves, but in and through them, rests on the glory of God himself. The works "declare" the glory of God. They point. But the final ground of our joy is God himself.

Learning from Light in a Toolshed

Lewis, whose greatest gift was his power to see what few see, described an experience that demonstrated how the physical world helps us see the glory of God.

> I was standing today in the dark toolshed. The sun was shining outside and through the crack at the top of the door there came a sunbeam. From where I stood that beam of light, with the specks of dust floating in it, was the most striking thing in the place. Everything else was almost pitch-black. I was seeing the beam, not seeing things by it. Then I moved so that the beam fell on my eyes. Instantly the whole previous picture vanished. I saw no toolshed, and (above all) no beam. Instead I saw, framed in the irregular cranny at the top of the door, green leaves moving on the branches of a tree outside and beyond that, 90 odd million miles away, the sun. Looking along the beam, and looking at the beam are very different experiences.[6]

So we can say that when we "look along" the heavens and not just "at" the heavens, they succeed in their aim of "declaring the glory of God." That is, we see the glory *of God*, not just the glory of the heavens. We don't just stand outside and analyze the natural world as a beam, but let the beam fall on the eyes of our heart, so that we see the source of the beauty—the original Beauty, God himself.

This is the essential key to unlocking the proper use of the physical world of sensation for spiritual purposes. All of God's creation becomes a beam to be "looked along" or a sound to be "heard along" or a fragrance to be "smelled along" or a flavor to be "tasted along" or a touch to be "felt along." All our senses become partners with the eyes of the heart in perceiving the glory of God through the physical world.

So on the one hand, Lewis has shown us that our more-than-physical spiritual emotions are incarnated in our physical sensations, transforming them so that they take on the quality of the emotion. And on the other hand he has shown us that the physical sensations are partners in perceiving the glory of God in the physical world and therefore are means of awakening and shaping those very spiritual emotions. Specifically, joy in God can be awakened by the physical display of God's glory, and that very joy enters and transforms the physical experience of it.

The Apostle Paul Helps Us Use the World in the Fight for Joy

Does the Bible itself give us any explicit help at this point to ensure, as much as possible, that our use of the physical world does in fact help us perceive the glory of God, so that our awakened emotions are not simply natural but spiritual? Yes, the apostle Paul addresses this issue in a fairly direct way in 1 Timothy 4:1-5.

> Now the Spirit expressly says that in later times some will depart from the faith by devoting themselves to deceitful spirits and teachings of demons, through the insincerity of liars whose consciences are seared, who *forbid marriage* and *require abstinence from foods* that *God created to be received with thanksgiving* by those who believe and know the truth. For everything created by God is good, and *nothing is to be rejected if it is received with thanksgiving, for it is made holy by the word of God and prayer.*

Notice that Paul predicts the coming of false teachers who have a very negative view of the physical world, particularly sex and food (which together involve all five of our senses). So these false teachers "forbid marriage" and "require abstinence from foods" (v. 3). Paul regards this as rebellion against God, because God's purpose for his good creation, Paul says, is that "nothing is to be rejected" (v. 4).

Instead of rejecting God's creation, Paul says there are two things we should do with it: receive it with thanksgiving (vv. 3-4), and sanctify it (sanctify = make holy, v. 5). Consider how each of these connects the physical world with our joy in God.

Gratitude for a Gift Involves Joy in a Giver

The sexual pleasures of the marriage bed and the culinary pleasures of good food, Paul says, are to be "received with thanksgiving." This is directly related to joy in God because of what thanksgiving is. First, gratitude is an emotion, not just a choice. You can make yourself say, "Thank you" when you do not feel gratitude, but everyone knows the difference between the words and the feeling. Gratitude is a spontaneous feeling of gladness because of someone's goodwill toward you. Their gift may not even arrive. It may get lost in the mail. But if you know that you were remembered, and that someone took the trouble to buy you something that you would have enjoyed, and that they sent it to you, you will feel gratitude, even if the gift never comes.

Which means, secondly, that the emotion of gratitude is directed toward a giver. Gratitude is *occasioned* by a gift, but is *directed* to the giver. Third, gratitude is a kind of joy. It is not a bad feeling or a neutral feeling. It is positive and pleasant. We do not regret feeling gratitude—unless we were deceived, and the gift turns out to be a trap. Begrudging gratitude is an oxymoron. There is no such thing. No one feels gratitude out of duty when they really don't want to. Gratitude is spontaneous and pleasant. It is joy in the goodwill of the giver.

The dominant link in the Bible between our gratitude and God is that God is good. "Oh give thanks to the LORD, for he is good, for his steadfast love endures forever!" (Ps. 106:1). This link between our thanks and God's goodness is repeated over and over (Ps. 107:1; 118:1, 29; 136:1; 1 Chron. 16:34; 2 Chron. 7:3; 5:13; Ezra 3:11). What is most significant about this link is that our gratitude is ultimately rooted in what God *is*, not in what he *gives*. It does not say,

"Give thanks to the Lord, for he *gives* good things." That is true. The good gifts, like sex and food, are occasions for the gladness of gratitude. But they are not the ultimate focus of our joy. The sensation of pleasure runs up the beam of God's generosity until it stops in the goodness of God himself.

I stress this because it is very easy for us to *say* we are thankful for the pleasures of sex and food, but never even take God into the picture. When that happens, the joy of sex and food is not joy in God, and is not spiritual, and is not an honor to God for his goodness. Enjoying God's gifts without a consciousness of God is no tribute to God himself. Unbelievers do this all the time. Therefore what Paul is teaching us here is that the proper use of physical pleasures in sex and food is that they send our hearts Godward with the joy of gratitude that finds its firmest ground in the goodness of God himself, not in his gifts. This means that if, in the providence of God, these gifts are ever taken away—perhaps by the death of a spouse or the demand for a feeding tube—the deepest joy that we had through them will not be taken away, because God is still good (see Hab. 3:17-18).

Sanctifying Sex and Food

Then, after saying that *gratitude* connects the physical world with joy in God, Paul goes on to say that this connection happens when the physical creation is *sanctified*. "Everything created by God is good, and nothing is to be rejected if it is received with thanksgiving, for *it is made holy by the word of God and prayer*" (1 Tim. 4:4-5).

The words "it is made holy" represent one Greek word (*hagiazō*), which sometimes means to set apart for holy use, as when Jesus said, "For which is greater, the gold or the temple that *has made the gold sacred?*" (Matt. 23:17). Here the use of gold in the temple sanctifies it (same word as in 1 Tim. 4:5). The gold is not itself changed, but it is given a God-exalting function by the way it is made part of God's temple. Other times the word *sanctify* means to transform something into a condition that will be suitable for God-exalting purposes, as when Jesus prayed for his disciples, asking that God would "sanctify them in the truth; your word is truth" (John 17:17). So when Paul says that sex and food are sanctified by the Word of God and prayer, it probably means that they are transformed and made suitable for their purpose of wakening and strengthening our God-exalting joy in Christ.

How do the Word of God and prayer bring about that sanctification of sex and food? The most obvious observation is that the *Word of God* is his speaking to us, and *prayer* is our speaking to him. So the general answer is that sex and food are made useful for God-exalting joy when we listen to what God has to say about them, and then speak back to him our affirmations of his truth and our need for help.

Sanctifying Physical Sensations by the Word of God

But we need to be specific. The relevant truth God speaks to us is (1) that he created sex and food (Gen. 1:27-28; 2:24-25; 3:16); (2) that they are good (Gen. 1:31); and (3) that they are intended not only to beget and sustain life, but also for our enjoyment. Paul says to Timothy about the wealthy in his congregation, "Charge them not to be haughty, nor to set their hopes on the uncertainty of riches, but on God, who *richly provides us with everything to enjoy*" (1 Tim. 6:17). (4) In addition God's Word tells us that the physical world of nature is declaring the glory of God (Ps. 19:1), so that the enjoyment it brings should rest finally in the beauty of God himself. (5) And the Word gives us many particulars about the proper use of sex (e.g., no fornication or adultery) and food (e.g., no addiction or excessive asceticism) and other natural pleasures. (6) Finally, the Word of God tells us that we are sinners and do not deserve anything but the wrath of God (Rom. 1:18; 3:9), and therefore the joy of seeing the glory of God in and through the pleasures of sex and food is an absolutely free gift bought with the blood of Jesus Christ (Rom. 8:32).

Knowing and affirming these truths from God's Word transforms sex and food from mere physical pleasures into partners in *revelation* and *rejoicing*. These physical sensations partner with the spiritual eyes of our hearts to perceive the *revelation* of God's glory in creation and to promote our *rejoicing* in him. When Paul said in Titus 1:15, "To the pure all things are pure," he had something like this in mind. He contrasts the pure with "the defiled and *unbelieving*." That links Titus 1:15 with 1 Timothy 4:3 where Paul says that sex and food are "to be received with thanksgiving by *those who believe* and know the truth."

In other words, sex and food are designed for *believers*, the pure in heart. For "to the pure all things are pure."

To those who submit gladly to the truth of God about themselves as sinners, and about Christ as the Savior, and about the Holy Spirit as the Sanctifier, and about God the Father as Creator—to them sex and food are sanctified. That is, they are pure. They are not unclean idols competing for our affections, which belong supremely to God. They are instead pure partners in the revelation of God's glory. They are beams of his goodness *along* which the pure in heart see God (Matt. 5:8).

Sanctifying Physical Sensations by Prayer

Thus sex and food and other natural physical delights are sanctified "by the word of God" (1 Tim. 4:5). But the same verse also says they are sanctified by "prayer." One way that prayer sanctifies sex and food and other physical sensations is by expressing to God our thanks for his goodness. But prayer has another role. Prayer also means asking God for the illumination of the eyes of our heart so that, in and through our physical sensations, we would see the glory of God. Prayer acknowledges that we cannot achieve our own purity. We cannot sanctify our own sensations. We cannot open our own eyes. And therefore we cannot enjoy God in all his gifts without the enabling grace that God gives in answer to prayer. Therefore we pray that the truth will have its sanctifying effect by the power of God's Spirit.

Thus prayer and the Word of God together sanctify sex and food—and every other good gift in this world. That is, the physical reality of food and human bodies, along with their physical sensations, become pure partners in the revelation of God's glory and the wakening of our joy in him.

The Direct Use of the World in the Fight for Joy

When we consider carefully how to use the physical world for the advancement of our joy in God, we realize that there is a *direct* use to be made of nature and an *indirect* use. The *direct* use is when we take steps to see and hear and smell and taste and touch God's creation (and man's representation of it in art) in order to perceive the glory of God more fully. The *indirect* use is when we take steps to keep our bodies and minds as fit as we can for spiritual use. Let's consider these in turn.

The *direct* use of the physical world in our fight for joy may be a trip to the Grand Canyon, or rising early enough to see a sunrise, or attending a symphony, or reading a historical novel, or studying physics, or memorizing a poem, or swimming in the ocean, or eating a fresh pineapple, or smelling a gardenia blossom, or putting your hand through your wife's hair, or watching Olympic gymnastics finals. All these and a thousand things like them are *direct* ways of using the natural world to perceive more of the glory of God.

The Glory of God Is an Overwhelmingly Happy Thing

And even though some encounters with God are terrible, it seems plain from Scripture that God wants us to rejoice in the glory we see in nature. I base this, for example, on Psalm 19. After saying, "The heavens declare the glory of God," David reaches for language to show the joy being communicated by the heavens. He says in verses 5-6 that the sun "comes out like a bridegroom leaving his chamber, and, like a strong man, runs its course with joy. Its rising is from the end of the heavens, and its circuit to the end of them, and there is nothing hidden from its heat."

Clearly this poet wants us to see and to feel that when the sun pours forth speech about the glory of God, the message is that the glory of God is an overwhelmingly happy thing. Why else would he say it is like a bridegroom coming out of his chamber? The point here is not merely that the bridegroom is decked out in the finest clothes and surrounded by his noble groomsmen. The point is that this is the happiest day of his life. This is the fulfillment of dreams. This is the beginning of a whole new kind of joy. That's what the glory of God is like. That's the message we should hear when we see the sun rise with lavish red and gold and lavender in the eastern sky. God's glory is a happy thing—like the happiness of a bridegroom on his wedding day.

This is even more explicit in the other picture David uses at the end of verse 5. When the sun rises and pours forth speech about the glory of God, it is like a strong man that runs his race *with joy*. How can we not think of Eric Liddell in that great scene from the film *Chariots of Fire* as he takes that last turn in the race for the glory of God, and his arms drive like living pistons, and his head goes back in that utterly unorthodox position, and every fiber in his body does just what it was made to do, and the smile breaks out across his face, and everything in Eric Liddell cries, "Glory to God!"

That's what the glory of God is like—it's like the happiest day of your life; it's like every muscle and every tendon and every ligament and every organ and all your mind and your emotions working just the way they were created to work on the day of triumph. The glory of God is the happiest reality in the universe.

Don't Neglect the Gift of Human Representations of God's Glory

In our fight for joy, we must not neglect the ministry of God to our souls in the world that he has made. We should make direct use of the world to see and savor the glory of God wherever he has displayed it. This includes the efforts of man, by his design and art, to represent something of God's glory. Even those who do not believe in God often sense that there is more to see in what they see. The Bible insists that every human being, even when suppressing the knowledge of God, does indeed "know God" and has "clearly perceived" his attributes in the things he has made.

> For what can be known about God is plain to them, because God has shown it to them. For his invisible attributes, namely, his eternal power and divine nature, have been clearly perceived, ever since the creation of the world, in the things that have been made. So they are without excuse. For although they knew God, they did not honor him as God. (Rom. 1:19-21)

This means that even the artistic works of unbelievers sometimes penetrate through the commonplace to the outskirts of the glory of God. Believers whose hearts are purified by the grace of Christ may see from this vantage point vastly more than the unbeliever. So even the unbelieving artist may unwittingly assist us in seeing and savoring the glory of God in the world he has made.

The Power of Human Words to Make the World a Cause of Joy

It is not a mistake that so much of the Bible is written in poetry. Nor is it a mistake that there are so many biblical metaphors and similes. The lesson is that God has ordained for language to pierce and portray what colorless language cannot do. The human heart moves irrepressibly toward poetry because it knows intuitively that the natural world is not all there is. The heart may not even believe that the heavens are telling the glory of God. But it knows, deep down, that they are telling something more than meets the physical eye.

Therefore, in our fight for joy it may often be helpful to read penetrating literature and see powerful drama. Not because they can ever rival or replace the Scriptures, but because they are part of the God-revealing creation and its reflection. God did not put us in the world to ignore it, but to use it wisely. From the beginning, human beings have discovered that the reflection of the world in human art wakens us to the world itself and what the world is saying about God. Echoes can waken us to the shout of reality, and poetry can give us eyes to see. If we weren't afflicted with persistent sleepiness of soul, we might see all the glory there is in nature. But as it is, we need help from creative artists. Richard Foster is justified in writing:

> I am concerned that our reading and our writing is gravitating to the lowest common denominator so completely that the great themes of majesty and nobility and felicity are made to seem trite, puny, pedestrian. . . . I am concerned about the state of the soul in the midst of all the cheap sensory overload going on today. You see, without what Alfred North Whitehead called "an habitual vision of greatness," our soul will shrivel up and lose the capacity for beauty and mystery and transcendence. . . .
>
> But it isn't just the substance of what we say (or write or read or hear or see) that concerns me. It is the way we say it. To write pedantically about radiance or infinity or ubiquity stunts the mind and cramps the soul. To find the right word, to capture the perfect image, awakens the spirit and enlarges the soul. Mark Twain noted that the difference between the right word and the almost right word is like the difference between the lightning and a lightning bug.[7] . . . The ancient Hebrew prophets cared enough about their message that

they frequently delivered it in poetic form. May new prophets arise in our day that will call us to faithful living in words that are crisp and clear and imaginative.[8]

And when they arise, one way that we fight for joy in God is to read what they write. The heavens are telling the glory of God. Seeing it is the ground of our joy. And often reading what others have seen wakens us to see what they saw, or even more.

Fighting for Joy with Sights and Sounds That Humans Make

And of course, words are not the only way that artists waken others to the glory of what they have seen. There is visual art (drawing, painting, sculpture, photography, film), and there is music. I will not say much here because I am out of my element. What I know about art and music I know from experience, not formal study. I am a witness, not a judge. And what I testify to is the power of visual art, and especially music. As it is with creative writing, so it is with these: they have the potential to awaken the mind and heart to aspects of God's glory that were not perceived before. Paintings or photographs of mountains and streams can call forth a sense of wonder and peace. If we are willing to "look along" (not just "at") these pictures, as Lewis taught us, our eyes will run up the beams to the Original Glory, and the wonder and peace will rest finally in the wonderful and peaceful mountains and streams of God's power and mercy.

Music, it seems to me, is the most complex art of all. Who can really explain what happens when music works its power? Its transforming effects are documented in cases ranging from Parkinson's disease to plants.[9] As with all things in nature and in the hands of fallen man, it can be used to reveal or conceal the glory of God—to corrupt the mind or illumine the mind. At its best, music echoes a true perception of some facet of God's glory. The ambiguity of the medium itself, combined with cultural and social and personal associations, complicates the display of that glory in sound.

I recall reading the story of a tribal person, with no exposure to Western culture, being flown to Europe and taken to a performance of Handel's *Messiah*. He sat almost the whole time covering his ears with his hands because, as he explained later, it was just so much noise to his ears. That is an extreme illustration of the complexity of communicating with music. Nevertheless, the power is there, and it works every day for good and for ill. My point is that in the fight for joy it is good and right to pursue a deeper sense of God's glory with the help of music.

Wielding the Weapon of Music in the Fight for Joy in God

If this were not right, the Bible would not command us so often to sing (e.g., Ex. 15:21; 1 Chron. 16:23; Ps. 96:1) or to play on instruments (e.g., Ps. 33:2-3; 57:8; 81:2; 150). Music seems to be woven into worship and the world of nature. Among the many creatures that God has made in his wisdom (Ps. 104:24) are the birds that God has taught to sing: "Beside [the springs] the birds of the heavens dwell; they sing among the branches" (Ps. 104:12). Surely God has not created music as a pointless distraction from rational apprehensions of God. Surely, this too is part of the creation that is "declaring the glory of God."

To wield music well in the fight for joy we should be filled with the Word of God, so that our minds are shaped by biblical truth. If our mind and heart have been molded by the contours of God's character and humbled by the grace of the gospel, we will discern better what sounds reveal and correspond to the varied glories of God. And since this depends so much on cultural contexts and personal backgrounds, we will need not only a grasp of musical richness, but also deep theological grounding in God-centered truth, and cultural sensitivity, and an awareness of the dynamics of the heart, and profound love for people of all kinds.

We must make it our aim that the joy awakened by music be joy in God. Not all pleasures of music are pleasures in God. Then the effort to delight in God through music will involve a prior shaping of the mind by the Word, so that structures of sound that do not conform to God's character are not pleasing in the first place. Then the effort to delight in God through music will also involve a thoughtful testing *after* the music has already awakened joy. Is this joy, we ask, rooted in something good about God? Is it shaping my emotions into a Christ-exalting configuration? Is it stirring my desires to know Christ better and love him more and show him to others at the cost of my own comfort? So *before* and *after* music has its immediate effect, we pursue the goal that music make us more glad in the glory of God.[10]

Fighting for Joy with the Wonder of the Commonplace

I don't want to give the impression that in our fight for joy one must always make special plans to pursue such revelations of God's glory—like a trip to the mountains or a theater. Most of the time we should simply open our eyes (and ears and noses and skin and taste buds). Not that this takes no effort. Clearly human beings have a strange malady that makes the ordinary glories of each day almost invisible, and certainly less interesting than their imitations in theaters and television. There are more *ooooh*'s and *ahhh*'s over the visual effects on a thirty-foot theater screen than over the night sky and the setting sun. Why is it so hard for us to feel wonder at the usual when clearly it is more spectacular than the man-made imitation?

Clyde Kilby, a former literature teacher at Wheaton College, who had a great influence on me when I was there, gave this answer:

> The fall of man can hardly be more forcefully felt than simply in noting what we all do with a fresh snowfall or the first buds of spring. On Monday they fill us with delight and meaning and on Tuesday we ignore them. No amount of shouting to us that this is all wrong changes the fact for very long. . . . Only some aesthetic power which is akin to God's own creativity has the capability for renewal, for giving us the power to see.[11]

This is a tragic condition captured by the proverb, "Familiarity breeds contempt"—or breeds blindness to ordinary and obvious beauty. But surely redemption through Jesus Christ means that we will be freed from that proverb someday. And since our redemption has already begun in this age, by the power of the Holy Spirit, Christians ought to have better eyes than people in general for seeing the wonders that day and night pour forth. We ought to be the kind of people who walk out of the house in the morning with the same sense of expectancy that we take into the theater—only more.

Chesterton's Elephantine Pursuit of the Obvious

Once when we were discussing in class this issue of human blindness to everyday wonders, Dr. Kilby recommended that we all read G. K.

Chesterton's book *Orthodoxy*. He said it would do more to help us see the glory of God in everyday life than anything he could say. I got it and read it. I recommend it, not because its theology is always right (he is Roman Catholic and does not like Calvinism), but because it holds out hope of seeing the divine glory of the obvious better than any book I know.

Chesterton says of the book that "it recounts my elephantine adventures in pursuit of the obvious."[12] He identifies one of the great causes of our blindness as self-absorption. He says that a person who is becoming morbid over fears and preoccupations about what others think of him needs the liberation from his illusion that anyone gives a hoot!

> How much happier you would be if you only knew that these people cared nothing about you! How much larger your life would be if your self could become smaller in it; if you could really look at other men with common curiosity and pleasure; if you could see them walking as they are in their sunny selfishness and their virile indifference! You would begin to be interested in them because they were not interested in you. You would break out of this tiny and tawdry theater in which your own little plot is always being played, and you would find yourself under a freer sky, in a street full of splendid strangers.[13]

In other words, what we need is a kind of childlikeness. And romantic tales are often used to awaken it.

> When we are very young children we don't need fairy tales: we only need tales. Mere life is interesting enough. A child of seven is excited by being told that Tommy opened a door and saw a dragon. But a child of three is excited by being told that Tommy opened a door. Boys like romantic tales; but babies like realistic tales— because they find them romantic. . . . This proves that even nursery tales only echo an almost pre-natal leap of interest and amazement. These tales say that apples are golden only to refresh the forgotten moment when we found that they were green. They make rivers run with wine only to make us remember, for one wild moment, that they run with water.[14]

The point is that Christ frees us from self-preoccupation and gives us— yes, only very gradually—a childlikeness that can see the sheer wonder of the staggering strangeness of the ordinary. Chesterton said that this discovery for him was captured in a riddle: "What did the first frog say?" Answer: "Lord, how you made me jump!"[15] In another place he says that he came to the point where what amazed him was not the strangeness of people's noses, but that they had noses in the first place. In becoming more childlike and more able to see glory in the wonder of the ordinary and the routine, he points out that we are becoming more like God.

> [Children] always say, "Do it again"; and the grown-up person does it again until he is nearly dead. For grown-up people are not strong enough to exult in monotony. But perhaps God is strong enough to exult in monotony. It is possible that God says every morning, "Do it again" to the sun; and every evening, "Do it again" to the moon. It may not be automatic necessity that makes all daisies alike; it may be that God makes every daisy separately, but has never got tired of making them. It may be that he has the eternal appetite of infancy; for we have sinned and grown old, and our Father is younger than we.[16]

I linger over this point—that seeing the glory of God may not require making a trip to the mountains or buying a ticket to the theater, but only opening our eyes—because I believe untold resources for mental health and spiritual joy in God lie all around us if we would but open our eyes.

Kilby's Prescription for Using the World in the Fight for Joy

At the end of his life my teacher, Clyde Kilby, came to Minneapolis and gave a lecture on how he intended to do just this. It was the last time I heard him, and the message that was bequeathed to us who listened was the same legacy he had left to me when I was in his college classes. He summed up his talk with eleven resolutions. I commend them to you as one way of overcoming our bent toward blindness for the wonders of the ordinary.

1. At least once every day I shall look steadily up at the sky and remember that I, a consciousness with a conscience, am on a planet

traveling in space with wonderfully mysterious things above me and about me.

2. Instead of the accustomed idea of a mindless and endless evolutionary change to which we can neither add nor subtract, I shall suppose the universe guided by an Intelligence which, as Aristotle said of Greek drama, requires a beginning, a middle and an end. I think this will save me from the cynicism expressed by Bertrand Russell before his death, when he said: "There is darkness without and when I die there will be darkness within. There is no splendor, no vastness anywhere, only triviality for a moment, and then nothing."[17]

3. I shall not fall into the falsehood that this day, or any day, is merely another ambiguous and plodding twenty-four hours, but rather a unique event filled, if I so wish, with worthy potentialities. I shall not be fool enough to suppose that trouble and pain are wholly evil parentheses in my existence but just as likely ladders to be climbed toward moral and spiritual manhood.

4. I shall not turn my life into a thin straight line which prefers abstractions to reality. I shall know what I am doing when I abstract,[18] which of course I shall often have to do.

5. I shall not demean my own uniqueness by envy of others. I shall stop boring into myself to discover what psychological or social categories I might belong to. Mostly I shall simply forget about myself and do my work.

6. I shall open my eyes and ears. Once every day I shall simply stare at a tree, a flower, a cloud, or a person. I shall not then be concerned at all to ask *what* they are but simply be glad *that* they are. I shall joyfully allow them the mystery of what [C. S.] Lewis calls their "divine, magical, terrifying and ecstatic" existence.

7. I shall sometimes look back at the freshness of vision I had in childhood and try, at least for a little while, to be, in the words of Lewis Carroll, the "child of the pure unclouded brow, and dreaming eyes of wonder."[19]

8. I shall follow Darwin's[20] advice and turn frequently to imaginative things such as good literature and good music, preferably, as Lewis suggests, an old book and timeless music.

9. I shall not allow the devilish onrush of this century to usurp all my energies but will instead, as Charles Williams suggested, "fulfill the moment as the moment." I shall try to live well just now because the only time that exists is just now.

10. If for nothing more than the sake of a change of view, I

shall assume my ancestry to be from the heavens rather than from the caves.

11. Even if I turn out to be wrong, I shall bet my life in the assumption that this world is not idiotic, neither run by an absentee landlord, but that today, this very day, some stroke is being added to the cosmic canvas that in due course I shall understand with joy as a stroke made by the architect who calls Himself Alpha and Omega.

Fighting for Joy by the Indirect Use of the World

I mentioned earlier that in our fight for joy there is a *direct* use to be made of nature and an *indirect* use. We've been talking mainly about the *direct* use—that is, when we take steps to see and hear and smell and taste and touch God's creation (and man's representation of it in art) in order to perceive the glory of God more fully. But with Kilby's eleven resolutions we have begun to cross over to the *indirect* use of nature. What I mean by the *indirect* use of nature is the steps we take to make our bodies and minds as proficient as possible in their role as physical partners in perceiving the glory of God.

Keep in mind that when the Bible says that "the heavens *declare* the glory of God" (Ps. 19:1), it is clear that the heavens are *not* the glory of God. They "declare" it or display it. They are the beam *along* which we look till our eyes run up to the spiritual beauty of God himself. Thus we see the heavens with our bodily eyes, and we experience the sensations of that sight in physical brains. Yet we perceive the glory of God with our spiritual eyes.

Jonathan Edwards describes this kind of joy (through creation) in God as he ponders what heaven will be like. Will we enjoy only God there, or will we enjoy other things as well? What does the psalmist mean when he declares, "I say to the Lord, 'You are my Lord; *I have no good apart from you*'" (Ps. 16:2), or "Whom have I in heaven but you? And *there is nothing on earth that I desire besides you*" (Ps. 73:25)? Edwards answers:

> The redeemed will indeed enjoy other things; they will enjoy the angels, and will enjoy one another: but that which they shall enjoy in

the angels, or each other, or in anything else whatsoever, that will yield them delight and happiness, will be what will be seen of God in them.[21]

This is what we pray toward even now—that all our joy in the things of this world would be because, in and through them, we see more of the glory of God. Spiritual beauty is perceived in and through physical beauty but is not identical with it. This is why I call the body with its sensations the physical *partner* in perceiving the glory of God in the natural world.

Edwards gives us an illustration of the indirect use of nature in the fight for joy. He writes:

> When the body enjoys the perfections of health and strength, the motion of the animal spirits [= physical responses] are not only brisk and free but also harmonious. There is a regular proportion in the motion from all parts of the body that begets delight in the inner soul and makes the body feel pleasantly all over. God has so excellently contrived the nerves and parts of the human body. But few men since the fall, especially since the flood, have health to so great a perfection as to have much of this harmonious motion. When it is enjoyed, one whose nature is not very much vitiated and depraved is very much assisted thereby in every exercise of body or mind. *And it fits one for the contemplation of more exalted and spiritual excellencies and harmonies, as music does.*[22]

What this means is that there are conditions of the body and the mind that are more conducive than others to the perception of spiritual beauty. This is the main reason for trying to handle our bodies with a wise measure of discipline. We want to see and savor the divine glory that God declares in the heavens and on the earth and in food and sexual intimacy and music and poetry and art. And Edwards is saying that there is a condition of the body that hinders or helps the perception of God's excellencies.

The Grace of Glory Revealed to Suffering Christians

Immediately I feel a qualification rising in my own mind. Beaten and battered prisoners for Christ often have extraordinary views of the beauty and sustaining sweetness of Christ. They are without food or warmth or cleanliness or any physical comfort. Yet they call persecution sweet names and put to shame most of us who are fit and hardy. They often have a superior spiritual sight in their broken health and simple meals.

So please don't interpret this final part of the chapter as a kind of chipper health and happiness regimen. The question is not whether God can reveal himself in precious ways to those who suffer. He can and does. It is possible, as the Bible says, to rejoice in tribulation (Rom. 5:3). "If you are insulted for the name of Christ, you are blessed, because the Spirit of glory and of God rests upon you" (1 Pet. 4:14). The question is what we should do during times when we can choose our own lifestyle of eating and exercising and resting. In what indirect ways can we improve the ability of our bodies and minds for their partnership in perceiving the glory of God?

Eating Right for the Sake of Joy in God

We have already touched on fasting in the previous chapter. There is a paradox here. By saying "No" to a physical appetite we say "Yes" to the body's ability to help us see the glory of God. A full stomach may say thanks for the food; but an empty stomach may see heavenly food more clearly. That's what Paul seems to imply about the sexual appetite when he says to Christian husbands and wives, "Do not deprive one another, except perhaps by agreement for a limited time, that you may devote yourselves to prayer" (1 Cor. 7:5). It really doesn't take much time to have sexual intercourse; so the issue is not to *save time* for prayer. The issue seems to be that fasting from legitimate sexual plea-sure tunes the body in a unique way for communion with God. I say this even while remembering how earnestly we contended earlier in this chapter for seeing the glory of God in the very act of sexual intimacy and in the very act of eating. Both are true.

Sereno Dwight tells us that Jonathan Edwards "carefully observed the effects of the different sorts of food, and selected those which best suited his constitution, and rendered him most fit for mental labor."[23] Thus he abstained from every quantity and kind of food that made him sick or sleepy. Edwards had set this pattern when he was twenty-one years old when he wrote in his diary, "By a sparingness in diet, and eat-

ing as much as may be what is light and easy of digestion, I shall doubt-
less be able to think more clearly, and shall gain time."[24] Hence he was
"Resolved, to maintain the strictest temperance in eating and drinking."[25]

The point here is not to commend the particulars of Edwards's
eating habits. The point is that we be intentional about how our eating
affects the ability of our body to be a helpful partner in seeing the glory
of God. We live in an era of eating disorders.[26] I am not eager to create
another one. I commend balance. Put the following two texts beside
each other. On the one hand, Paul made food and drink clearly secondary: "The kingdom of God is not a matter of eating and drinking but of
righteousness and peace and joy in the Holy Spirit" (Rom. 14:17). But
on the other hand, he said, in regard to food, "I will not be enslaved
by anything" (1 Cor. 6:12 RSV). In the balance of those two truths we
can find a way to eat that will provide both the denial and the delight
that will fit us for seeing the glory of God in the Word and in the world.

Exercise as an Indirect Fight for Joy

The Bible has little to say about physical exercise, not because it's not
important for modern sedentary people, but mainly because, in the biblical world of walking and farming and manual labor, the lack of physical exercise was not a problem. The call today is for spiritual wisdom
based on biblical principles and contemporary medical knowledge.

The biblical principles would include the following: our bodies
belong to Christ and are meant to glorify him (1 Cor. 6:19-20); laziness is wrong and self-destructive (Prov. 21:25); Christians should be
free from any enslaving habits (1 Cor. 6:12); hard work is a virtue and
brings rewards (2 Tim. 2:6); advance usually comes through affliction
(Acts 14:22); and all Christ-exalting efforts to be healthy flow from
faith in the gospel of Jesus Christ (Gal. 6:14). "No pain, no gain" is an
idea that could be documented from all over the Bible, especially the
sacrifice of Christ.

Contemporary medical knowledge would include the fact that
obesity kills and contributes to dozens of ailments. Not all obesity is
self-inflicted. Some medical conditions make it virtually impossible to
avoid it. But most of it *is* self-inflicted, and this kind of self-destruction
does not enhance the ability of the body or the mind to see and savor

the glory of God in this world, or the glory of Christ who endured the cross by postponing the feast till the age to come (Heb. 12:2).

Another aspect of medical knowledge that should shape our wisdom about exercising is that consistent exercise has refining effects on our mental and emotional stability. One medical report sums up the benefits like this:

> The psychological and emotional benefits from exercise are numerous, and many experts now believe that exercise is a viable and important component in the treatment of emotion disorders. A 1999 review of multiple studies found, across the board, that exercise advances the treatment of clinical depression and anxiety. . . . Yet another study found that regular brisk walking cut the incidence of sleep disturbances in half in people who suffer from them. . . . Either brief periods of intense training or prolonged aerobic workouts raise levels of chemicals in the brain, such as endorphins, adrenaline, serotonin, and dopamine, that produce feelings of pleasure. . . . Aerobic exercise is also linked with improved mental vigor, including reaction time, acuity, and math skills. Exercising may even enhance creativity and imagination. According to one study, older people who are physically fit respond to mental challenges just as quickly as unfit young adults.[27]

Again keep in mind that the aim of this chapter and this book is not maximal physical health. Nor is it to help you find ways to get the best buzz for your brain. None of that is of any interest to me. My aim is that you will find a way of life that enables you to use your mind and your five senses as effective partners in seeing the glory of God, and that you be so satisfied in him that you are willing to risk your health and your life to make him known. It may seem paradoxical, but that's the way it is: the right use of your body and your mind may enable you to see so much of God that you would sacrifice your life for Christ.

Rest as a Weapon in the Fight for Joy

Finally, if we would see the glory of God, we must rest. For all his talk about spending and being spent, Charles Spurgeon, the nineteenth-century London pastor, counsels us to fight for joy by resting and taking a day off and opening ourselves to the healing powers that God has put in the world of nature.

For us pastors, he says, "Our Sabbath is our day of toil, and if we do not rest upon some other day we shall break down."[28] Spurgeon himself kept, when possible, Wednesday as his day of rest.[29] More than that, Spurgeon said to his students,

> It is wisdom to take occasional furlough. In the long run, we shall do more by sometimes doing less. On, on, on for ever, without recreation may suit spirits emancipated from this "heavy clay," but while we are in this tabernacle, we must every now and then cry halt, and serve the Lord by holy inaction and consecrated leisure. Let no tender conscience doubt the lawfulness of going out of harness for a while.[30]

And when we take time away from the press of duty, Spurgeon recommends that we breathe country air and let the beauty of nature do its appointed work. He confesses that "sedentary habits have a tendency to create despondency . . . especially in the months of fog." And then he counsels:

> He who forgets the humming of the bees among the heather, the cooing of the wood-pigeons in the forest, the song of birds in the woods, the rippling of rills among the rushes, and the sighing of the wind among the pines, needs not wonder if his heart forgets to sing and his soul grows heavy. A day's breathing of fresh air upon the hills, or a few hours' ramble in the beech woods' umbrageous calm, would sweep the cobwebs out of the brain of scores of our toiling ministers who are now but half alive. A mouthful of sea air, or a stiff walk in the wind's face, would not give grace to the soul, but it would yield oxygen to the body, which is the next best. . . . The ferns and the rabbits, the streams and the trouts, the fir trees and the squirrels, the primroses and the violets, the farm-yard, the new-mown hay, and the fragrant hops—these are the best medicine for hypochondriacs, the surest tonics for the declining, the best refreshments for the weary. For lack of opportunity, or inclination, these great remedies are neglected, and the student becomes a self-immolated victim.[31]

Getting Older in the Fight for Joy

We must keep an eye on the apostolic command, "Keep a close watch on yourself" (1 Tim. 4:16). One reason we must watch ourselves closely is that we change over the years. What was wise eating and exercising and resting in the early years is no longer wise. As I write, I am finishing my twenty-fourth year at the church I serve. I am moving toward my fifty-ninth birthday. I have watched my body and my soul with some care over these years and have noticed some changes. They are partly owing to changing circumstances, but much is owing to a changing body.

I cannot eat as much as I used to without gaining unhelpful weight. My body does not metabolize the same way it used to. Another change is that I am emotionally less resilient when I lose sleep. There were early days when I could work without regard to sleep and feel energized and motivated. In more recent years my threshold for despondency is lower on less sleep. For me, adequate sleep is not just a matter of staying healthy. It's a matter of staying in the ministry—I'm tempted to say it's a matter of persevering as a Christian. I know it is irrational that my future should look so bleak when I get only four or five hours of sleep several nights in a row. But rational or irrational, that is a fact. And I must live within the limits of facts. Therefore we must watch the changes in our bodies. In the fight for joy we must be wise in the adjustments we make. Spurgeon was right when he said:

> The condition of your body must be attended to. . . . [A] little more . . . common sense would be a great gain to some who are ultra spiritual, and attribute all their moods of feeling to some supernatural cause when the real reason lies far nearer to hand. Has it not often happened that dyspepsia [indigestion] has been mistaken for backsliding, and bad digestion has been set down as a hard heart?[32]

I once struggled with the truth that joy is a fruit of the Holy Spirit (Gal. 5:22), because I knew from experience that it is also a "fruit" of a good night's rest. In other words, I was more gloomy on little rest and more happy on good rest. What brought light to this perplexity is that one of the ways the Spirit produces his fruit in our lives is by humbling us enough to believe we are not God and that God can run the world without our staying up too late and getting up too early. God has united the body and the spirit in such a way that careless uses of the body will ordinarily diminish our sight of the hope-giving glory of God. Not surprisingly, therefore, our joy in God usually decreases with inadequate rest.

All the World a Witness to the Glory of God

Joy in God is not the same as joy in sex or a sizzling steak or deep ravines or powerful music. But God's will is that all these—and every part of his good creation—declare the glory of God. All the world, and even the imperfect representations of it in human art, is a witness to the glory of God. That glory is the ultimate ground of all human gladness. Therefore, the created world is a holy weapon in the fight for joy. But it must be "made holy by the word of God and prayer" (1 Tim. 4:5). To help you do that has been my aim in this chapter.

I waited patiently for the Lord.

P S A L M 4 0 : 1

Weeping may tarry for the night,
but joy comes with the morning.

P S A L M 3 0 : 5

Ah my deare angrie Lord,
Since thou dost love, yet strike;
Cast down, yet help afford;
Sure I will do the like.
I will complain, yet praise;
I will bewail, approve:
And all my sowre-sweet dayes
I will lament, and love.

G E O R G E H E R B E R T
"Bitter Sweet"[1]

When the Darkness Does Not Lift

*Doing What We Can While We Wait
for God—and Joy*

A s this book comes to a close, I am aware that I have put my oar in a very large sea. I rise from my desk and walk past a wall of books that have spoken more wisely than I on the care and cure of sad Christian souls. Just opening these volumes reminds me of how many wise and valuable things remain to be said—and cannot be said in one book. It will always be so. The Word of God is inexhaustible, and the world he made holds countless treasures waiting to be found by clear eyes in search of Christ-exalting joy. And the needs of embattled people who fight for joy will always be as diverse as the people themselves. So I content myself with rowing out into this sea as far as my limits allow, and I pray that you will search out some of these great old books[2] and go farther in your quest for joy than I have been able to take you.

To Help Those for Whom Joy Stays out of Reach

My aim in this last chapter is to give some guidance and hope to those for whom joy seems to stay out of reach. Virtually all Bible-saturated physicians of the soul have spoken about long seasons of darkness and desolation. In the old days they called it melancholy. Richard Baxter, for example, who died in 1691, wrote with astonishing relevance about the complexities of dealing with Christians who seem unable to enjoy God. "Delighting in God, and in his word and ways," he said, "is the flower and life of true religion. But these that I speak of can delight in nothing—neither God, nor in his word, nor any duty."[3]

How can we help Christians who seem unable to break out of darkness into the light of joy? Yes, I call them Christians, and thus assume that such things happen to genuine believers. It happens because of sin, or because of Satanic assault, or because of distressing circumstances, or because of hereditary or other physical causes. What makes these old books so remarkable is the way they come to terms with all these causes and their many combinations, and how they address each condition appropriately. The Puritan pastor never seemed to give up on anyone because of discouraging darkness.

Long before the rise of psychiatry and contemporary brain electrophysiology, Bible-saturated Puritan pastors recognized the complexity of causes behind the darkness of melancholy. In fact, the first answer Baxter mentions to the question, "What are the *causes* and *cure* of it?" is, "With very many there is a great part of the CAUSE in distemper, weakness, and diseasedness of the body; and by it the soul is greatly disabled to any comfortable sense. But the more it ariseth from such natural necessity, it is the less sinful and less dangerous to the soul; but never the less troublesome."[4]

In his sermon on the causes and cures of melancholy he has an entire section on "medicine and diet." He says, in his quaint but remarkably accurate language, "The disease called 'melancholy' is formally in the spirits, whose distemper unfits them for their office, in serving the imagination, understanding, memory, and affections; so by their distemper the thinking faculty is diseased, and becomes like an inflamed eye, or a foot that is sprained or out of joint, disabled for its proper work."[5]

The Physical Side of Spiritual Darkness

I will not go further discussing the physical treatment of melancholy— and its severe form, depression—than I have gone in the previous chapter. This is the work of a medical doctor, which I am not. What we should be clear about, though, is that the condition of our bodies makes a difference in the capacity of our minds to think clearly and of our souls to see the beauty of hope-giving truth. Martyn Lloyd-Jones, the great preacher at Westminster Chapel in London in the mid-twentieth century, began his helpful book *Spiritual Depression* by waving the flag of warning that we not overlook the physical. It is significant that Lloyd-Jones was a medical doctor before he was called to the ministry of preaching.

> Does someone hold the view that as long as you are a Christian it does not matter what the condition of your body is? Well, you will soon be disillusioned if you believe that. Physical conditions play their part in all this. . . . There are certain physical ailments which tend to promote depression. Thomas Carlyle, I suppose, is an outstanding illustration of this. Or take that great preacher who preached in London for nearly forty years in the last century—Charles Haddon Spurgeon—one of the truly great preachers of all time. That great man was subject to spiritual depression, and the main explanation in his case was undoubtedly the fact that he suffered from a gouty condition which finally killed him. He had to face this problem of spiritual depression often in a most acute form. A tendency to acute depression is an unfailing accompaniment of the gout which he inherited from his forebears. And there are many, I find, who come to talk to me about these matters, in whose case it seems quite clear to me that the cause of the trouble is mainly physical. Into this group, speaking generally, you can put tiredness, overstrain, illness, any form of illness. You cannot isolate the spiritual from the physical for we are body, mind and spirit. The greatest and the best Christians when they are physically weak are more prone to an attack of spiritual depression than at any other time and there are great illustrations of this in the scriptures.[6]

Gaius Davies, a psychiatrist in Britain who knew Lloyd-Jones well, observed,

> Before 1954, when the series of sermons on depression was completed, no effective antidepressant had been on the market, though some progress was made towards that in 1954. Later, in 1955-6 when new forms of medication were available freely, I know how concerned Dr. Lloyd-Jones was to know which kinds of antidepressants were most effective, because he asked me about them a good deal when I was beginning my medical career, and talked to other

doctors in a similar way. He wanted to know enough to be able to advise those who asked his opinion.[7]

The Place of Medication in the Fight for Joy

I do not want to give the impression that medication should be the first or main solution to spiritual darkness. Of course, by itself medicine is *never* a solution to *spiritual* darkness. All the fundamental issues of life remain to be brought into proper relation to Christ when the medicine has done its work. Antidepressants are not the decisive savior. Christ is. In fact, the almost automatic use of pills for child misbehavior and adult sorrows is probably going to hurt us as a society.

David Powlison, who edits *The Journal of Biblical Counseling*, counsels at the Christian Counseling and Educational Foundation, and lectures at Westminster Seminary, wrote of a sea change in the mental sciences in the mid-1990s:

> Have no doubt, the world did change in the mid-90s. The *action* is now in your body. It's what you got from Mom and Dad, not what they did to you. The *excitement* is about brain functions, not family dysfunctions. The *cutting edge* is in hard science medical research and psychiatry, not squishy soft, philosophy-of-life, feel-your-pain psychologies. . . . Biology is suddenly hot. Psychiatry has broken forth, a *blitzkrieg* sweeping away all opposition. . . . Medicine is poised to claim the human personality. . . . The biopsychologizing of human life is having a huge effect, both in culture and the church.[8]

His conclusion is that this preoccupation with biopsychiatry will pass, and as it does,

> biopsychiatry will cure a few things, for which we should praise the God of common grace. But in the long run, unwanted and unforeseen side effects will combine with vast disillusionment. The gains will never live up to the promises. And the lives of countless people, whose normal life problems are now being medicated, will not be qualitatively changed and redirected. Only intelligent repentance, living faith, and tangible obedience turn the world upside down.[9]

Powlison refers sympathetically to Ed Welch's book, *Blame It on the Brain?*—where Welch is willing to employ medication in cases of persistent debilitating depression. Welch says:

> If the person is not taking medication but is considering it, I typically suggest that he or she postpone that decision for a period of time. During that time, I consider possible causes, and together we ask God to teach us about both ourselves and him so that we can grow in faith in the midst of hardship. If the depression persists, I might let the person know that medication is an option to deal with some of the physical symptoms.[10]

To many, this may seem excessively cautious. But widespread scientific evidence is already reining in the initial enthusiasm about the unique effectiveness of antidepressants. One summary article in *The Washington Post* in May 2002 put the situation starkly like this:

> After thousands of studies, hundreds of millions of prescriptions and tens of billions of dollars in sales, two things are certain about pills that treat depression: Antidepressants like Prozac, Paxil and Zoloft work. And so do sugar pills. A new analysis has found that in the majority of trials conducted by drug companies in recent decades, sugar pills have done as well as—or better than—antidepressants.[11]

The point of Welch's caution and the *Post's* skepticism is not that depression or spiritual darkness is disconnected with our physical condition. They are deeply connected. The point is that the relationship between the soul and the brain is beyond human comprehension and should be handled with the greatest care and with profound attention to the moral and spiritual realities of human personhood that may exert as much influence on the brain as vice versa.

In other words, if someone reading this book is on medication, or is thinking about it, I do not condemn you for that, nor does the Bible. It may or may not be the best course of action. I commend you to the wisdom of a God-centered, Bible-saturated medical doctor. If there was imperfection in the choice to use medication, the imputed righteousness of Christ will swallow it up as you rest in him. Don't forget the lesson of "gutsy guilt" from Chapter Six.

Waiting in Darkness, We Are Not Lost and Not Alone

With or without medication there are other things that can be done in the midst of prolonged darkness. And I would love to encourage you in some of these. It will be of great advantage to the struggling Christian to remember that seasons of darkness are normal in the Christian life. I don't mean that we should not try to live above them. I mean that if we do not succeed, we are not lost, and we are not alone, as the fragment of our faith cleaves to Christ. Consider the experience of David in Psalm 40:1-3.

> I waited patiently for the LORD; he inclined to me and heard my cry. He drew me up from the pit of destruction, out of the miry bog, and set my feet upon a rock, making my steps secure. He put a new song in my mouth, a song of praise to our God. Many will see and fear, and put their trust in the LORD.

The king of Israel is in "the pit of destruction" and "the miry bog"—descriptions of his spiritual condition. The song of praise is coming, he says, but it is not now on his lips. It is as if David had fallen into a deep, dark well and plunged into life-threatening mud. There was one other time when David wrote about this kind of experience. He combined the images of mud and flood: "Save me, O God! For the waters have come up to my neck. I sink in deep mire, where there is no foothold; I have come into deep waters, and the flood sweeps over me" (Ps. 69:1-2).

In this pit of mud and destruction there is a sense of helplessness and desperation. Suddenly air, just air, is worth a million dollars. Helplessness, desperation, apparent hopelessness, the breaking point for the overworked businessman, the outer limits of exasperation for the mother of three constantly crying children, the impossible expectations of too many classes in school, the grinding stress of a lingering illness, the imminent attack of a powerful enemy. It is good that we don't know what the experience was. It makes it easier to see ourselves in the pits with the king. Anything that causes a sense of helplessness and desperation and threatens to ruin life or take it away—that is the king's pit.

How Long, O Lord, How Long!

Then comes the king's cry: "I waited patiently for the LORD; he inclined to me and heard my cry." One of the reasons God loved David so much was because he cried so much. "I am weary with my moaning; every night I flood my bed with tears; I drench my couch with my weeping" (Ps. 6:6). "You have kept count of my tossings; put my tears in your bottle. Are they not in your book?" (Ps. 56:8). Indeed they are! "Blessed are those who mourn" (Matt. 5:4). It is a beautiful thing when a broken man genuinely cries out to God.

Then after the cry you wait. "I waited patiently for the LORD." This is crucial to know: saints who cry to the Lord for deliverance from pits of darkness must learn to wait patiently for the Lord. There is no statement about how long David waited. I have known saints who walked through eight years of debilitating depression and came out into glorious light. Only God knows how long we must wait. We saw this in Micah's experience in Chapter Six. "I sit in darkness . . . until [the Lord] pleads my cause and . . . will bring me out to the light" (see Micah 7:8-9). We can draw no deadlines for God. He hastens or he delays as he sees fit. And his timing is all-loving toward his children. Oh, that we might learn to be patient in the hour of darkness. I don't mean that we make peace with darkness. We fight for joy. But we fight as those who are saved by grace and held by Christ. We say with Paul Gerhardt that our night will soon—in God's good timing—turn to day:

> *Give to the winds thy fears,*
> *Hope and be undismayed.*
> *God hears thy sighs and counts thy tears,*
> *God shall lift up thy head.*
>
> *Through waves and clouds and storms,*
> *He gently clears thy way;*
> *Wait thou His time; so shall this night*
> *Soon end in joyous day.*
>
> *Far, far above thy thought,*
> *His counsel shall appear,*
> *When fully He the work hath wrought,*
> *That caused thy needless fear.*

> *Leave to His sovereign sway*
> *To choose and to command;*
> *So shalt thou, wondering, own that way,*
> *How wise, how strong this hand.*[12]

The Ground of Our Assurance[13] When We Cannot See Our Faith

It is utterly crucial that in our darkness we affirm the wise, strong hand of God to hold *us*, even when we have no strength to hold *him*. This is the way Paul thought of his own strivings. He said, "Not that I have already obtained this or am already perfect, but I press on to make it my own, *because Christ Jesus has made me his own*" (Phil. 3:12). The key thing to see in this verse is that all Paul's efforts to grasp the fullness of joy in Christ are secured by Christ's grasp of him. Never forget that your security rests on Christ's faithfulness first.

Our faith rises and falls. It has degrees. But our security does not rise and fall. It has no degrees. We *must* persevere in faith. That's true. But there are times when our faith is the size of a mustard seed and barely visible. In fact the darkest experience for the child of God is when his faith sinks out of his own sight. Not out of God's sight, but his. Yes, it is possible to be so overwhelmed with darkness that you do not know if you are a Christian—and yet still be one.

All the great doctors of the soul have distinguished between faith and its full assurance. The reason for this is that we are saved by the work of God causing us to be born again and bringing us to faith. "The wind blows where it wishes, and you hear its sound, but you do not know where it comes from or where it goes. So it is with everyone who is born of the Spirit" (John 3:8). We are not saved by producing faith on our own and then making that the basis of our new birth. It is the other way around. Which means that God is at the bottom of my faith, and when it disappears for a season from my own view, God may yet be there sustaining its root in the new birth and protecting the seed from destruction. This was crucial in Richard Baxter's soul care.

> Certainty of our faith and sincerity is not necessary to salvation, but the sincerity of faith itself is necessary. He shall be saved that giveth up himself to Christ, though he know not that he is sincere in doing

it. Christ knoweth his own grace, when they that have it know not that it is sound.

An abundance are cast down by ignorance of themselves, not knowing the sincerity which God hath given them. Grace is weak in the best of us here; and little and weak grace is not very easily perceived, for it acteth weakly and unconstantly, and it is known but by its acts; and weak grace is always joined with too strong corruption; and all sin in heart and life is contrary to grace, and doth obscure it; . . . And how can any under all these hindrances, yet keep any full assurance of their own sincerity?[14]

Baxter's aim here is not to destroy a Christian's comfort. On the contrary, he wants to help us in the times of our darkness to know that we can be safe in Jesus, even when we have lost sight of our own sincerity. The witness of the Holy Spirit that we are the children of God (Rom. 8:16) may be clear or faint. But the reality is unshakable. "God's firm foundation stands, bearing this seal: 'The Lord knows those who are his'" (2 Tim. 2:19). "God is faithful, by whom you were called" (1 Cor. 1:9). "He who began a good work in you will bring it to completion at the day of Jesus Christ" (Phil. 1:6). Baxter's words are crucial counsels if we are to survive the dark night of the soul. And that night will come for almost every Christian. And when it comes, we must wait for the Lord, cry to him, and know that our own self-indictment, rendered in the darkness, is not as sure as God's Word spoken in the light.

When a Child of God Is Persuaded That He Is Not

Christians in the darkness of depression may ask desperately, How can I know that I am truly a child of God? They are not usually asking to be reminded that we are saved by grace through faith. They know that. They are asking how they can know that their faith is real. God must guide us in how we answer, and knowing the person will help us know what to say.[15]

The first and best thing to say may be, "I love you. And I am not letting you go." In those words a person may feel God's keeping presence that they may not feel in any other way. Or, second, we might say,

218 When I Don't Desire GOD

"Stop looking at your faith, and rivet your attention on Christ. Faith is sustained by looking at Christ, crucified and risen, not by turning from Christ to analyze your faith. Let me help you look to Christ. Let's read Luke 22—24 together." Paradoxically, if we would experience the joy of faith, we must not focus much on it. We must focus on the greatness of our Savior.

Third, we might call attention to the evidences of grace in their life. We might recount our own sense of their authenticity when we were loved by them, and then remind them of their own strong affirmations of the lordship of Christ. Then say, "No one can say 'Jesus is Lord' except in the Holy Spirit" (1 Cor. 12:3). This approach is not usually successful in the short run, because a depressed person is prone to discount all good assessments of his own condition; but it can be valuable in the long run, because it stands as an objective hope and act of love over against his own subjective darkness.

Fourth, we might remind the sufferer that his demand for a kind of absolute, mathematical certainty about his right standing with God is asking for too much. None of us lives with that kind of certainty about any relationships in life, and this does not destroy our comfort. As Baxter says, "No wife or child is certain that the husband or father will not murder them; and yet they may live comfortably, and not fear it."[16] In other words, there is a kind of certainty that we live by, and it is enough. It is, in the end, a gift of God.

One can imagine a wife obsessed with fear that her husband will kill her, or that during the night one of her children will kill another one. No amount of arguing may bring her away from the fear of this possibility. Rationally and mathematically it *is* possible. But millions of people live in complete peace about these things, even though there is no absolute 2 + 2 = 4 kind of certainty. The certainty is rooted in good experience and the God-given stability of nature. It is a sweet assurance—and a gift of God. So we say to our suffering friend: don't demand the kind of certainty about your own relationship to God that you don't require about the other relationships in your life.

It follows from this that we should all fortify ourselves against the dark hours of depression by cultivating a deep distrust of the certainties of despair. Despair is relentless in the certainties of its pessimism. But we have seen again and again, from our own experience and others', that absolute statements of hopelessness that we make in the dark are notoriously unreliable. Our dark certainties were not sureties. While we have the light, let us cultivate distrust of the certainties of despair.

Fold Not the Arms of Action

Waiting for the Lord in a season of darkness should not be a time of inactivity. We should do what we can do. And *doing* is often God's appointed remedy for despair. Wise Christian counselors, ancient and modern, have given this advice. George MacDonald, whom C. S. Lewis called "his master,"[17] wrote:

> He changes not because you changest. Nay, He has an especial tenderness of love towards thee for that thou art in the dark and hast no light, and His heart is glad when thou dost arise and say, "I will go to my Father." . . . Fold the arms of thy faith, and wait in the quietness until light goes up in thy darkness. Fold the arms of thy Faith I say, but not of thy Action: bethink thee of something that thou oughtest to do, and go to do it, if it be but the sweeping of a room, or the preparing of a meal, or a visit to a friend. Heed not thy feelings: Do thy work.[18]

Richard Baxter gave the same counsel three hundred years earlier than MacDonald and traced it back to the Bible.

> Be sure that you live not idly, but in some constant business of a lawful calling, so far as you have bodily strength. Idleness is a constant sin, and labour is a duty. Idleness is but the devil's home for temptation, and for unprofitable, distracting musings. Labour profiteth others and ourselves; both soul and body need it. Six days must thou labour, and must not eat "The bread of idleness" (Prov. xxxi. 13-27). God hath made it our duty, and will bless us in his appointed way. I have known grievous, despairing melancholy cured and turned into a life of godly cheerfulness, principally by setting upon constancy and diligence in the business of families and callings.[19]

What Matters Is Your Duty, Not Your Joy?

This counsel from MacDonald and Baxter raises a critical question: they both seem to make feelings negligible. They seem to say: what matters is that you do your duty, not that you feel joy. But that may not be what they mean, and if it were, I would strongly disagree. When MacDonald says, "Heed not thy feelings, do thy work," he means: don't let *wrong* feelings govern you. Act against them. If your feelings are telling you that staying in bed is the best thing today, preach to your feelings and tell them how foolish they are. Don't lose sight of the gospel in this preaching! Don't forget that defeating these wrong feelings and getting out of bed is enabled by the Spirit and is *becoming what you are in Christ*. But then exert your will and get up! I certainly agree with this.

But the question is deeper: If joy in God is the fountain of love and the root of right living—as I believe it is—can behavior that proceeds without joy be virtuous? I will answer the question at two levels.

First, I would say that a Christian, no matter how dark the season of his sadness, never is completely without joy in God. I mean that there remains in his heart the seed of joy in the form, perhaps only of a remembered taste of goodness and an unwillingness to let the goodness go. This is not the "joy that is inexpressible and filled with glory" (1 Pet. 1:8). It's not the joy that we have known at times and fight to regain. But it is a fragment of such joy—like a man who sits in prison and pulls out a tattered picture of his wife, or a paralyzed victim of a car accident who watches a video of the day he could dance. Or even more fragmentary, the joy may only lie there in the cellar of our soul in the form of penitent sadness that we cannot desire God as we ought. Inside that sadness is the seed of what we once knew of joy.

Duty Includes the Duty of Joy

The other answer I would give is that we should never say to ourselves or another person in the season of darkness, "Just do your work. Just do your duty. Just act like a Christian, even if you don't feel like one." That's almost good advice. But the problem is in the word *just*. Instead of only saying, "Just do your duty," we must say four other things as well.

First, we must say that joy is part of your duty. The Bible says, "Rejoice always" (1 Thess. 5:16). And in regard to the duty of giving, it says, "God loves a *cheerful* giver" (2 Cor. 9:7). In regard to the duty of service, it says, "Serve the LORD *with gladness*" (Ps. 100:2). In regard to the duty of mercy it says do it *"with cheerfulness"* (Rom. 12:8). In regard to the duty of afflictions, it says, *"Count it all joy"* (Jas. 1:2). We simply water down the divine command when we call someone to half their duty.

The second thing we must say when we tell a disconsolate person to "do their job" is that while they do their job, they should probably be repenting and confessing the sin of gloomy faith. I say "probably" because even in cases where the main cause is physical, there is probably some element of sinful pride or self-pity mingled with it. I am aware that this may sound like an added burden to the one who is in spiritual darkness. But it is not an *added* burden. If it is a burden at all, it is already there and not *added* by calling it what it is. Failing to rejoice in God when we are commanded to rejoice is sin. False comforts lead to artificial healing. But the truest diagnoses lead to the deepest cures. So, yes, we tell the disconsolate: "If you can, get up from your bed and make a meal, or sweep a room, or take a walk, or visit a friend, or go to work. But it is not a matter of indifference whether you do this with joy in God; if you can't, then tell him so, and that you are sorry. He will hear you mercifully and forgive."

Will You Be a Hypocrite If You Obey without Joy?

Which leads to the third thing we say along with "Do your duty." We say: as you are able to do some of your duty, ask God that the joy be restored. That is, don't sit and wait for the joy, saying, "I will be a hypocrite if I do an act of mercy today, since I do not feel the joy of mercy." No, you will not be a hypocrite, *if* you know that joy is your duty, and repent that you don't have it, and ask God earnestly to restore the joy even as you do the deed. That is *not* the way a hypocrite thinks. That is the way a true Christian thinks in the fight for joy.

And the fourth thing we say, when we counsel the depressed Christian to be up and doing something good, is, "Be sure to thank God as you work that he has given you at least the will to work." Do not say, "But it is hypocritical to thank God with my tongue when I don't *feel* thankful in my heart." There is such a thing as hypocritical thanksgiving. Its aim is to conceal ingratitude and get the praise of men. That is not your aim. Your aim in loosing your tongue with words of gratitude is that God would be merciful and fill your *words* with the *emotion* of true gratitude. You are not seeking the praise of men; you are seeking the mercy of God. You are not hiding the hardness of ingratitude, but hoping for the inbreaking of the Spirit.

Thanksgiving with the Mouth Stirs Up Thankfulness in the Heart

Moreover, we should probably ask the despairing saint, "Do you know your heart so well that you are sure the words of thanks have no trace of gratitude in them?" I, for one, distrust my own assessment of my motives. I doubt that I know my good ones well enough to see all the traces of contamination. And I doubt that I know my bad ones well enough to see the traces of grace. Therefore, it is not folly for a Christian to assume that there is a residue of gratitude in his heart when he speaks and sings of God's goodness even though he feels little or nothing.

To this should be added that experience shows that *doing* the right thing, in the way I have described, is often the way toward *being* in the right frame. Hence Baxter gives this wise counsel to the oppressed Christian:

> Resolve to spend most of your time in thanksgiving and praising God. If you cannot do it with the joy that you should, yet do it as you can. You have not the power of your comforts: but have you no power of your tongues? Say not, that you are unfit for thanks and praises unless you have a praising heart and were the children of God: for every man, good and bad, is bound to praise God, and to be thankful for all that he hath received, and to do it as well as he can, rather than leave it undone. . . . Doing it as you can is the way to be able to do it better. Thanksgiving stirreth up thankfulness in the heart.[20]

Does Unconfessed Sin Clog Our Joy?

It may be that part of the cause of spiritual darkness is cherished sin that we are unwilling to let go. I have assumed all along in this book that the pursuit of joy implies hatred for sin. Sin destroys joy. It offers deceptive delights, but it kills in the end. In dealing with our sin we can make two mistakes. One is to make light of it. The other is to be overwhelmed by it. In the fight for joy we must take it seriously, hate it, renounce it, and trust Christ as our only Savior from its guilt and power.

One of the reasons that some people suffer from extended times of darkness is the unwillingness to renounce some cherished sin. Jesus and the apostle Peter and King David all spoke of how unconfessed sin hinders our joy in God. Jesus said, "If you are offering your gift at the altar and there remember that your brother has something against you, leave your gift there before the altar and go. First be reconciled to your brother, and then come and offer your gift" (Matt. 5:23-24). We quench the joy of fellowship with God while we refuse to confess our offenses to man. Peter related this to marriage and said that if a husband sins against his wife, his prayers will be hindered (1 Pet. 3:7). If we want the joy of seeing and savoring God in Christ, we must not make peace with our sins. We must make war.

Listen to the experience of David that comes from unconfessed and unforsaken sin in his life: "Blessed is the man against whom the LORD counts no iniquity, and in whose spirit there is no deceit. For *when I kept silent, my bones wasted away through my groaning* all day long" (Ps. 32:2-3). These words are full of hope. We can hold fast to our sin, keep it secret, and "groan all day long" in darkness—or we can confess it and experience the stunning experience of "the man against whom the LORD counts no iniquity."

The almost incredible hope of confessing and renouncing sin is that the Lord does not then rub it in our face but cancels it. He does not count it against us. From this side of Calvary, we know how God can do that with justice. Christ bore the wrath of God for that sin (Gal. 3:13). We don't have to. The accounts are settled. Therefore, we should not fear to confess and let go of any cherished sin. The shame will not haunt us. Christ clothes us with his own righteousness (2 Cor. 5:21).

Confessing to God and to Man Is Sweet Freedom

As we ponder both the deep, unconscious depravity of our souls and the presumptuous sins of our wills, we should pray the words of Psalm 19:12-13: "Who can discern his errors? Declare me innocent from hidden faults. Keep back your servant also from presumptuous sins;

let them not have dominion over me!" We have *hidden* faults that we cannot even confess, because we don't know what they are. And we have sins that we know about. It is good news to realize there is a biblical prayer that covers both. "Declare me innocent" of the ones I don't know about (because of Christ's blood), and "keep back your servant" from the ones I do know about (by Christ's power). If you hold fast to sin instead of renouncing it and fighting it, the darkness will remain as a severe, but merciful witness to the outcome of cherishing idols.

Do not be content with whispering your sin to God. That is good. Very good. But he offers us something more: "Confess your sins *to one another* and pray for one another, that you may be healed" (Jas. 5:16). There is a release and healing that flows from confessing not only to God in the secret place of your heart, but also to a trusted friend, or to the person you have offended. The tender words, "I'm sorry; will you forgive me?" are one of the surest paths to joy.

Give the Devil His Due, but No More

If you ask about the devil's role in your darkness, I answer: give him his due, but no more. He and his demons are *always* at work, not just sometimes. There is nothing extraordinary about the *fact* of his harassment. Paul considers it a normal part of Christian warfare to "take up the shield of faith, with which you can extinguish all the flaming darts of the evil one" (Eph. 6:16). Peter counsels us, "Be sober-minded; be watchful. Your adversary the devil prowls around like a roaring lion, seeking someone to devour. Resist him, firm in your faith" (1 Pet. 5:8-9). All this is normal. But the quality of his harassment varies from mild temptation to murder. Jesus calls him "a murderer from the beginning" (John 8:44). He has the power to inspire painful persecution and even kill Christians (Rev. 2:10).

But there are three great comforts in the face of Satan's attacks. One is that Satan cannot do anything apart from God's sovereign permission (Job 1:12; 2:6), which is governed by God's infinite wisdom and covenant love. Thus Satan's servants become God's sanctifying envoys (2 Cor. 12:7-10). So even if Satan has a hand in your darkness, he is not free to do more than your loving Father permits, and God will turn it for your good (Luke 22:31-32).

Second, the decisive blow against Satan's destructive power was delivered by the death of Jesus for our sins (Col. 2:15; Heb. 2:14). This means that Satan can harass us and even kill us, but he cannot destroy us. Only unforgiven sin can damn the human soul. If Christ has covered all our sin by his blood, and if God imputes to us the perfect righteousness of Christ, then Satan has no grounds for any damning accusation, and his case against us fails in the court of heaven. "Who shall bring any charge against God's elect? It is God who justifies. Who is to condemn? Christ Jesus is the one who died" (Rom. 8:33-34).

The Devil Cannot Abide with the Light of Cherished Truth

Third, deliverance from Satan's oppressing, darkening, and deceiving work in the life of the Christian comes most often by the power of truth, and only rarely by exorcism. I have seen demon-possession and have been a part of one very dramatic exorcism. I don't believe the person was a Christian till after the deliverance. The complete takeover of the personality by a demon is not something the Holy Spirit would allow in the Christ-indwelt heart. But that distinction may not matter much to the Christian who is being attacked and harassed from without on every side. The battle can be fierce. What is called for usually is the ministry of 2 Timothy 2:24-26.

> The Lord's servant must not be quarrelsome but kind to everyone, able to teach, patiently enduring evil, correcting his opponents with gentleness. God may perhaps grant them repentance leading to a knowledge of the truth, and they may escape from the snare of the devil, after being captured by him to do his will.

Gentle, loving, teaching of the *truth* is the process in which God himself grants repentance and a knowledge of the *truth*, which results in an escape from the captivity of the devil. The devil cannot abide truth and light. He is by nature a liar and deceiver. He thrives in darkness. Therefore, if, by God's grace we can bring the full force of truth to shine in the believer's darkness, the devil will not survive the light. Good, solid Bible teaching is a crucial part of deliverance from the darkening power of the devil.[21]

The Darkness That Feeds on Self-Absorption

Sometimes the darkness of our souls is owing in part to the fact that we have drifted into patterns of life that are not blatantly sinful but are constricted and uncaring. Our world has shrunk down to mere prudential concerns about ourselves and our families. Ethics has diminished from global concerns of justice and mercy and missions down to little lists of bad things to avoid. We find ourselves not energized for any great cause, but always thinking about the way to maximize our leisure and escape pressure. Unconsciously we have become very self-absorbed and oblivious and uncaring toward the pain and suffering in the world that are far worse than our own.

Paradoxically, depressed persons may say that they must care for themselves and cannot take on the problems of the world, when in fact part of the truth may be that their depression is feeding on the ingrown quality of their lives. This hit home to me when Bill Leslie came to Minneapolis some years ago and told his story. Bill Leslie was the pastor of LaSalle Street Church in Chicago, Illinois, from 1961 to 1989. He died of a heart attack at the age of sixty-one in 1993. His ministry was marked by concern for the whole person in the context of Chicago urban life. In an article on "Compassionate Evangelicalism," *Christianity Today* listed Leslie among the "early holistic ministry leaders."[22]

How Bill Leslie Became a Watered Garden and a Spring

He told of a near breakdown that he had, and how a spiritual mentor directed him to Isaiah 58. He said it was verses 10-11 that rescued him from a season of darkness marked by feelings of exhaustion, burnout, and a dead-end ministry. The text says:

> If you pour yourself out for the hungry and satisfy the desire of the afflicted, then shall your light rise in the darkness and your gloom be as the noonday. And the LORD will guide you continually and satisfy your desire in scorched places and make your bones strong; and you shall be like a watered garden, like a spring of water, whose waters do not fail.

What struck Pastor Leslie so powerfully was the fact that if we pour ourselves out for others, God promises to make us like "a watered garden"—that is, we will receive the water we need for refreshment and joy. But even more, we will thus be "a spring of water" that does not fail—for others, for the demanding, exhausting, draining ministry of urban self-giving. He saw that God's way of lifting gloom and turning it into light was to "pour yourself out for the hungry and satisfy the desire of the afflicted." This gave him a pattern of divine life that got him through his crisis and kept him going for the rest of his days.

God has made us to flourish by being spent for others. Jesus said, "It is more blessed to give than to receive" (Acts 20:35). Most of us do not *choose* against this life of outpouring; we *drift* away from it. We confuse pressured family life and stresses at work with Christian sacrifice, when in fact much of it has little to do with meeting the needs of the hungry and afflicted and perishing.

Please hear me carefully. This is not the diagnosis for all depression or discouragement. If it were, such self-giving servants would never be depressed. But they are. My point is that *one* of the causes of some people's darkness is a slowly creeping self-absorption and small-mindedness. And the cure may be the gradual embrace of a vision of life that is far greater than our present concerns. Some things may have to be taken out of our schedule. But as health and joy return, we may be capable of more than we ever dreamed.

What My Eighty-Five-Year-Old Father Said Was Missing

I would mention in particular the life-giving, joy-producing effect of sharing your faith with unbelievers by word and deed. A few days ago I called my eighty-five-year-old father and said, "Daddy, I am writing a book on how to fight for joy. What one thing comes to your mind from sixty years of ministry as to what Christians could do to increase their joy?" Almost without hesitation he said, "Share their faith." Joy in Christ thrives on being shared. That is the essence of Christian joy: it overflows or dies.

Millions of Christians live with a low-grade feeling of guilt for not openly commending Christ by their words. They try to persuade themselves that keeping their noses morally clean is a witness to Christ. The problem with this notion is that millions of unbelievers keep their noses morally clean. Christians will—and should—continue to feel bad for not sharing their faith. Christ is the most glorious person in the world. His salvation is infinitely valuable. Everyone in the world needs it. Horrific consequences await those who do not believe on Jesus. By grace alone we have seen him, believed in him, and now love him. Therefore, not to speak of Christ to unbelievers, and not to care about our city or the unreached peoples of the world is so contradictory to Christ's worth, people's plight, and our joy that it sends the quiet message to our souls day after day: this Savior and this salvation do not mean to you what you say they do. To maintain great joy in Christ in the face of that persistent message is impossible.

The Aim Is That Our Words Would Be the Overflow of Joy in Christ

I am aware, again, that this will feel like added guilt for the depressed person. It is not added. It is already there. Hiding it is like hiding part of the diagnosis of a person's disease. Jesus said shocking things, and hiding them will serve no one well in the long run. "Everyone who acknowledges me before men, I also will acknowledge before my Father who is in heaven, but whoever denies me before men, I also will deny before my Father who is in heaven" (Matt. 10:32-33). This is not meant by Jesus as a heavy burden or a hard yoke. "Come to me, all who labor and are heavy laden, and I will give you rest. Take my yoke upon you, and learn from me, for I am gentle and lowly in heart, and you will find rest for your souls. For my yoke is easy, and my burden is light" (Matt. 11:28-30).

What makes the gospel good news is not that Christ can be buried in our TV-saturated lives without the loss of joy. What makes it good news is that God is long-suffering and willing to forgive and start over with us again and again. The depressed person cannot simply go out and proclaim the joy of the Lord. But little by little a life can be built on grace and forgiveness that comes to the point where to be an advocate and a witness to Jesus is like breathing—and just as life-giving. The fight is to enjoy Christ so much that speaking of him is the overflow and increase of that enjoyment.[23]

Is the Cause You Live for Large Enough for Your Christ-Exalting Heart?

J. Campbell White, secretary of the Laymen's Missionary Movement, said in 1909:

> Most men are not satisfied with the permanent output of their lives. Nothing can wholly satisfy the life of Christ within his followers except the adoption of Christ's purpose toward the world he came to redeem. Fame, pleasure and riches are but husks and ashes in contrast with the boundless and abiding joy of working with God for the fulfillment of his eternal plans. The men who are putting everything into Christ's undertaking are getting out of life its sweetest and most priceless rewards.[24]

In the midst of darkness saints may have no strength to pursue such global dreams. But it may be, in the mercy of God, that as we wait for the light to go up, we can do poorly what we would love to do well. Perhaps we can read a short article about the church in China. Or listen online about a missionary who suffered much for the gospel. Or write a note to a missionary family with a few lines about how we are hanging on to grace, and include a brief prayer for them.

Loving Those Who Cannot See the Light

For most people who are passing through the dark night of the soul, the turnaround will come because God brings into their lives unwavering lovers of Christ who do not give up on them. Throughout Richard Baxter's sermon on the causes and cures of melancholy are strewn counsels to the church on how to carry the burdens of the depressed. He says things like, "Often set before them the great truths of the gospel which are fittest to comfort them; and read them informing, comforting books; and live in a loving, cheerful manner with them."[25] If depressed saints cannot read the Bible or a good book, we should read it to them.

The Amazing Grace of John Newton's Care for William Cowper

One great example of persevering love for a depressed friend is John Newton,[26] the English pastor who wrote "Amazing Grace." He was one of the healthiest, happiest pastors in the eighteenth century. This proved to be life-giving—to a point—for a suicidal poet named William Cowper, who wrote some of our best-known hymns. Newton had drunk deeply at the fountain of grace, the cross of Jesus Christ. He was filled with joy and overflowing for those who weren't. To taste the kind of person Newton was, listen to this testimony he wrote about how he lived his days.

> Two heaps of human happiness and misery; now if I can take but the smallest bit from one heap and add to the other, I carry a point. If, as I go home, a child has dropped a halfpenny, and if, by giving it another, I can wipe away its tears, I feel I have done something. I should be glad to do greater things, but I will not neglect this. When I hear a knock on my study door, I hear a message from God; it may be a lesson of instruction; perhaps a lesson of penitence; but, since it is his message, it must be interesting.[27]

In 1767, at the age of thirty-six, William Cowper entered Newton's life while Newton was pastor at Olney. Cowper had already had a total mental breakdown and had attempted suicide three different times. He had been institutionalized at St. Alban's Insane Asylum, where God met him in a powerful way through the loving care of Dr. Nathaniel Cotton, and by a converting encounter with the gospel in Romans 3:25.

> Immediately I received the strength to believe it, and the full beams of the Sun of Righteousness shone upon me. I saw the sufficiency of the atonement He had made, my pardon sealed in His blood, and all the fullness and completeness of His justification. In a moment I believed, and received the gospel.[28]

After his release from St. Alban's, Cowper moved in with the Unwin family in a parish near Olney. When the father of the family died, Newton came to console them. Cowper was so helped by what he heard that he and Mrs. Unwin moved to Olney to be a part of Newton's church. For the next thirteen years Newton tended the tangled garden of Cowper's soul. Cowper said, "A sincerer or more affectionate friend no man ever had."[29]

While there, Cowper entered a time of spiritual despair that made him feel utterly God-forsaken and lost. This lasted most of the rest of his life until he died in 1800. Again there were repeated attempts at suicide, and each time God providentially prevented him. Newton stood by him all the way through this, even sacrificing at least one vacation so as not to leave Cowper alone.

In 1780, Newton left Olney for a new pastorate in London, where he served for the next twenty-seven years. It is a great tribute to him that he did not abandon his friendship with Cowper, though this would, no doubt, have been emotionally easy to do. Instead there was an earnest exchange of letters for twenty years. Cowper poured out his soul to Newton as he did to no one else.

The last days of Cowper's life brought no relief. There was no happy ending. In March 1800, Cowper said to the visiting doctor, "I feel unutterable despair." On April 24 Miss Perowne offered some refreshment to him, to which he replied, "What can it signify?" He never spoke again and died the next afternoon.[30]

To the end Newton remained Cowper's pastor and friend, writing and visiting him again and again. He did not despair of the despairing. After one of these visits in 1788 Cowper wrote:

> I found those comforts in your visit, which have formerly sweetened all our interviews, in part restored. I knew you; knew you for the same shepherd who was sent to lead me out of the wilderness into the pasture where the Chief Shepherd feeds His flock, and felt my sentiments of affectionate friendship for you the same as ever.[31]

There Is No Wasted Work in Loving Those without Light

You cannot persuade a depressed person that he is not reprobate if he is utterly persuaded that he is. But you can stand by him. And you can keep soaking him, as Newton did for Cowper, in the "benevolence, mercy, goodness, and sympathy" of Jesus, and "the sufficiency of the atonement," and "the fullness and completeness of Christ's justification."[32] He may say that they are wonderful, but that they do not belong to him—as Cowper did. But in God's time these truths may yet be given the power to awaken hope and beget a spirit of adoption. Or, even in the absence of evidence that peace is given, they may be used in some mysterious way to sustain the mustard seed of faith that is so small it cannot be seen.

I do not know the outcome of Cowper's fight for joy. But I do know that true saints enter dark seasons, and should they die in the midst of one, it is no sure sign that they were not born again, nor that they were not sustained in their darkness by the sovereign hand of grace. God has his reasons why he would leave one of his children feeling so forsaken—just as he has his reasons for martyrdom (John 21:19). Sometimes we can see these reasons, and sometimes we can't.

Gaius Davies tells the following story:

> Winston Churchill used to speak of his "black dog": he survived though he was dogged by depression for much of his life. It is said that only because Churchill had faced his own black periods was he able, at sixty years of age, to rally those who felt overwhelmed by the Nazi threat. His own experience of adversity enabled him to be a leader who helped to save the world from the darkness of tyranny.[33]

But Cowper did not live to lead a nation into triumphant war. He died miserable. What was his "black dog" good for? It is not for us to render this final judgment. But I bear one small testimony. Without his struggles he probably would not have written, "There Is a Fountain Filled with Blood" and brought hope to thousands of sinners who fear they have sinned their lives away.

> *The dying thief rejoiced to see that fountain in his day;*
> *And there have I, though vile as he, washed all my sins away.*
> *Washed all my sins away, washed all my sins away;*
> *And there have I, though vile as he, washed all my sins away.*[34]

And he would not have written "God Moves in a Mysterious Way" and by it helped me and many others through a hundred thickets of discouragement.

> *God moves in a mysterious way*
> *His wonders to perform;*
> *He plants his footsteps in the sea*
> *And rides upon the storm.*

Deep in unfathomable mines
Of never failing skill
He treasures up his bright designs
And works his sovereign will.

You fearful saints, fresh courage take;
The clouds you so much dread
Are big with mercy and shall break
In blessings on your head.

His purposes will ripen fast,
Unfolding every hour;
The bud may have a bitter taste,
But sweet will be the flower.

Blind unbelief is sure to err
And scan his work in vain;
God is his own interpreter,
And he will make it plain.[35]

There is a legacy of severe mercy in writings such as these. The words are costly. And so they prove precious. So it is with everyone who stands beside a melancholy saint and helps him fight for joy.

William Cowper testified that the legacy had been left to him by another embattled poet and pastor, George Herbert, who had died at the age of thirty-nine in 1633. Cowper said, "This was the only author I had any delight reading. I pored over him all day long; and though I found not here what I might have found—a cure for my malady, yet it never seemed so much alleviated as while I was reading him."[36] Not surprisingly, therefore, a poem by Herbert wonderfully sums up this chapter and this book. It's called "Bitter-Sweet." I hope you will read it twice, once to get the flow, and once aloud (as poetry is meant to be read) for the beauty and the meaning. Please don't stumble over the old-fashioned spelling. Herbert would be very happy if you were encouraged in your fight for joy.

Ah my deare angrie Lord,
Since thou dost love, yet strike;
Cast down, yet help afford;
Sure I will do the like.

I will complain, yet praise;
I will bewail, approve:
And all my sowre-sweet dayes
I will lament, and love.[37]

Or as the apostle Paul put it for all the saints who fight for joy in this fallen world of pain and suffering, we live and minister "as sorrowful, yet always rejoicing" (2 Cor. 6:10).

Notes

Chapter One
Why I Wrote This Book

1. C. S. Lewis, *The Problem of Pain*. (New York: Macmillan, 1962), 145.

2. Augustine, *Confessions*, trans. R. S. Pine-Coffin (New York: Penguin, 1961), 152 (VII.17).

3. John Piper, *Desiring God: Meditations of a Christian Hedonist*, 3rd ed. (Sisters, Ore.: Multnomah, 2003). This is the book in which Christian Hedonism, as I understand it, is most fully developed.

4. Augustine, *Confessions*, 181 (IX.1), emphasis added.

5. John Calvin, *The Institutes of the Christian Religion*, ed. John T. McNeill (Philadelphia: Westminster Press, 1960), 192-193 (I.15.6).

6. Thomas Watson, *Body of Divinity* (1692; repr. Grand Rapids, Mich.: Baker, 1979), 10.

7. Quoted from an unpublished sermon, "Sacrament Sermon on Canticles 5:1" (circa 1729), edited version by Kenneth Minkema in association with *The Works of Jonathan Edwards*, Yale University.

8. Jonathan Edwards, "The Spiritual Blessings of the Gospel Represented by a Feast," in *The Works of Jonathan Edwards*, vol. 17, *Sermons and Discourses, 1723-1729*, ed. Kenneth P. Minkema (New Haven, Conn.: Yale University Press, 1996), 286.

9. Charles Hodge, "The Excellency of the Knowledge of Christ Jesus Our Lord," in *Princeton Sermons: Outlines of Discourses, Doctrinal and Practical* (London: Thomas Nelson and Sons, Paternoster Row, 1870), 214.

10. Geerhardus Vos, *The Pauline Eschatology* (1930; repr. Grand Rapids, Mich.: Eerdmans, 1966), 71, emphasis added.

11. For more on this, see Chapter 11.

12. C. S. Lewis, *Letters to Malcolm Chiefly on Prayer* (New York: Harcourt Brace Jovanovich, 1963), 89-90.

13. This is an excerpt from a letter to "Joan," a child who wrote him on July 18, 1957, in *C. S. Lewis: Letters to Children*, ed. Lyle W. Dorsett and Marjorie Lamp Mead (New York: Simon & Schuster, 1995), 276.

Chapter Two
What Is the Difference between Desire and Delight?

1. C. S. Lewis, *Till We Have Faces* (New York: Harcourt, Brace, and World, 1956), Book 1, Chapter 7.

2. C. S. Lewis, *Surprised by Joy* (New York: Harcourt, Brace and World, 1955), 166.

3. Jonathan Edwards, *The Works of Jonathan Edwards*, vol. 2, *The Religious Affections*, ed. John E. Smith (New Haven, Conn.: Yale University Press, 1959), 266-267.

4. C. S. Lewis, *Surprised by Joy,* 218, 220-221.

5. Jeremy Taylor, quoted in C. S. Lewis, *George MacDonald: An Anthology* (London: Geoffrey Bles, 1946), 19.

Chapter Three
The Call to Fight for Joy in God

1. Flannery O'Connor, *The Habit of Being*, ed. Sally Fitzgerald (New York: Farrar, Straus, Giroux, 1979), 126.

2. Lest it appear that we have created an artificial paradox here, take note that there are others like it in the Bible. This paradox is woven into the very fabric of biblical revelation: we are responsible creatures (and therefore God commands); and God is sovereign (and therefore he gives what he commands). Neither his sovereignty nor our responsibility cancels out the other. Consider these examples:

    Responsibility: Deuteronomy 10:16, "Circumcise . . . your heart."
    Gift: Deuteronomy 30:6, "The Lord your God will circumcise your heart."
    Responsibility: Ezekiel 18:31, "Make yourselves a new heart and a new spirit!"
    Gift: Ezekiel 36:26, "I will give you a new heart, and a new spirit I will put within you."

Responsibility: Mark 11:22, "Have faith in God."

Gift: Ephesians 2:8 "You have been saved through faith . . . it is the gift of God."

Responsibility: Acts 2:38, "Repent."

Gift: 2 Timothy 2:25, "God may perhaps grant them repentance."

Responsibility: John 3:7, "You must be born again."

Gift: John 3:8, "The wind blows where it wishes. . . . So it is with everyone who is born of the Spirit."

3. Georg Neumark, "If Thou But Suffer God to Guide Thee" (1641).

4. Karolina W. Sandell-Berg, "Day by Day" (1855), trans. Andrew L. Skoog (1855).

Chapter Four
Joy in God Is a Gift of God

1. C. S. Lewis, *Surprised by Joy* (New York: Harcourt, Brace and World, 1955), 18.

2. Matthew Henry, *Matthew Henry's Commentary on the Whole Bible*, 6 vols. (Old Tappan, N.J.: Fleming Revell Company, n.d.), 6:744.

3. N. P. Williams, *The Ideas of the Fall and of Original Sin* (1926), cited in Edward T. Oakes, "Original Sin: A Disputation," *First Things* 87 (November 1998): 24.

4. Augustine, *Confessions*, trans. R. S. Pine-Coffin (London: Penguin Books, 1961), 236 (X.31).

Chapter Five
The Fight for Joy Is a Fight to See

1. Jonathan Edwards, "Born Again," in *The Works of Jonathan Edwards*, vol. 17, *Sermons and Discourses, 1730-1733*, ed. Mark Valeri (New Haven, Conn.: Yale University Press, 1999), 192.

2. Quoted from Jonathan Edwards, *The End for Which God Created the World*, in John Piper, *God's Passion for His Glory: Living the Vision of Jonathan Edwards* (Wheaton, Ill.: Crossway, 1998), 242.

3. I have argued extensively from the Scriptures for this truth in several other places. See *Desiring God: Meditations of a Christian Hedonist*, 3rd ed. (Sisters, Ore.: Multnomah, 2003), 308-320; *Let the Nations Be Glad: The Supremacy of God in Missions*, 2nd ed. (Grand Rapids, Mich.: Baker, 2003), 21-28.

4. Jonathan Edwards, *The Works of Jonathan Edwards*, vol. 13, *The "Miscellanies," a-500*, ed. Thomas Schafer (New Haven, Conn.: Yale University Press, 1994), 495 (#448). For Edwards's extended development of this truth see *The End for Which God Created the World*, in Piper, *God's Passion for His Glory: Living the Vision of Jonathan Edwards*, 117-251.

5. Edwards, *The End of Which God Created the World*, 247.

6. Jonathan Edwards, "A Divine and Supernatural Light," in *The Works of Jonathan Edwards*, vol. 17, *Sermons and Discources, 1730-1733*, ed. Mark Valeri, 413.

7. Ibid., 413.

8. Quoted from Thomas Binney's "Sermons," in Charles Haddon Spurgeon, *The Treasury of David*, 3 vols. (Mclean, Va.: Macdonald Publishing Company, n.d.), 1:131, emphasis added. Thomas Binney (1798-1874) was an English Congregationalist pastor and hymn-writer.

9. Edwards, "A Divine and Supernatural Light," 414.

Chapter Six
Fighting for Joy like a Justified Sinner

1. John Bunyan, *Grace Abounding to the Chief of Sinners* (Hertfordshire: The Evangelical Press, 1978), 90-91.

2. For an explanation of why our joy will be ever-increasing, see John Piper, "Can Joy Increase Forever? Meditation on Ephesians 4:29 and 5:4," *A Godward Life, Book Two* (Sisters, Ore.: Multnomah, 1999), 162-164.

3. Christopher Catherwood, *Five Evangelical Leaders* (Wheaton, Ill.: Harold Shaw Publishers, 1985), 170-171. Interested readers can visit the Martyn Lloyd-Jones Trust Recordings website (http://www.mljtrust.org) to listen to the audio sermons online.

4. Jonathan Edwards, *The Works of Jonathan Edwards*, vol. 13, *The "Miscellanies," a-500*, ed. Thomas Schafer (New Haven, Conn.: Yale University Press, 1994), 495, Miscellany #448; see also #87, 251-252; #332, 410.

> Because [God] infinitely values his own glory, consisting in the knowledge of himself, love to himself, [that is,] complacence [contentment] and joy in himself; he therefore valued the im-

age, communication or participation of these, in the creature. And it is because he values himself, that he delights in the knowledge, and love, and joy of the creature; as being himself the object of this knowledge, love and complacence. . . . [Thus] God's respect to the creature's good, and his respect to himself, is not a divided respect; but both are united in one, as the happiness of the creature aimed at, is happiness in union with himself. (*Dissertation Concerning the End for Which God Created the World*, in *The Works of Jonathan Edwards*, ed. Paul Ramsey, 8:532-533, emphasis added)

5. Jonathan Edwards, "Some Thoughts Concerning the Revival," in *The Works of Jonathan Edwards*, vol. 4, *The Great Awakening*, ed. C. Goen (New Haven, Conn.: Yale University Press, 1972), 387.

6. Martyn Lloyd-Jones, *Spiritual Depression: Its Causes and Cures* (Grand Rapids, Mich.: Eerdmans, 1965), 5, 11-12.

7. Ibid., 20.

8. Ibid., 21.

9. The historic *Westminster Confession of Faith* expresses well how faith alone justifies but is never alone and always gives rise to love.

Those whom God effectually calleth He also freely justifieth; not by infusing righteousness into them, but by pardoning their sins, and by accounting and accepting their persons as righteous: not for anything wrought in them, or done by them, but for Christ's sake alone: nor by imputing faith itself, the act of believing, or any other evangelical obedience, to them as their righteousness; but by imputing the obedience and satisfaction of Christ unto them, they receiving and resting on Him and His righteousness, by faith: which faith they have not of themselves; it is the gift of God. (11.1)

Faith, thus receiving and resting on Christ and His righteousness, is the alone instrument of justification; yet is it not alone in the person justified, but is ever accompanied with all other saving graces, and is no dead faith, but worketh by love. (11:2)

10. Andrew Thomson, "Life of Dr. Owen," in *The Works of John Owen*, ed. W. H. Goold, 24 vols. (1850-1853; repr. Edinburgh: Banner of Truth, 1965), 1:XCII.

11. Bunyan, *Grace Abounding to the Chief of Sinners*, 55-59.

12. Ibid., 90-91.

13. John Dillenberger, ed., *Martin Luther: Selections from His Writings* (Garden City, N.Y.: Doubleday and Co., 1961), 11-12.

14. Dietrich Bonhoeffer, *The Cost of Discipleship* (1937; repr.: New York: The Macmillan Co., 1949), 47, 55, 57.

15. John Piper, *Fifty Reasons Jesus Came to Die* (Wheaton, Ill.: Crossway, 2004).

16. Edith Cherry, "We Rest on Thee" (1895).

17. Jim Elliot, quoted in Elisabeth Elliot, *Shadow of the Almighty: The Life and Testament of Jim Elliot* (New York: Harper & Brothers, 1958), 19.

Chapter Seven
The Worth of God's Word in the Fight for Joy

1. John Owen, *On Indwelling Sin in Believers,* in *The Works of John Owen*, ed. W. H. Goold, 24 vols. (1850-1853; repr. Edinburgh: Banner of Truth, 1967) 6:250-251.

2. See Chapter Five for a fuller discussion of the relationship between seeing the glory of God and hearing the Word of God.

3. Edward Welch, "Self-Control: The Battle Against 'One More,'" *The Journal of Biblical Counseling* 19 (Winter 2001): 30.

4. Jonathan Edwards, "The Pleasantness of Religion," in *The Sermons of Jonathan Edwards: A Reader,* ed. Wilson H. Kimnach, Kenneth Minkema, and Douglas A. Sweeney (New Haven, Conn: Yale University Press, 1999), 23-24.

5. There are two different words for "blessed" in the New Testament. *Eulogetos* usually means "praised," while *makarios*—used in the Beatitudes of Matthew 5—means "happy" or "fortunate." Paul himself uses it in other places to refer to the happiness of the person whose sins are forgiven (Rom. 4:7) or the person whose conscience is clear (Rom. 14:22).

6. I have tried to show how this battle is fought in *Future Grace* (Sisters, Ore.: Multnomah, 1995).

7. John Owen, *Mortification of Sin in Believers,* in *The Works of John Owen* (Edinburgh: Banner of Truth, 1965) 6:9.

8. Owen, *On Indwelling Sin in Believers,* in *The Works of John Owen,* 6:250-251, emphasis added.

9. See above in this chapter where I compared Colossians 3:16, which speaks of the word of Christ dwelling richly in us, and Ephesians 5:18-19, which speaks of the Spirit dwelling in us. The parallel is similar to what we are seeing here in John 15:5, 7.

10. Martin Luther, "A Mighty Fortress Is Our God," (1529).

Chapter Eight
How to Wield the Word in the Fight for Joy

1. John Wesley, "Preface to Sermons on Several Occasions, 1746," *The Works of John Wesley,* vol. 1, 104-106.

2. Quoted in John R. Stott, *The Preacher's Portrait* (Grand Rapids, Mich.: Eerdmans, 1961), 30-31.

3. For further thoughts on why the early morning is best, see Chapter Ten.

4. This plan can be downloaded from www.Navigators.org.

5. Some ministries will email you the reading for the day (http://www.bible-reading.com/bible-plan.html). I suggest that you simply type "Bible Reading Plans" into your Internet search engine and find the one suited best to your needs. Another plan to consider is the "M'Cheyne Reading Plan," which guides you through the New Testament and Psalms twice and the rest of the Old Testament once. It can be found—with insightful commentary—in D. A. Carson, *For the Love of God: A Daily Companion for Discovering the Riches of God's Word,* 2 vols. (Wheaton, Ill.: Crossway, 1998-1999). According to the U.S. Census Bureau the average person has about a twenty-five-minute commute to work. If that means that people spend on average fifty minutes in the car each workday, then the entire Bible on CD could be listened to during that time in three months. One edition completes the reading of the Bible in seventy-two hours. This could have a profound effect on the mind for the glory of Christ and the joy of the listener.

6. George Müller, *A Narrative of Some of the Lord's Dealing with George Müller, Written by Himself, Jehovah Magnified. Addresses by George Müller Complete and Unabridged,* 2 vols. (Muskegon, Mich.: Dust and Ashes, 2003), 1:646.

7. Ibid., 2:732.

8. Ibid., 2:740.

9. Ibid., 2:834.

10. Ibid., 1:271.

11. Ibid., 1:272-273.

12. Dallas Willard, "Spiritual Formation in Christ for the Whole Life and the Whole Person," *Vocatio* 12 (Spring 2001): 7.

13. "[Bunyan] had studied our Authorized Version . . . till his whole being was saturated with Scripture; and . . . his writings . . . continually make us feel and say, 'Why, this man is a living Bible!' Prick him anywhere; and you will find that his blood is Bibline, the very essence of the Bible flows from him. He cannot speak without quoting a text, for his soul is full of the Word of God." Charles Haddon Spurgeon, *Autobiography*, ed. Susannah Spurgeon and Joseph Harrald, 2 vols. (1897-1900; repr. Edinburgh: Banner of Truth, 1973), 2:159.

14. John Bunyan, *The Pilgrim's Progress*, ed. Barry Horner (North Brunswick, N.J., 1997), 72.

15. John Brown, *John Bunyan: His Life, Times, and Work* (London: The Hulbert Publishing Co., 1928), 364.

16. One way would be to use the Fighter Verse program developed at our church. See it at http://www.childrendesiringGod.org; also available as an app.

17. You can purchase an inexpensive eBook edition onine.

18. Davis puts a very heavy stress on saying the verse chapter and numbers with each verse when you memorize long passages. He has good reasons. Take them seriously, and make your own decision. I do not say the verse numbers before each verse when I memorize a paragraph or a chapter. One reason is that I want to be able to recite the words in times of ministry and devotion and worship when verse numbers would sound very artificial and be distracting for others (as they are for me) in the flow of the passage.

19. Wesley L. Duewel, *Let God Guide You Daily* (Grand Rapids, Mich.: Francis Asbury Press, 1988), 77.

20. Thomas Goodwin, "The Vanity of Thoughts," in *The Works of Thomas Goodwin*, 12 vols. (Eureka, Calif.: Tanski Publications), 3:526-527.

21. C. S. Lewis, "On the Reading of Old Books," in *God in the Dock* (Grand Rapids, Mich.: Eerdmans, 1970), 205.

22. Ibid., 200.

23. Wayne Grudem, *Systematic Theology: An Introduction to Biblical Doctrine* (Grand Rapids, Mich.: Zondervan, 1994).

24. You can find a line of Puritan classics that are being republished today by checking The Banner of Truth Trust.

25. Michael S. Horton, "What Still Keeps Us Apart?" in *Roman Catholicism: Evangelical Protestants Analyze What Divides and Unites Us*, ed. John H. Armstrong (Chicago: Moody, 1994), 253.

26. C. S. Lewis, *Surprised by Joy* (New York: Harcourt Brace and World, 1955), 207.

27. John Piper, *God's Passion for His Glory: Living the Vision of Jonathan Edwards* (Wheaton, Ill.: Crossway, 1998).

28. Jonathan Edwards, *The Works of Jonathan Edwards*, vol. 16, *Letters and Personal Writings*, ed. George S. Claghorn (New Haven, Conn.: Yale University Press, 1998), 753-755.

29. Ibid., 801.

30. Quoted in Ewald M. Plass, comp., *What Luther Says: An Anthology in Three Volumes* (St. Louis: Concordia Publishing House, 1959), 3:1360.

31. Heiko A. Oberman, *Luther: Man Between God and the Devil* (New York: Doubleday, 1992), 323.

Chapter Nine
The Focus of Prayer in the Fight for Joy

1. Anselm, *Proslogion*, Chapter 26.

2. E. G. Rupp and Benjamin Drewery, eds., *Martin Luther: Documents of Modern History* (New York: St. Martin's Press, 1970), 72-73.

3. B. B. Warfield, "Is the Shorter Catechism Worth While?" in *Selected Shorter Writings of Benjamin B. Warfield*, ed. John E. Meeter, 2 vols. (Phillipsburg, N.J.: P & R, 1980), 1:382-383.

4. J. I. Packer, *My Path of Prayer*, ed. David Hanes (Worthing, West Sussex: Henry E. Walter, 1981), 56.

5. See John Piper, *The Dangerous Duty of Delight* (Sisters, Ore.: Multno-

244   Notes pp. 141–63

mah, 2001) for a fuller explanation of how the pursuit of and prayer for joy is dangerous.

6. See Chapter 12 where I discuss how to act against your feelings in a way that is not hypocritical or legalistic. The key is never to say that feelings don't matter. They do. You may have to act when they are missing, but the aim in all our acting and praying is that they return.

7. Augustine, *Confessions*, in *Documents of the Christian Church*, ed. Henry Bettenson (London: Oxford University Press, 1967), 54.

8. Robert Robinson, "Come, Thou Fount of Every Blessing" (1758).

9. George Croly, "Spirit of God, Descend upon My Heart" (1854).

Chapter Ten
The Practice of Prayer in the Fight for Joy

1. *Autobiography of George Müller*, comp. Fred Bergen (London: J. Nisbet Co., 1906), 152-154.

2. See in Philippians 4:3-6 the same sequence of thought from fruitful people-helping that is rooted in joy that is rooted in prayer. "Yes, I ask you also, true companion, help these women, who have labored side by side with me in the gospel together with Clement and the rest of my fellow workers, whose names are in the book of life. Rejoice in the Lord always; again I will say, rejoice. Let your reasonableness be known to everyone. The Lord is at hand; do not be anxious about anything, but in everything by prayer and supplication with thanksgiving let your requests be made known to God."

3. For other instances of planned discipline in prayer see Psalm 55:17; Mark 1:35; Luke 22:39-40.

4. G. W. Bromiley, "Introduction," in William Law, *A Serious Call to a Devout and Holy Life* (Grand Rapids, Mich.: Eerdmans, 1966), vi.

5. William Law, *A Serious Call to a Devout and Holy Life*, 147.

6. Ibid., 144.

7. Ibid., 149-150.

8. George Müller, *A Narrative of Some of the Lord's Dealing with George Müller, Written by Himself, Jehovah Magnified. Addresses by George Müller Complete and Unabridged*, 2 vols. (Muskegon, Mich.: Dust and Ashes Publications, 2003), 2:731.

9. Ibid., 1:273.

10. Ibid., 1:272-273.

11. I have tried to unfold in Chapter Eight of *Don't Waste Your Life* how secular jobs can be pursued to the glory of Christ (Wheaton, Ill.: Crossway, 2003, 131-154). I would also commend Gene Edward Veith's *God at Work: Your Christian Vocation in All of Life* (Wheaton, Ill: Crossway, 2002).

12. Three other examples of how prayer is designed by God to keep us for eternal life: (1) In Luke 21:36 Jesus says, "But stay awake at all times, *praying that you may have strength to escape all these things that are going to take place, and to stand before the Son of Man.*" (2) Jesus prayed in Luke 22:32 for God to keep Peter from utter apostasy. After saying that Peter would deny him three times, Jesus said, "*But I have prayed for you that your faith may not fail.* And when you have turned again, strengthen your brothers." This is the way we should pray for ourselves and each other. It is God the Father who decisively *keeps*, but we have a dependent role to play: we pray. (3) In John 17:11 Jesus prays, "Holy Father, keep them in your name, which you have given me" (see also vv. 12-15).

13. Ed. Johannes E. Huther, *Meyer's Critical and Exegetical Handbook to the General Epistles of James, Peter, John, and Jude,* trans. Paton J. Gloag (1883; repr. Winona Lake, Ind.: Alpha Publications, 1980), 697, italics added. See also John Calvin's excellent comment on Jude 20:

> This order of perseverance depends on our being equipped with the mighty power of God. Whenever we need constancy in our faith, we must have recourse to prayer, and as our prayers are often perfunctory, he adds, "in the Spirit," as if to say, such is the laziness, such the coldness of our makeup, that none can succeed in praying as he ought without the prompting of the Spirit of God. We are so inclined to lose heart, and be diffident that none dares to call God "Father," unless the same Spirit puts the Word into us. From the Spirit, we receive the gift of real concern, ardor, forcefulness, eagerness, confidence that we shall receive—all these, and finally those groanings which cannot be uttered, as Paul writes (Romans 8:26). Jude does well indeed to say that no one can pray as he ought to pray, unless the Spirit direct him. (John Calvin, *A Harmony of the Gospels Matthew, Mark and Luke and the Epistles of*

James and Jude, vol. 3, trans. A. W. Morrison [Grand Rapids, Mich.: Eerdmans, 1972], 334-335)

14. I think this "becoming more real to us" is what Paul teaches us to pray for in Ephesians 3:17-19 when he prays "that you, being rooted and grounded in love, may have strength to comprehend with all the saints what is the breadth and length and height and depth, and to know the love of Christ that surpasses knowledge, that you may be filled with all the fullness of God."

15. Law, *A Serious Call to a Devout and Holy Life*, 154.

16. We might enlarge on this first petition with words like these: "O Lord, please grant that your glory be honored . . . your holiness be reverenced . . . your greatness be admired . . . your power be praised . . . your truth be sought . . . your wisdom be esteemed . . . your beauty be treasured . . . your goodness be savored . . . your faithfulness be trusted . . . your commandments be obeyed . . . your promises be relied on . . . your justice be respected . . . your wrath be feared . . . your grace be cherished . . . your presence be prized . . . your person be loved."

17. Law, *A Serious Call to a Devout and Holy Life*, 153.

18. Ibid.

19. Ibid., 154.

20. William Wordsworth, "The World Is Too Much With Us: Late and Soon," in *An Anthology of Romanticism*, ed. Ernest Bernbaum (New York: The Ronald Press Company, 1948), 236. "Sordid boon" is an ironic phrase that describes the windfall of the world as sadly dirty and disillusioning.

21. A rich source of prayers that can have the effect of deepening and enriching and focusing our fight for joy through prayer is Arthur Bennett, ed., *The Valley of Vision: A Collection of Puritan Prayers and Devotions* (Edinburgh: Banner of Truth, 1975).

22. John Piper, *A Hunger for God* (Wheaton, Ill.: Crossway, 1997).

23. Similarly Phillips Brooks said, "The more we watch the lives of men, the more we see that one of the reasons why men are not occupied with great thoughts and interest is the way in which their lives are overfilled with little things." Phillips Brooks, "Fasting" (a sermon for

Lent), in *The Candle of the Lord and Other Sermons* (New York: E. Dutton and Company, 1881), 207.

24. Piper, *A Hunger for God*, 21-23.

25. Law, *A Serious Call to a Devout and Holy Life*, 112. Don't take the word *comfortable* here to mean luxurious and easy. The biblical and eighteenth-century meaning of *comfort* is inner peace and strength that may in fact lead us to endure some very uncomfortable circumstances for Christ's sake.

26. "For each other" means that the benefit of joy goes both ways: praying *for* others can often help to lift your own darkness. In our depression and dark seasons the greatest temptation is to become increasingly alone and isolated. Turning ourselves outward in prayer for others, even when we don't feel we have anything to give, can have a wonderful effect on the soul, and the clouds may soon lift.

Chapter Eleven
How to Wield the World in the Fight for Joy

1. C. S. Lewis, "Meditation in a Toolshed," in *God in the Dock* (Grand Rapids, Mich.: Eerdmans, 1970), 212.

2. Some philosophers of science, like Michael Ruse, *say* they believe morality is no more than a biological survival development, but I doubt that they live that way. Ruse writes, "The position of the modern evolutionist is that . . . morality is a biological adaptation no less than are hands and feet and teeth. Considered as a rationally justifiable set of claims about an objective something, ethics is illusory. I appreciate that when somebody says 'Love thy neighbor as thyself,' they think they are referring above and beyond themselves. Nevertheless, such reference is truly without foundation. Morality is just an aid to survival and reproduction . . . and any deeper meaning is illusory." Michael Ruse, "Evolutionary Theory and Christian Ethics," in *The Darwinian Paradigm* (London: Routledge, 1989), 262-269.

3. C. S. Lewis, "Transposition," in *The Weight of Glory and Other Addresses* (Grand Rapids, Mich.: Eerdmans, 1949), 26. "I suspect that, save by God's direct miracle, spiritual experience can never abide introspection. If even our emotions will not do so, (since the attempt to find out what we are now *feeling* yields nothing more than a physical sensation) much less will the operations of the Holy Ghost. The at-

tempt to discover by introspective analysis our own spiritual condition is to me a horrible thing which reveals, at best, not the secrets of God's spirit and ours, but their transposition in intellect, emotion and imagination, and which at worst may be the quickest road to presumption or despair."

4. Lewis, "Transposition," 24.

5. Ibid., 28.

6. Lewis, "Meditation in a Toolshed," 212.

7. The exact quote is, "The difference between the almost right word and the right word is really a large matter—it's the difference between the lightning bug and the lightning." It is taken from a letter from Mark Twain to George Bainton (October 15, 1888), first printed in *The Art of Authorship: Literary Reminiscences, Methods of Work, and Advice to Young Beginners, Personally Contributed by Leading Authors of the Day*, comp. and ed. George Bainton (New York: D. Appleton and Company, 1890), 85-88.

8. Richard Foster, "A Pastoral Letter from Richard Foster" in the November 1996 issue of *Heart to Heart*, a publication of Foster's ministry, *Renovaré*, 1-3.

9. "One minute would see Miss D. compressed, clenched, and blocked, or jerking, ticcing, and jabbering—like a sort of human bomb; the next, with the sound of music from a wireless or a gramophone, the complete disappearance of all these obstructive-explosive phenomena and their replacement by a blissful ease and flow of movement as Miss D., suddenly freed of her automatisms, smilingly 'conducted' the music, or rose and danced to it." Quoted from Oliver Sachs, *Awakenings*, in Robert Jourdain, *Music, the Brain, and Ecstasy: How Music Captures Our Imagination* (New York: William Morrow and Company, 1997), 301.

10. I am aware that so much more could be said about the possibilities and perils of music in the spiritual life. I would like to recommend that you pursue this further in Harold M. Best, *Music Through the Eyes of Faith* (San Francisco: HarperCollins, 1993). This is the most helpful and provocative book I know of on the spiritual function of music.

11. I do not recall the source for this quote. It is simply there in my memo-

rabilia, and may have been a letter or recollection from class. If anyone finds it published, let me know, and I will give due credit.

12. G. K. Chesterton, *Orthodoxy* (1924; repr. Garden City, N.Y.: Image Books, 1959), 12.

13. Ibid., 20-21.

14. Ibid., 54.

15. Ibid., 55.

16. Ibid., 60.

17. The quote is from Bertrand Russell, *The Autobiography of Bertrand Russell*, 3 vols. (London: George Allen and Unwin, 1968), 2:159.

18. What he means by abstracting is taking concrete examples and reducing them to the abstraction of generalities. For example, dealing in concrete specifics means seeing and savoring a particular oak tree in your front yard where you climbed as a child and where you carved your initials when you fell in love. But dealing in abstractions means lumping this tree into a category and speaking abstractly of all oak trees.

19. The quote comes from the prefatory verse to Lewis Carroll's *Through the Looking Glass*.

20. Darwin gave this advice out of great regret looking back over his life. Near the end of his life, in the autobiography that he wrote for his children, he said:

> Up to the age of 30 or beyond it, poetry of many kinds . . . gave me great pleasure, and even as a schoolboy I took intense delight in Shakespeare. . . . Formerly pictures gave me considerable, and music very great, delight. But now for many years I cannot endure to read a line of poetry: I have tried to read Shakespeare, and found it so intolerably dull that it nauseated me. I have also almost lost any taste for pictures or music. . . . I retain some taste for fine scenery, but it does not cause me the exquisite delight which it formerly did. . . . My mind seems to have become a kind of machine for grinding general laws out of large collections of facts, but why this should have caused the atrophy of that part of the brain alone, on which the higher tastes depend, I cannot conceive. . . . The loss of these tastes is a loss of happiness, and may possibly be injurious to the intellect, and more probably to the moral character, by enfeebling the emotional part of our nature.

Cited in Virginia Stem Owens, "Seeing Christianity in Red and Green as Well as Black and White," *Christianity Today* 2 (September 2, 1983): 38.

21. Jonathan Edwards, "God Glorified in the Work of Redemption, by the Greatness of Man's Dependence upon Him, in the Whole of It (1731)" (sermon on 1 Corinthians 1:29-31), in *The Sermons of Jonathan Edwards: A Reader*, ed. Wilson H. Kimnach, Kenneth Minkema, and Douglas A. Sweeney (New Haven, Conn.: Yale University Press, 1999), 75.

22. Jonathan Edwards, "Miscellanies" no. 95, in *The Works of Jonathan Edwards*, vol. 13, *The "Miscellanies," a-500*, ed. Thomas Schafer (New Haven, Conn.: Yale University Press, 1994), 263, emphasis added.

23. Sereno E. Dwight, "Memoirs of Jonathan Edwards," in *The Works of Jonathan Edwards*, ed. Edward Hickman (1834; repr. Edinburgh: Banner of Truth, 1974), 1:xxxviii.

24. Ibid., xxxv.

25. Ibid., xxi.

26. For guidance from a biblical perspective, see Elyse Fitzpatrick, *Love to Eat, Hate to Eat: Breaking the Bondage of Destructive Eating Habits* (Eugene, Ore.: Harvest House, 1999).

27. See http://www.endovascular.net/EXERCIZE.html. Accessed 5-26-04. The online article this was quoted from is no longer available.

28. Charles Haddon Spurgeon, *Lectures to My Students* (1875, 1877; repr. Grand Rapids, Mich.: Zondervan, 1972), 160.

29. Eric W. Hayden, *Highlights in the Life of C. H. Spurgeon* (Pasadena, Tex.: Pilgrim Publications, 1990), 103.

30. Spurgeon, *Lectures to My Students*, 161.

31. Ibid., 158.

32. Ibid., 312.

Chapter Twelve
When the Darkness Does Not Lift

1. George Herbert, "Bitter Sweet," from his collection titled *The Temple* (1633), quoted from: http://home.ptd.net/~gherbert/Bittersweet.html, accessed on 6-3-2004.

2. Willem Teellinck, *The Path of True Godliness*, trans. Annemie God-

behere, ed. Joel R. Beeke (repr. Grand Rapids, Mich: Baker, 2003); Richard Sibbes, *The Bruised Reed* (1630; repr. Edinburgh: Banner of Truth, 1998); William Bridge, *A Lifting Up for the Downcast* (1649; repr. Edinburgh: Banner of Truth, 1979); Jeremiah Burroughs, *The Rare Jewel of Christian Contentment* (1648; repr. Edinburgh: Banner of Truth, 1979); John Owen, *The Mortification of Sin* (1656; repr. Ross-shire, Scotland: Christian Focus, 2002); Owen, *Communion with God* (1657; repr. Edinburgh: Banner of Truth, 1992); Richard Baxter, "The Cure of Melancholy and Overmuch Sorrow by Faith and Physic," in *Puritan Sermons 1659-1689*, vol. 3, ed. Samuel Annesley (Wheaton, Ill.: Richard Owen Roberts Publishers, 1981 [available to read at http://www.puritansermons.com/baxter/baxter25.htm]); Walter Marshall, *The Gospel Mystery of Sanctification* (1692; repr. Grand Rapids, Mich.: Reformation Heritage Books, 1999); Henry Scougal, *The Life of God in the Soul of Man* (1739; repr. Ross-shire, Scotland: Christian Focus, 1996); Jonathan Edwards, *The Religious Affections* (1746; repr. Edinburgh: Banner of Truth, 1986); Martyn Lloyd-Jones, *Spiritual Depression: Its Causes and Cures* (Grand Rapids: Eerdmans, 1965); Gaius Davies, *Genius, Grief and Grace: A Doctor Looks at Suffering and Success* (Ross-shire, Scotland: Christian Focus, 2001); J. I. Packer, *Faithfulness and Holiness: The Witness of J. C. Ryle* (Wheaton, Ill.: Crossway, 2002).

3. Baxter, "The Cure of Melancholy," 257.

4. Ibid., 258.

5. Ibid., 286.

6. Lloyd-Jones, *Spiritual Depression*, 18-19.

7. Davies, *Genius, Grief and Grace*, 354.

8. David Powlison, "Biological Psychiatry," in *The Journal of Biblical Counseling* 17 (Spring 1999): 3-4.

9. Ibid., 6.

10. Edward T. Welch, *Blame It on the Brain? Distinguishing Chemical Imbalances, Brain Disorders, and Disobedience* (Phillipsburg, N.J.: P&R, 1998), 126.

11. Shankar Vedantam, "Against Depression, a Sugar Pill Is Hard to Beat," in *The Washington Post* (May 7, 2002): A01.

12. Paul Gerhardt, "Give to the Winds Thy Fears" (1656), trans. John Wesley (1737), www.cyberhymnal.org/htm/g/i/givetotw.htm, accessed on 7-15-04.

13. For a biblical and balanced treatment of assurance, see Donald S. Whitney, *How Can I Be Sure I'm a Christian? What the Bible Says About Assurance of Salvation* (Colorado Springs: NavPress, 1994).

14. Baxter, "The Cure of Melancholy," 266, 278.

15. For two helpful articles on depression and how to help those who struggle, see Edward T. Welch, "Counseling Those Who Are Depressed" and "Words of Hope for Those Who Struggle with Depression," *The Journal of Biblical Counseling* 18, no. 2 (2000): 5-31; 40-46.

16. Baxter, "The Cure of Melancholy," 278.

17. C. S. Lewis, ed., *George MacDonald: An Anthology* (London: Geoffrey Bles, The Centenary Press, 1946), 20.

18. Ibid., 36. See the quote in its context from the sermon "The Eloi," at http://www.johannesen.com/SermonsSeriesI.htm. The online article this was quoted from is no longer available.

19. Baxter, "The Cure of Melancholy," 282.

20. Ibid., 281.

21. For a careful and wise biblical assessment of the devil's role in the Christian life and how Jesus and we should make war, see David Powlison, *Power Encounters: Reclaiming Spiritual Warfare* (Grand Rapids, Mich.: Baker, 1995).

22. Joel Carpenter, "Compassionate Evangelicalism," *Christianity Today* 47, no. 12 (December 2003). http://www.christianitytoday. com/ct/2003/012/2.40.html.

23. For biblical and encouraging help in personal evangelism, see Will Metzger, *Tell the Truth: The Whole Gospel to the Whole Person by Whole People*, revised and expanded edition (Downers Grove, Ill.: InterVarsity Press, 2002).

24. J. Campbell White, "The Laymen's Missionary Movement," in *Perspectives on the World Christian Movement*, ed. Ralph D. Winter and Steven C. Hawthorne (Pasadena, Calif.: William Carey Library, 1981), 222.

25. Richard Baxter, "The Cure of Melancholy," 284.

26. For the fuller story of Cowper and Newton from which this material

is taken see John Piper, "'The Clouds Ye So Much Dread Are Big with Mercy': Insanity and Spiritual Songs in the Life of William Cowper," in *The Hidden Smile of God: The Fruit of Affliction in the Lives of John Bunyan, William Cowper, and David Brainerd* (Wheaton, Ill.: Crossway, 2001), 81-122. For more on Newton, see John Piper, "John Newton: The Tough Roots of His Habitual Tenderness," in *The Roots of Endurance: Invincible Perseverance in the Lives of John Newton, Charles Simeon, and William Wilberforce* (Wheaton, Ill.: Crossway, 2002), 41-75.

27. Gilbert Thomas, *William Cowper and the Eighteenth Century* (London: Ivor Nicholson and Watson, Ltd., 1935), 202.

28. Ibid., 132.

29. Ibid., 192.

30. Ibid., 384.

31. Ibid., 356.

32. Ibid., 131-132.

33. Davies, *Genius, Grief and Grace*, 13.

34. William Cowper, "There Is a Fountain Filled with Blood" (1772).

35. William Cowper, "God Moves in a Mysterious Way" (1774).

36. Davies, *Genius, Grief and Grace*, 103-104.

37. Herbert, "Bitter Sweet."

Scripture Index

Person Index

Subject Index

❄ desiringGod

Everyone wants to be happy. Our website was born and built for happiness. We want people everywhere to understand and embrace the truth that *God is most glorified in us when we are most satisfied in him*. We've collected more than thirty years of John Piper's speaking and writing, including translations into more than forty languages. We also provide a daily stream of new written, audio, and video resources to help you find truth, purpose, and satisfaction that never end. And it's all available free of charge, thanks to the generosity of people who've been blessed by the ministry.

If you want more resources for true happiness, or if you want to learn more about our work at Desiring God, we invite you to visit us at www.desiringGod.org.

www.desiringGod.org

A Passionate Call to
Make Your Life Count

"God created us to live with a single passion to joyfully display his supreme excellence in all the spheres of life. The wasted life is the life without this passion. God calls us to pray and think and dream and plan and work not to be made much of, but to make much of him in every part of our lives."

—JOHN PIPER

What do you crave?

In this classic meditation on fasting, John Piper helps Christians apply the Bible's teaching on this long-standing spiritual discipline, highlighting the profound contentment that comes from delighting in God above all else. Piper helps readers put self-indulgence to death by directing them to the all-satisfying, sin-conquering glory of Christ.

Now available with a foreword by best-selling authors David Platt and Francis Chan.
